NATHAN COHEN

The Making of a Critic

NATHAN COHEN

The Making of a Critic

Wayne E. Edmonstone

Lester and Orpen Limited

Canadian Cataloguing in Publication Data
Edmonstone, Wayne E
    Nathan Cohen

Bibliography: p.
Includes index.
ISBN 0-919630-94-4

1. Cohen, Nathan, 1923-1971.   2. Critics—
Canada—biography.

PN1708.C64E34   792/092/4   C77-001439-9

Printed in Canada

CONTENTS

Photographs appear after page *124*.

FOREWORD

Throughout his career as a professional journalist and broadcaster, the late Nathan Cohen made a unique contribution to Canadian journalism, not only as a theatrical critic, but as a social critic as well. However, Cohen, who is today primarily remembered for his work as drama critic of the Toronto *Star*, in fact first gained his formidable reputation as a national critic long before he joined that paper.

Beginning as a university newspaper editor, and during a subsequent career as a labour journalist, Communist Party writer, freelance contributor to Jewish newspapers and broadcaster for the Canadian Broadcasting Corporation, Cohen developed and polished the critical standards and national viewpoint that were to continue for his entire career in the media.

From the outset, Cohen insisted that the creation of indigenous works of art was essential to the development of a distinctive Canadian cultural identity, that informed criticism itself was absolutely necessary to both Canadian artistic and political life, that critical *audiences* must be developed in Canada before the country could reach national maturity, and that higher standards of Canadian journalistic criticism than had prevailed were a necessity in assisting this national development. And, as the writing of this young journalist/critic, a man barely out of his teens, was to have an almost immediate and controversial effect on theatre in English Canada, the work of his formative years deserves particular attention.

As much as possible, I have let Mr. Cohen do the talking, to make his own case. I hold the view that a writer's ideas are best served by the clear presentation of what he has written, rather than someone else's interpretation of that writing. Cohen's material, most of which is presented here for the first time since it was written and/or broadcast, in itself makes a considerable contribution to Canadian journalistic history, and should prove invaluable to future students of his work. It should also provide anyone with an interest in Canadian culture with some stimulating and controversial reading. Many of his articles and broadcasts, long-lost to even the memory of his readers or listeners, still remain a valid legacy to Canadian culture — and, in addition, they point to the value of art as well as criticism, in creating a national identity.

On another level, I have tried to present what I have come to think of as a "documentary" or "narrative" biography of the critic and, to some extent, of the period in which he developed as a journalist. Needless to say, many of the "participants" in the narrative have been dead for a number of years, yet their posthumous contributions have been invaluable in helping to add flavour and perspective to the period under discussion.

*

Foreword

On the critic's death in March, 1971, at the age of 47, his widow, Mrs. Gloria Cohen, donated Mr. Cohen's papers to the National Archives in Ottawa, with the stipulation that they not be made accessible to the public until her death. In November of 1975, Mrs. Cohen graciously allowed me access to her late husband's papers from the Archives, giving me carte blanche to use whatever material I deemed necessary, although she had not herself examined the papers before donating them. One cannot thank her enough for her assistance and enthusiasm.

The research materials consisted of photocopies of Mr. Cohen's articles for the Mount Allison *Argosy Weekly*, and microfilmed documents spanning his thirty-year career as a journalist. The microfilmed material included correspondence relating to the Toronto *Star*, *Fighting Words*, and personal letters, scrapbooks containing articles, clippings and playbills, and preponderantly, radio broadcast scripts prepared for both the CBC and radio station CKFM.

The broadcasts and articles I have selected for use here were taken from the literally thousands of such items in the Cohen archives. In addition to the archival materials used, I have also drawn on articles written about Mr. Cohen after his death, my own reminiscences of the critic when we worked together at the Toronto *Star* and those of a number of his colleagues, as well as a variety of other works on theatre and culture in general.

I am also indebted to Professor G. Stuart Adam, director of Carleton University's School of Journalism for suggesting the project, Dr. Roger Bird, who gave invaluable assistance with the original manuscript, and Ms. Marijane Gilbody, who valiantly typed and proofread the copy.

It may be the opinion of some people who read the pages which follow that I have not been critical enough of

Nathan Cohen — although I have not gone out of my way to avoid it. However, in the process of carrying out the research necessary for this project, I was inevitably forced to consider my own period of reviewing art, architecture and sometimes films for the Toronto *Star* during 1972 and 1973, as well as my current work with the Vancouver *Sun*, and am astounded at how many of my own attitudes and value judgements are the result of the influence of Mr. Cohen, not only in the area of the arts, but in the practice of journalism as a craft. He taught me that both good journalism and superior culture are interdependent, and that both rely on a coherent philosophical point of view. I began the book with a profound respect for the man and his work, and have ended it with that respect undiminished.

Finally, the writing of this volume was interrupted by the death of the man to whom I owe my first introduction to the arts, my father, Elgin Wright Edmonstone, and it is to him that it is respectfully dedicated.

Wayne E. Edmonstone
Ottawa: *November 1975* — Vancouver: *July 1977*

NATHAN COHEN
The Making of a Critic

1

CAPE BRETON

If, as Wordsworth once suggested, the child is the father of the man, it may be well worth our while to take at least a brief look at the early years and early writings of Nathan Cohen. Although education, erudition, opportunity and a genuine love for the arts can help make a critic, more than anything else it is a rather unusual sort of temperament that will sustain him over the years.

In fairness to those who spend their lives doing original rather than interpretative work, perhaps at bottom it is the temperament of the artist *manqué*, but there may be more to it than that.

To the American poet and literary critic John Crowe Ransom, the critical temperament was one which used a work of art as the opportunity to create "a little work of art in its honor" — but more often than not the critic serves as a midwife to the arts rather than a creator in any sense of the word. Yet the critic exhibits and, with luck, retains, an ability to be impressed — and at times even awed — by the creative efforts of others, while at the same time holding on to a desire for perfection which insists that those efforts can and should be improved.

To Nathan Cohen, the critical instinct, and the desire to express it, came early.

Most children, faced with something as awe-inspiring as the images of their first shoot-em-up western on the giant screen of the local popcorn emporium, come blinking out of the theatre at full gallop, with pistol-pointed fingers, identifying with the characters whose adventures they've just shared on the big screen. It was typical of the six-year-old Nathan Cohen that he came out of the theatre identifying with the screenwriter.

By his own account[1] Cohen decided then and there that the western to which he'd been taken that Saturday afternoon in 1930 was "simply awful." As a result, he went home and decided he could improve on the Hollywood product by writing a story of his own called *Buffalo Bill and the Wild Horses*. That laboriously printed, misspelled little copybook exercise in improving on the original did accomplish two things, one of which was unexpected. It outraged his mother, who decided it was "blasphemy" for the son of staunchly Jewish parents to be working on the Sabbath, and it planted the seed in the child's mind that he would become a writer.[2]

Cohen's first exposure to live theatre — in the mid-1930's — was also something of a mixed blessing:

"Some actors from Boston came to my home town with *Uncle Tom's Cabin*," Cohen later reminisced, "and I went to see them.

"They were terrible. Uncle Tom didn't know his lines, the buxom lady that was Little Eva sipped at a bottle and hiccupped all through her death scene, and at one point Simon Legree sneezed so hard his wig flew off, his braces broke, and he ran off the stage with his trousers flapping about his knees. Still, bad as the show was, I have fond memories of it.

"After all, it did introduce me to the theatre . . . and even now I can't help but be grateful."[3]

Nathan Cohen was born April 16, 1923 in Sidney, Nova Scotia. Cohen's parents had come to Nova Scotia from a small "shtetl" in Eastern Europe. His father was a grocer, but a learned man, and had founded a synagogue in Sidney and later one in Los Angeles where he died in the early sixties. Cohen's mother died of cerebral hemorrhage at age fifty-three. Ironically, Cohen thought she was forty-seven when she died, and believed that he too would die at the same age — a prediction which proved all too true.

The boyhood of a large, ungainly, precocious Jewish boy in the restricted Scots Presbyterian atmosphere of this Cape Breton city in the 1920's and 1930's undoubtedly had its difficult moments, and possibly created a feeling of "being different," which may have had a bearing on Cohen's later aggressive individuality. Yet Cohen himself seems to have felt that the combination of influences to which he was exposed (he spoke frequently of "my Jewish-Presbyterian background")[4] in that sprawling east coast city was salutary and he recalled the place and people with affection.

Cohen credited a grade school teacher, Ann Farquarson, with encouraging him in his writing, for which he had "a certain flair,"[5] and another unnamed grade school teacher for inadvertently directing his thinking toward a concept of Canadian nationalism that was to last a lifetime.

Here's how he explained it in a radio broadcast on the eve of Canada's Centennial Year:

"In public school in Sydney, Nova Scotia, I had a

teacher who was an ardent recessionist — and who, as the end of the school year impinged and he talked of July 1 and Dominion Day and Confederation, would virtually grow tearful because our province had joined Canada.

"It was a great mistake, he said. We should have remained a separate colony or joined the United States, where our markets were.

"Now I have no idea what effect his remarks had on the other students — this was in grade five or grade six — but what it did for me was to get me to read Canadian history . . . and get a notion in my head of how this country was formed, what it looks like, and what its various elements were and how they had been made to fit.

"Of course, like every other Canadian, I make a big point of my regional origin — I am, I say proudly, not even a Nova Scotian, — I am a Cape Bretoner — but I have never truly thought of myself that way.

"Rather, I have always seen myself simply as a Canadian — and it has always bothered me that so few of us genuinely feel that way . . . and have regional rather than national loyalties.

"This regionalism has been a handicap to our evolution and unification in any true sense — and it is the essence of the Canadian structure.

"So it is only by finding ways and means to unite our regional and national loyalties that we can achieve a true nationhood.

"That is so easy to say — and so hard to achieve.

"Part of the solution is for those of us who are commentators, opinion makers, to be more forceful in our Canadianism, not to apologise for it, and to work unceasingly for good will among our various peoples and for the expression of genuine national feeling in our literary and performing arts.

"We have an exciting history.

"We need to see that history dramatized, and dramatized both colourfully and accurately. We need to have more imaginative awareness among our own artists of what's happening in the country now. We need acting and dancing and opera companies to play on a circuit that will expose them to people all the way from St. John's, Newfoundland to the Northwest Territories.

"We need radio and TV programs that will point out, entertainingly, what the things are we have in common. I am not saying these things will be decisive in making us feel more like members of the one country, the one community. But they will help — which makes them worthwhile.

"We have lasted 100 years. That's encouraging. We can become a truly unified state with a voice the world will know and welcome. That's something to work for. In a demagogue's hands patriotism can be vulgarized and prostituted. But patriotism is one of the noblest emotions people can experience — and I hope in this second century we are entering every one of us will feel an upsurge of pride and exultation and deem it an honour and privilege to be Canadian.

"As indeed, and with all my heart — I do."[6]

Here we have the perfect synthesis of Cohen's methodology: searching out his roots, looking back over his own history and tracing what he had learned and applying it to his present craft and position as a critic, and using his own lesson-learned to express a hope for the future.

That he did so, publicly, with the unabashedly sentimental passion of the Maritimer, the almost religious zeal of the "Jewish-Presbyterian," and the sometimes embarrassing simplicity of a man who is unafraid to express what he truly feels, is testimony to just how strong those roots were. Cohen learned from his life, and he wanted to share what he had learned with as wide an audience as he could find.

And oh how he *wanted* to learn, in those restricted, impatient days back in Nova Scotia. In 1936, at high school, more doors began to open:

"When I hit high school I had an English professor, a man named Willie Mould who in those days seemed like a giant to me," Cohen remembered. "He was a very proper Englishman with a little Neville Chamberlain moustache. He taught Shakespeare and the first time I heard that man reciting — badly, I suspect now — an excerpt from *Henry V*, I got terribly excited.

"I went after class and asked him to tell me more about Henry V and to tell me more about Shakespeare. You can imagine the excitement of the teacher being suddenly presented with a student who was actually interested in what he was talking about."[7]

The dapper little English teacher also introduced Cohen to the leading show business journal *Variety*, which became lifelong reading, and he and other teachers were soon inviting the intellectually inclined student to their homes and giving him access to their libraries.

In his high school years, Cohen seems to have even avoided the stigma often attached to "bright" students who get too close to their teachers and loathe high school jockstrapping — perhaps because of his formidable size, and perhaps because he found time to manage the school softball team.

By the time Cohen entered Mount Allison University, a small, liberal arts university at Sackville, New Brunswick, in the fall of 1939 at the very youthful age of sixteen, he was already beginning to show signs that although he was almost fanatically eager to learn, he didn't always enjoy being taught. He recalled that he told his faculty advisor what courses he wanted to take, rather than asking for guidance, and he rarely attended formal lectures.[8]

"But that wasn't because I didn't study," Cohen explained. "I went wild when I hit university because there were all these books — all these doors suddenly open to me — all this learning suddenly available to me."[9]

An excerpt from the university paper, the *Argosy Weekly* — which Cohen (who in a piece of self-editing insisted on being known as Nathan Cohn — at a young age, he was experimenting with different spellings of his name) joined as a staffer in November of 1940 and of which he became managing editor in 1942 — gives us a picture of his activity:

"Has played prominent roles in dramatics and debating. President of Mount Allison Players, member of Eurhetorian Debating Committee, advisor to junior debaters.

"Likes variety in his acting. Has been: income tax collector (*You Can't Take It With You*), Mexican spy (*Soldadera*), middle-aged philanderer-writer (*Hay Fever*), and a sea captain (*Ile*). Has been in winning festival dramas in last two years.

"Is particular about the spelling of his name (without an 'e') and his age (he's not allowed to vote yet).

"First senior in several years to be *Argosy* Editor-in-Chief, position usually going to a post-graduate.

"Is originator and producer of a series (it is hoped) of radio dramas from Mount Allison beginning a week from today.

"Likes to talk, isn't overly modest, hates gossip columns, and thinks Hedy Lamarr is perfect."

Two other items of interest from the paper of the same date — March 7, 1942 — are a photograph of Cohen as a pudgy, crew-cut, rather Prussian-looking young man, and a column which praises his acting ability, but chides him for being inaudible at times during a performance — a criticism he was himself to apply to many an actor.

Before Cohen became editor-in-chief, the paper was a typical student publication of the time, devoted mostly to literary contributions: prose, poetry and essays. Cohen moved to make it more of a newspaper, with emphasis on features, sports and editorials,[10] and because he found it "impossible" to "take the concept of so-called editorial neutrality seriously," he relied heavily on "the editorial privilege of expressing my individual opinion"[11] in the *Argosy's* pages.

Teenage undergraduate writing, perhaps any early writing, can return to haunt the mature writer at a later date, causing at best acute embarrassment and at worst a sort of nausea ("How in God's name could I ever have written *that?*"); and yet, in Cohen's case, the pieces which follow give an indication of the style and attitudes he was to continue to develop in later life. Written by a young man "not yet old enough to vote," they show a highly developed sense of the necessity for social criticism in national development, and a hard edge of realism under the mass of wartime rhetoric that was common to even much more sophisticated writing during the 1940's. Looked at in retrospect — and leavened by some of the author's later memories — they still make interesting, if at times somewhat florid, reading today:

"Every once in a while," Cohen wrote in an editorial dated November 29, 1941, "we become convinced that man learns nothing from the past, and adds only to the burden of his troubles.

"The symptoms are a total optimism, wreathed in platitudes about the brotherhood of man and the basic goodness of human nature.

"No one knows what this world will be like after the present war is over. We can only surmise. We take it all for granted that we will win. But that does not mean that we are going to live in a paradise.

"All hell may break loose. Few agree on how we shall act. Each has his own idea, the right idea of course, and each *knows* that if what he advocates is not done life won't be worth the cost of a penny bar.

"The League of Nations Society in Canada has chosen this time to come back into circulation, offering panaceas for our bidding. Students are urged to do their part in the rebuilding of civilization. This is our chance to save the world again. And so on, until we become dazzled by the wealth of promises lavished on us. It sounds so easy, so wonderful.

"Assert our strength, point out our elders' mistakes.

"Apparently college students have an affinity for this kind of fad.

"But it would be well to pause a minute and take stock. And if we do, then we will be faced by a very disillusioning fact: we ourselves are as much responsible for the mess today as any politician or so-called statesman that you would like to mention. We had our chance the last time and all we did was talk. Some of the faculty will remember when students here pledged solemnly, dramatically, that they would never go to war again because war is evil.

"What a pathetic farce! What an ignoble dream! How we enjoyed feeling like pioneers who were reconstructing the tottering edifice. Pipe dreams, enchanting, and alluring, but thin as air and insubstantial as vapor.

"And when the cloudburst came we retired into our shells, and only lately have we begun to come out again.

"But not any wiser. We are planning to build the world on the same old post-1918 basis. Conferences where nothing is achieved and weeks taken in saying so. Societies with flowery names and without purpose. A potpourri of worthlessness that will only shove us back into the mire.

"It is our opinion that it is time to get wise to ourselves. The League of Nations, which did achieve some good, should restrict itself to things other than political for here it failed ignominiously.

"Let's stop saying that we are the future. We are no such thing.

"We are the present, and it is only by improving the present that the future is ensured. If ever we begin signing peace petitions and world benefit conferences again, then we will have to share a major part of the blame for the ensuing disaster. . ."

Jerky, tentative, and florid as it is, that little piece does show some insight in a teenager during a period when the style of undergraduate discourse, and most writing for the public in general as well, was centred around propaganda and grand Churchillian phrases about how great the world would be after the war.

In fact, for those of us who are old enough to remember, the world *was* to be reconstituted on "the same old post-1918 basis," with the imperialistic powers recovering their lost territories and the traditional power blocs regaining and retaining their challenged authority — as a result of this last great "war to end wars." Subsequent history, and a backward look at the utterances of public figures of the time, confirm how not only naive but deliberately distorted such a world view was, and it is to his credit that the eighteen-year-old Cohen was already questioning it.

Later that month, Cohen published his first piece of arts criticism, an evaluation of a Canadian poet who was a former student of Mount Allison:

"Charles Bruce graduated from Mount Allison in, I believe, the fall of 1928. While here some of his verse was published in pamphlet form, and he has had more published of late.

"Very wisely he has escaped the insidious disease which permeates most writers in this country — the conviction that he is expressing in a new and startling manner the great truths of all ages.

"In short he makes no pretense toward being a poet and is, consequently, much more of one than some of our more loquacious pedants. He writes pleasantly, charmingly, without any slipshod characteristics. If he is not of the substance of Shakespeare or Wordsworth, then neither is he a mill-of-the-grist versifier.

"'Personal Notes' is a slight poem which as he himself observes was written to express the belief of one individual . . . and is meant to apply to living generally. In construction the aim is clarity. Mr. Bruce has succeeded admirably. His poem is crystal clear, so clear that at times 'Personal Notes' is more of a prose essay than a poetic expression of faith. The opening passage establishes the mood and purpose:

> Between the written word and the typed reply,
> Between the phone's ring and the key's question,
> I have set down a statement of belief;
> This is for myself — not argument or protest—
> But simple care to get my thinking straight
> On the rough content of its casual faith.

"To me this is the real beauty of Bruce's work. Here is, he says, what I think, not what I *should* think and most certainly not what you *should* think. Despite all that has happened he maintains that survival is the keynote of our existence, and those things survive which are the finest expressions of mankind — love, beauty, discipline of mind. In Britain these qualities exist, and this is why Britain will survive, not the empire but the ideal.

"Canadian poetry is a nebulous thing. In some ways it is similar to a woman a friend once described to me. Beautiful, yes. Talented, he wasn't sure. But she thrived on uncompromising adoration and the man who began to balk her own will soon found himself at outs with her.

"'Which is why,' he said cynically, 'her husband has been living a hell on earth.' So Canadian poets at one time scorned all critical advice, and created a crippled maladjusted literature from which only Lampman escaped.

"Bruce to be sure is no Lampman, but he makes no pretence of it.

"If his poem is not an epic, it is sincere and sensitive, not too trite and at times the lines are noble and eloquent. . ."[12]

Oddly enough, this little piece, written once again at the age of eighteen, already contains two of Cohen's most important concepts as a critic of the arts, and more particularly of the arts in Canada.

First — and this was to be repeated constantly in columns, broadcasts, and even personal correspondence throughout his career — that the writer should tell his readers what he really thinks, rather than what conventional (or for that matter, unconventional) wisdom indicates he should be thinking; but on no account should he ever tell those readers what they should think.

And second, that unequivocal praise, without a leavening of critical appreciation and advice, ultimately stunts the growth of both the artist and his art. To Cohen, even at that early age, those who worshipped the arts in Canada were always in danger of becoming mere idolators.

*

Just before Christmas of 1941, during that dark period of national anxiety when the Allies were retreating before the advancing Nazis in Europe and the Middle East, and the British Crown Colony of Hong Kong (including two battalions of Canadians) was about to fall to the Japanese, Cohen found himself involved in a stark, flaming, near-fatal tragedy of his own.

Here's how he remembered it in a 1966 radio broadcast:

"In my mind Christmas is associated with an event that happened a quarter of a century ago, when I was going to university in Sackville, New Brunswick.

"On December 21, the day before classes broke up for the Christmas holidays, fire broke out in the men's residence.

"It shot up from the elevator shaft and spread unchecked.

"There were no fire escapes and no ropes to let ourselves down to safety.

"Several boys burned to death ... five, I think, altogether — a couple of dozen of us were injured. I was, relatively speaking, lucky.

"Although I was one of the last to jump, from the ledge of my fourth floor room, and though I was burned from head to foot, I escaped without a single broken bone.

"They found me, I am told, wandering around on the football grounds below the residence, in the snow, and all I could think of was that I had left my thesis on the Romantic Poets of Canada in my room — and three years work had gone up in smoke.

"There were no hospitals in Sackville — the ambulance rushed us to Amherst nearby and we were put up in the public wards.

"Most of us had no idea how badly hurt we were — we were in our late teens — we couldn't grasp the enormity of what had happened — and it wasn't until our families came, and told us, or passed out when they saw us, that we began to get some glimmering.

"But the thing that I remember most vividly is that on Christmas eve the head of the university, a minister, Dr. George J. Trueman came to visit us in a ward which held ten of us. I can't tell you what time it was — in the evening I know that — and he went from bed to bed and shook hands with each of us and tried to say something to cheer us up and of course the words stuck in his mouth and he couldn't talk.

"He stopped at the door and said — he was a tall man, very thin, with a shock of white hair — 'Boys, is there anything you would like me to do?'

"And one of the fellows, 'Dud' Desbrisse, who is now a Minister in the New Brunswick government said 'Sir, would you sing something with us?'

"It was such an unexpected request. He stood there a moment with his coat over his sleeve, and he opened and closed his mouth several times, and then he began to sing, not very well, 'Silent Night, Holy Night.' The others picked it up and were still singing it when he left.

"And when it was over we started on 'Good King Wenceslaus,' and when that was over, something else.

"We just sang until the nurse came in and told us that we were disturbing the rest of the hospital and would have to be quiet. At which we began to laugh and we just couldn't stop."[13]

That hurriedly written, conversational broadcast, incidentally, is another facet of the mature Cohen's popularity with the public. He was constantly stepping out of his role as The Critic, to offer bits and pieces of himself, his own experience, to his readers and listeners and emerged as a person, rather than a disembodied voice from on high.

It's also typical that the story should end on, even emphasize, a note of almost lighthearted optimism, sentimentality, and affection. Cohen was — although a lot of people never understood it — a very warm and loving man.

Shortly after the fire, he was back at work on the *Argosy*, writing a scathing attack on British diplomat Anthony Eden, over the latter's comments on the fall of Hong Kong on December 25th. The Japanese had indulged in an orgy of rape and murder after capturing the island, and Eden took pains to point out that the depredations had been carried out "without regard to race or nationality."

Cohen took exception to the comment, arguing that if British authorities were only concerned about what happened to whites in their territories — giving the impression that the rape and murder of other orientals by the Japanese didn't matter — then they were disregarding the very values for which they claimed to be fighting.[14]

He also turned his attention to Canadian politics and the need for a critical attitude to government policy, and to divisive regional and religious attitudes in the country.

"The defeat of Arthur Meighen in the recent by-election," Cohen wrote on February 14, 1942, "is as much to be regretted as it was surprising.

"Whatever his defects may have been, no matter whom he represented, he would have been a vigorous and severe government critic, acquainted with his subjects and aware of their importance.

"It seems unnecessary to add that the lack of this critical quality in our parliament has not helped the war effort any. The capricious howling of Mitchell Hepburn smacks and stings with personal hatred; but there is no solid foundation in what he and men of the Paul Bouchard ilk say.

"Yet the fact remains: we need constructive critical interference with the government's policy and we haven't got it. There is no initiative among our representatives. They debate indifferently topics so vital that to the outsider it is incredible. In short, we are still fighting a party war.

"The great majority of people who have been elected to govern us are still shifting the brakes along Liberal or Conservative lines.

"Do you doubt that? Can you doubt it when you look at Ottawa, when you read your daily newspaper, when you see industrial and labour leaders still trying to outsmart each other, when everything shows that Canadians are still complacent about the outcome of the war? Never was Canadian unity more needed; never was it more lacking. We are being high pressured in every direction by people who want to convince us of everything contradictory; that we need conscription, that we don't need conscription; that the French-Canadians are loyal, that the French-Canadians are treacherous, and so on ad infinitum.

"If we had nothing else good to say about Mr. Meighen at least he adhered strictly to the policy of a war program, which he advocated upon being nominated for the Conservative leadership. It may have been undiplomatic but it was sincere. And sincerity among our leaders is not too prominent a trait.

"Our unity is a war unity. Let regionalism take care of itself after the war. Let us promote this war to the full. No government is impervious to attack. Mr. Churchill has much to answer for, despite his golden flow of rhetoric; and the British war effort far outdistances ours. If men like Shinwell, yes, and British Conservatives, can attack Churchill then we can attack King. But note the reason for their attack; it is because he is not doing enough. There is no desire for party achievement, for party triumph.

"Our plight, while less spectacular, is serious. There are raiders right up the Jersey Coast; we have virtually lost Singapore; we are still having strikes. Yet people say smugly that everything is fine. . ."

Although he was already writing like a man rehearsing for middle-age, the young Cohen was, in these editorials, beginning to develop a more cutting phrase, and trying to find a viable political philosophy. Underneath the ebullient idealism, there lies a genuine frustration at the political game-playing and overall complacency of Canadians, which as a Jew, may have particularly disturbed Cohen, given the plight of Jews in Europe. Cohen's attitude anticipates by decades the "New Left" attitudes of later college journalists, but it was unusual in the 1940's.

Cohen applied his criticism directly to the causes of the Second World War — in which, it must be remembered, he was watching his older classmates go off to fight, and perhaps die — thus making the issue more than an intellectual abstraction.

"This war arose from malice, ignorance and fear," Cohen wrote in the *Argosy*. "It was inspired by groups who lulled us to believe in material progress above spiritual integrity. It was developed by cliques more concerned with their own welfare than the interest of their own country. It was nurtured by our own narrow-mindedness and complacency.

"Hitler and Mussolini precipitated no war; they are the products of our own sloth and shame. The democratic countries are paying dearly in lives and honour for the unhappy horrors which they let loose.

"You may, if you will, accuse me of abstract ideas. You may say that combat has been forced upon us because of economic conditions, political maneuvers, geographical necessities.

"You may point to England of the 1920's and 30's, to France and America, and assert that none of these countries wanted war. And I say that you are right. But I say further that they did nothing to prevent it, and that is why we are guilty. Because none of us, none of the common ordinary people wanted war, we did not believe it could come.

"But where has there been peace in this troubled era? War is not only strife between large nations; it is more than colossal regimented armies wiping each other out; it is the tears and suffering of the gentle people, the little people, the misdemeanours of our governments, the inability to overcome prejudice, and see eye-to-eye for the common good.

"This does not produce war. This is war. . ."[15]

True, the ideas Cohen expressed during this period were not original but, given the time, the environment, and the age of the author, they do indicate considerable independence in thinking, a growing sophistication of expression and vivid clarity of content.

Cohen's independence of mind, and his confidence in his own ability to understand complex problems proved to be too much for at least one member of the Mount Allison faculty, and earned him a public rebuke after he had written an editorial on the controversy then raging around French Canada and the conscription question.

The editorial read:

"We are not among those who stand by the belief that French Canada is the element disturbing the Canadian war effort. The more we see, hear and learn about that situation the more we are convinced that this issue is trumped-up and fabricated from beginning to finish.

"The French-Canadian situation is one which demands some patient examination but not these hot words of hatred and contempt which are filling many of our editorial pages today.

"We have never been in complete agreement with many of the sentiments expressed in the editorial columns of the Sackville *Tribune*.

"The *Tribune* does, however, deserve much credit for its stand on the French-Canadian issue. And we distrust greatly the motives of those who, in these most crucial of all times, take time out to fulminate against the French-speaking elements and stir up conflict between the Protestant and Catholic portions of the country.

"And if you look into the thing carefully, that is all that is being accomplished. One religious creed is being played against the other to the benefit of neither and to the disadvantage of all.

"The irony is self-apparent. Those people claiming that their only desire is to see unity in Canada are doing their best to wreck it, to precipitate dissension. There is unity in Canada, more unity than there has ever been. What benefit will it accrue to our self-appointed patriots, our Hepburns and MacCulloughs to take advantage of the rantings of a few men like Camillien Houde to make political spoil, unless they are so eager to get party leadership that they are willing to split the country wide open for it?"[16]

Now, while it was presumably all right for a student editor to pontificate critically on wide general questions like the nature of liberalism, the political process and national issues *per se*, this was hitting a little close to home, particularly in New Brunswick which had a large French-speaking population, and at a time when religious feelings were so divided that when people spoke of "a

mixed marriage," they were referring to a wedding between Protestant and Catholic.

One of Cohen's history professors took violent exception to the editorial, and evidently decided to put the
young know-it-all in his place. The argument ended with
the teacher telling him, in effect, that a foreign-born Jew
couldn't possibly understand the French-English problem in Canada.

Cohen could take criticism as well as dish it out — in
fact, he deliberately invited it by writing about controversial issues. But the slur against his origins was
unexpected — particularly coming from a teacher in
what he idealistically saw as an enlightened university
environment — and it hurt.

He retaliated with a follow-up editorial:

"We have, in our day, been accused of many things,
some of them unpleasant and some of them true," Cohen
began. "And we admit to the undiplomatic, but often
worthwhile, crime of being tactless.

"But we hardly expected a faculty member, many
years older than ourself, to exhibit a lack of tact which
she did in referring to an editorial which had been written in this paper the week before.

"We take it for granted that people know from our
name that we are not of the Christian faith. But, unlike
the faculty member, we are unable to see why this should
prevent us from being able to look at the French-
Canadian situation any more honestly than, let us say,
one reared in the Protestant or Catholic tradition. And
we most definitely do not think it to the advantage of the
university to have a person's ancestry or faith, made the
subject of criticism.

"In short, we were informed, and this in the presence of
another faculty member, a much wiser one, that because
we had not been born in Canada (which we were) we were

unable to understand the French-Canadian problem except in a trifling off-hand manner.

"It strikes us, (tactless creature that we are) that if we did not understand the problem it would be for another reason: ignorance.

"And we admit that our knowledge is limited to what many people from Quebec have told us, and what we have learned from the less prejudiced newspapers, and what certain students of that question have told us.

"We have tried to look at the question objectively, and the point which we made was simply that wartime is not the best occasion to go into such a vexatious issue.

"We do not question that this person, who is a member of the history department, is much better acquainted with the situation than we.

"We would certainly imagine that she knows more about it than we. And we would not deny that the reason she is being paid to teach in a university is because she is supposed to know about such matters.

"But we do most categorically question her right, either as a person or a teacher, to make a person's religion the standard for judgement.

"We could if we wished make an issue of this. But we are positive the good lady's intentions were not malicious. Indeed, the contrary.

"We would only point out for her benefit that her remark was extraordinarily tactless, that knowledge, and nothing else, is the criterion for criticism."[17]

Having delivered himself of this little homily — which contains in its last sentence another criterion which was to be a permanent Cohen standard — he did let the matter drop.

Oddly enough, though, directly below the column containing the editorial sits this little humorous "filler" of the kind normally used to fill in white space on newspapers; but it reads:

CUSTOMER: This coat isn't a very good fit.
ABIE, THE TAILOR: Vell, vat do you expect for $5 . . .
an attack of epilepsy?[18]

Did Cohen (or Cohn)-the-editor include this cliché dialect joke to show his readers that he wasn't overreacting simply because he was a Jew? Quite likely, he did.

Cohen's penchant for tussling with issues well beyond the bounds of the university on the *Argosy's* pages also brought him some criticism from alumni readers that the paper was not reflecting the school "as it is."

This, he felt, was unfair. "Mount Allison is not the same as it was in 1930," he wrote in his final editorial, "it will be different in 1960. If the *Argosy* attitude is not the same, it is because the campus itself is not the same. That is a point well worth keeping in mind.

"Some old graduates forget that university customs, like fashions, change. Mount Allison is today a college devoted to a practical consideration of life. The days of the 'art' college alone, or the 'rah-rah' outlook are over. Altogether the change is not a bad one. . ."[19]

And altogether, the experience of Mount Allison was a seminal one for Cohen. Despite the trauma of incidents such as the fire and his confrontation with a bigoted staff member, it was an horizon-expanding time in which he developed social and aesthetic attitudes and standards which were to last him a lifetime.

In a small university Cohen thrived on the attention he attracted by his multiple activities: the acting and debating, the directing and the campus bull-sessions, the editing and, perhaps most of all, the writing,* all of which strengthened his sense of his own significance.

* During his time at Mount Allison, Cohen also turned his hand to fiction: writing twenty-eight short stories and selling three of them.

He was also influenced by other social factors.

Until the comparatively recent period of mass-education, university graduates, even students, were regarded as something of an intellectual elite in Canada. At least they were the thinking man's apprentice, destined for what were then thought of as "the professions" — medicine, law, teaching and so forth — and imbued with the concepts of culture rather than the mass of purely specialized technical data which is more common today. They were, in a sense, *expected* to make a cultural contribution to their environment by virtue of their opportunities in "getting a good education," rather than simply becoming workable and workmanlike cogs in a vast social machine — and Cohen was very conscious of that responsibility.

After he had established his reputation as a renowned and respected critic, Cohen summed up what he had learned from his university days and what they continued to teach him:

"It was in Mount Allison, a small, liberal arts university which adhered to the philosophy of the small university that I received my first serious and meaningful exposure to the performing arts — especially to dramatic literature and theatre — and to the nature of appreciation and analysis," he explained in a 1967 broadcast.

"Of course in those days becoming a critic was the furthest thing from my mind. My thoughts didn't run in that direction at all.

"I was taking an arts degree and thinking of becoming a professor or a lawyer. If someone had suggested that I might become a critic I would have hooted with laughter.

"But it is curious to discover the extent to which one prefigures in one's adolescence — and I was in my teens when I entered and graduated from university — one's adult activities and attitudes.

"The student paper in Sackville is called the *Argosy*, and when I was there this week* the current managing editor produced for me an article I had written when I was the editor in 1941 ... and do you know what it was about? 'What's wrong with theatre at Mount Allison University.'

"So what I found out, by this return to Sackville, was that in fact I am now essentially the same as I was then.

"Just as passionate about excellence, but hopefully a little wiser, a little more mature."[20]

---

* Cohen returned to Mount Allison in May of 1967 to receive an honorary doctor of laws degree.

2

POLITICS

After graduating from Mount Allison with a Bachelor of
Arts degree in 1942, Cohen moved to Toronto, where he
began, as planned, to study law at Osgoode Hall, but was
forced to drop out of the course because of the ill health
that was to plague him intermittently for the rest of his
life: ill-health due partly to the burns and fall he suffered
when he jumped out of the dormitory window to escape
the fire and partly to a diabetic strain in his family which
he inherited. He returned to the Maritimes, and after an
extended period of recuperation, went to work as the
one-man reporting staff of the *Glace Bay Gazette*, a
labour paper financed by the United Mine Workers of
America.[21]

Cohen's entry into journalism was unusual for the
time only in that he possessed a university degree and
was ostensibly qualified for a better job. The working
journalist was involved in a business that resembled
casual labour more than a "profession" — for that mat-

ter, it still does — and the educational level of the majority of its practitioners was a high school diploma, at best. They learned their trade on-the-job, sometimes beginning as a copy boy, or a cub reporter, or as Cohen was to do over the next two years, as a jack-of-all-trades on a small paper; and if their formal education was slender, the necessity of learning a great deal about an unending variety of subjects forced them to continue their self-education.

But if the base from which they operated was limited, they learned from within those very limitations of time and space, and even often of viewpoint, to communicate easily and clearly — if at times superficially. As the British reporter and author James Cameron once pointed out, few of that older breed of newspapermen ever "cold-bloodedly set out on a career" in the business as college-educated journalism students do today:

"God knows, we are mostly tramps," Cameron explained. "One knew someone, one scratched out a piece . . . and lo, one had 'entered journalism.'"

Such people also generally saw themselves as "writers" (with a great piece of creative work somewhere in the future) to whom journalism gave the opportunity to earn a living by writing, a point of view shared by Cohen. Labour journalism in particular must have appealed to Cohen as it gave him scope to exercise his still-developing social conscience. He could, within the confines of the labour movement, write in his distinctive and highly editorial style without having to adhere to the allegedly objective style of the commercial press, and the job held the promise of producing some active, union-sponsored response to his political criticism.

Ultimately, this initial experiment in practical journalism seems to have ended in a certain disillusionment for Cohen. Certainly, he was effective for a time, and he gained a brief prominence — not to say notoriety — in Nova Scotia after writing a scathing series of editorials condemning conditions in the province's mining industry, which resulted in a call for a national conference on mining and his being publicly denounced in the provincial legislature by the minister of mines.[22]

However, internal dissension within the union and the eccentricities of editor Robert Reeds slowly strangled the *Gazette*, leading Cohen to remark on the paper's death, in 1947:

"It is estimated that the experiment in labour journalism cost district 26 approximately $100,000. How much it cost in grief and aggravation cannot be calculated. From personal observation, I can vouch that it was considerable. Publishing a daily labour newspaper is an enterprise filled with risk. In view of what happened to the *Gazette* it is probable that those trade unions, which consider embarking on similar projects, will definitely desist from doing so."[23]

Cohen left the paper in 1945.

Perhaps, like many another young idealist since, Cohen, at the age of 21, had decided that the *Gazette* simply wasn't radical enough; for his growing distaste for political liberalism had been reinforced by his exposure to the left wing of the labour movement, and he was rapidly moving towards Marxism.

Personally, he was still very much at loose ends:

"I had no idea what I was going to do with myself," Cohen recalled in later years. "I had a vague idea of perhaps going back to law, but in the meantime I had to earn a living."[24]

He worked briefly for the National Film Board in Ottawa,[25] and later in Toronto he tried and failed to land a job as a reporter on the *Globe and Mail*.[26]

Instead of looking for another job on a regular paper,

Cohen made one more attempt to enlist in the class struggle by joining the Communist Party and going to work for the party's paper, the *Canadian Tribune*.

This period of his career is generally glossed over rather quickly in the available biographical material written on Cohen. A recent writer, for example, simply states that he "flirted briefly with joining the Communist Party"[27] before moving on to more important things. Cohen himself frequently spoke of that time as one of youthful idealistic folly. He once asserted that while he enjoyed doing intellectual work for the party, he tore up his card in high-dudgeon and stalked out after being told he was expected to stand on street corners passing out propaganda leaflets.*

However, there is evidence in Cohen's writings in a number of Jewish publications for which he freelanced in Toronto after he had officially broken with the party, to show that his interest in Marxism outlasted his short spell as a Communist Party member. Writing under the byline of "Nat" Cohen — and a number of pseudonyms — he turned out articles for the *Wochenblatt*, *New Voice*, and the *Canadian Jewish Weekly* during the late 1940's covering a variety of topics: Jewish culture, international politics, features on prominent Jews, and reviews of books, films and theatre.

Cohen's articles during this period — from 1946 until 1948 when he began working as a regular drama critic for the Canadian Broadcasting Corporation — were still mostly political, particularly those for the *Wochenblatt*, which Cohen described in May of 1947 as: " . . . a Jewish

---

*On another occasion, some twenty years later, when I returned from a stint in Cuba as a correspondent for the Toronto *Star*, one of the first persons I met was Cohen, who then described himself as "a small-l liberal":

"Ah, Wayne, just back from Cuba I see. . ." he said. "Another disillusioned socialist, eh? Well, don't worry m'boy. . . We've all been through it. . ."

newspaper whose policy and program is Marxist to the core. The principles of Marxism," he added, "which have already liberated a sixth of Europe, contain the solution to Jewish problems that face Jewry today."[28]

And although he was increasingly turning to arts criticism at every available opportunity, that too was showing a clearly Marxist orientation, as witness this glowing film review written in August of 1946:

"Of all the new artistic media which have enriched the spacious firmaments of human achievement, none is bolder, more exciting in possibility and potentially great than the motion picture.

"We use the term motion picture, deliberately drawing a line between it and the movie, that mass assembly product of *Gilda* and *Easy to Wed* and *Without Reservations*, which reduces visual film to the level of sexual vulgarity.

"But the motion picture is an art now certainly and unquestionably popular. Not everyone can create it but almost everyone can view it.

"It is an art capable of projecting onto a flat screen the language, conscience, feeling and drama which gives life a greater purpose and beauty, the motive for all expression.

"In temper with the times, its art is co-operative. No one person is responsible for it: the director, the photographer, the screenwriter are inseparable. For this reason and because it is new, there are many who ridicule any description of the motion picture as an art. They will say it cannot equal staged drama. They exaggerate its faults and blemishes. One normally intelligent critic dismissed it with the cry 'It has not produced one play like *Othello* nor one writer like Shakespeare!'

"But the motion picture in the short space of some twenty-five years has contributed such remarkable films as *Thunder Rock, Long Voyage Home, Grapes of Wrath, The Informer, Zola, Alexander Nevsky, Make Way for Tomorrow, The Baker's Wife*, and *Potemkin*. Such an art does not require a defence.

"As an artistic medium it has proved itself. The magnitude of its scope raises breathtaking opportunities immediately apparent to the discriminating objective observer.

"Recently we saw a motion picture which moved us to a fresh glimpse of this infant art. By Hollywood standards (Hollywood being the most important maker of movies, although the British capitalist producers are beginning to run it a good second) it is certainly not successful.

"It is an old picture made during the war and a commercial failure.

"Sex has no part in its plot, although there is a beautiful love story.

"The Hollywood producers would sneer at such stupidity. Yet *They Came to the City*, written by J.B. Priestley and produced in Britain, towers so far above most motion pictures that it deserves to be heralded, even belatedly, for what it is: an adult film that assumes for itself an intelligent audience and discusses some of the problems that people will be facing in the post-war world.

"In *They Came to the City* several Englishmen representing a cross-section of the population are transferred bodily to an unknown region. One is a member of the landed gentry, another a financier, and the third a bank manager; the women consist of an aged aristocrat and her unhappy daughter, a charlady, the bank manager's wife, and a waitress.

"Finally there is a merchant seaman. As we wait for them to enter a walled city barely visible thousands of feet below we become acquainted with these nine people. They descend into the city: a city which the audience is never permitted to see. Two remain — the charlady and the unhappy daughter.

"The remainder leave.

"That is all. Nothing else happens. Yet what has transpired is a daring story about real people and how they behave when confronted with the world emerging from the war, with all its difficulties, confusions, disappointments, promise and boundless inevitability.

"For the city is a symbol: it is the new world, successor of the world of yesterday, the tomorrow of centuries that is becoming today.

"The theme of *They Came to the City* is that people will react to new conditions much according to their established circumstances.

"The characters are typical. The charlady, an amalgamation of the poor and oppressed, enters it confidently. The unhappy daughter synthesizing the millions of professional and white collar individuals who find living futile discovers new vitality and purpose.

"But the aristocrats and the financier are terrified. They have seen their own security struck a death blow. The baronet who hates 'people' is mortally afraid. The businessman is goaded to fury when he learns that the inhabitants of the city consider profit-making a crime. The bank manager, thrilled as he is, turns his back because he is reluctant to give up his present profitable income.

"Far different reasons influence the last two — the waitress and the seaman. They would like to remain but they know someone must tell the world what the city is really like. Intuitively they know that the vicious reports of the others will have to be counteracted. The task they undertake is not easy, even in contemplation.

"They know that there will be dark days ahead, that they will be rebuffed by many and misunderstood by more, that there will be days when they themselves will doubt what they saw.

"Nonetheless they return. They have seen a city, a world where social justice is a profound reality. Fortified by that supreme fact, they are prepared to take any risks.

"There is no such thing, and never was, as an 'art for art's sake.' All art is a product of its times and the peoples of that time. It is a multi-coloured expression of what people want, see, believe, and think. It is the reflection and explanation of the present and the accumulations of yesterday that make up the present and a preview of the future.

"When an artist praises a moribund way of life in order to stave off its successor he is, wittingly or not, betraying the principles of artistic integrity that he espouses.

"When, perplexed by human weakness and angered by human imperfections, he seeks sanctuary in an 'ivory tower,' he harms himself, not humanity.

"When he gives the people what profit-gorging bosses order him to give instead of what they know is right, he is corrupting himself even more than he corrupts the people.

"All the more reason, therefore, to salute an achievement, which, despite its many weaknesses, does not compromise with the integrity of art.

"Its heroes are the 'little people' whom it is all the fashion to scorn these days. Its strength is derived from its recognition of the 'little people' as the invincibles of society, the only ones able to greet the new world.

"*They Came to the City* courageously grapples with the realities of this sadly confused world of ours. Not many motion pictures, even the better ones, have done so with such basic clarity and confidence.

"Our hope is that it will reach broader audiences than it has hitherto done and that it will serve as an inspiration to the many fine artists in the motion picture business who are manufacturing the glossy, trivial fare which passes for art in Hollywood and other film centres today."[29]

In some respects, posthumous exhumation of a writer's early work and exposure of it to detailed examination smacks more of autopsy than criticism, and yet, if one agrees with John Simon's dictum that all criticism may reveal as much about the writer as it does his subject, it has a definite value.

The above review, for example, while it contains a number of stock dialectical phrases about "profit-gorging bosses" and some easy moralizing, gives the unmistakable impression of the Marxist tail wagging the cultural dog.

For one thing, it contains an early and excellent little defence of the value of "film" over that of "the movies"* and it is written in a way that makes one curious about the picture: after reading the review, you'd still like to see it. Also, one clearly gets the impression that Cohen was writing about something that was on his mind, rather than simply reviewing a film for the edification of the masses; he does not, among other things, bother to mention where it can be seen.

The real keynote of his piece, in fact, seems to be an increasing concern with the integrity of art, and of the artist; a concern which in all likelihood mirrors his own increasing struggle with the problem of how one places one's own "art" at the service of a worthwhile social end while at the same time retaining one's individuality.

And there is little doubt that for this young man who was fiercely determined to express himself individualistically, his working life since leaving school — first

* See John Simon's introduction to *Movies Into Film*, The Dial Press, New York, 1971 for further expansion of this idea.

within the confines of the labour movement, then under the stultifying discipline of the Communist Party, and now, locked into the ethnocentricity of the Jewish press — was becoming a problem.

Temperamentally, Cohen was always inclined towards expressing a universal, rather than a particular, viewpoint. Of course, like all men, he had to begin from his own starting points of birthplace, tradition and religion, before he could move on to more universal concerns. His university days, his work with the Cape Breton miners, and even his working in one of Canada's major cities had all expanded his horizons — but it is perhaps still within the religious traditions of his Jewish boyhood that we can find a clue to something of his temperament.

Judaism, although in some of its forms as bigoted and restrictive as any other religion, also contains a beautiful and vital sense of universality. Author Herbert Tarr, for example, cites the exquisite *Midrash* in which, according to ancient rabbinical tradition, God reproaches His angels for breaking into songs of celebration when the Egyptians were drowning in the Red Sea. (Pointing to the drowned Egyptians, God thunders: "How *dare* you celebrate when my children are lying dead upon the seashore!"); and the traditional answer to the question of why God created only one man, Adam, at the beginning of the world is: "in order that no man afterwards should be able to say, 'My ancestors were better than yours.' As all human beings are traced back to one parent, all human beings must necessarily be brothers."[30]

Such a universal outlook most likely had become an intrinsic part of Cohen's character, transcending the boundaries of both religion and politics. As a result, he felt as restricted in the role of a "professionally Jewish" writer as he did as a professional Marxist. Only when he began to review theatre, was he able to resolve at least some of these conflicts, and discover his own distinctive voice.

Cohen's first theatrical review appeared in the *Wochenblatt* in 1946. A review of Eugene O'Neill's *Ah, Wilderness!*, it was typical of his early efforts in that it praised the Toronto cast and production but took exception to the weakness of the play:

"Eugene O'Neill's *Ah, Wilderness!* as performed by members of the New Play Society in Toronto last week, was a brisk, professional affair that Broadway producers would have envied.

"It was the best-acted, best-directed amateur production we have ever seen in Toronto. Directed by the CBC luminary Andrew Allan and acted by a cast taken largely from radio, it was handsomely costumed and paced.

"The success of the production was all the more remarkable when one considers that the stage of the Royal Ontario Museum is small and cramped for a play. Nonetheless, the actors carried off their assignments in fine style.

"Bud Knapp as Nat Miller was easily the outstanding character actor, although Tom Tweed and Glen Burns gave him stiff competition.

"O'Neill women rarely being impressive, the female cast did well with stereotyped roles.

"It is a pity, though, that a group of such obvious talents as the New Play Society should waste them on a play as weak as *Ah, Wilderness!*

"O'Neill is a playwright whose contempt for humanity, sombre hatred for the modern world, and craving for the past has endeared him to pessimists the world over. His melancholia prevails in what is purported to be a humorous story about American 'plain people' around the turn of the century.

"All of the characters who are supposed to be genuine and plain are exaggerated by O'Neill. They fall into his regular mold: that is to say, they are types and symbols, never real people. One does not laugh with them, one laughs at them."[31]

This early, rather tentative review, while probably accurate enough, was also in its own way quite clever. By its kudos to the cast and production, it was almost certain to bring Cohen to the attention of Toronto's rather small, quasi-professional theatre community of the time, yet by attacking O'Neill, a major playwright, he may have felt he had preserved both his critical integrity and independence of thought. His dislike of O'Neill's attitude as a dramatist was genuine, and it is doubtful that Cohen's comments were merely designed to get him attention.

But while his views as a theatre critic were rather quickly to establish a growing reputation, his political writing could be incredibly non-critical, especially when it came to the Soviet Union, in the late 1940's. In January of 1947, for example, he began an article which dealt with the importance of socialism to Jews, with the following:

"V.I. Lenin had a mind as sharp as the honed edge of a blade, a heart as all-embracing as humanity, and a vision issuing from the hopes of mankind, which he saw being realized in his lifetime...

"Like the man who succeeded him, Joseph Stalin, Lenin was brilliant as a strategist, an enemy of everything which endangered or was not in the interest of the people..."

The article ended: "Today the Soviet Union is a mighty

skyscraper amid a host of slums . . . it is the future — and it works."[32]

In another article, he praised the Russian magazine *Heymland*, which, he argued, "truly expresses the character of Soviet Jewry."

"In not one issue of the magazine," Cohen wrote, "were the following subjects discussed: local anti-Semitism, job discrimination, social prejudice, or the pressing need for Jewish unity within the borders of the country. . .

"The reason Heymland ignores them is because these problems do not exist in the U.S.S.R.[*]

"The Jewish citizen of the Soviet Union is consequently a prototype of the Jew of Tomorrow. Because of that he seems strange to many of us. We are not accustomed to the idea that the future should co-exist with the present."[33]

Given the genuinely incredible nature of passages such as those quoted above, it is small wonder that Cohen felt himself restricted in writing within the orthodox Marxist viewpoint. After all, the time was the late 1940's, not the early 1930's, and despite the fact that Cohen was only in his early 20's, he had already shown himself to have a good grasp of international affairs, and there was ample evidence to contradict the utopian picture he was painting. The charitable view is that rather than "flirting with Communism," Cohen vigorously embraced it and was writing out of genuine conviction. Be that as it may, he was not even "doing intellectual work for the Party," but simply hacking out propaganda; and given his character, it's hard to believe he didn't know it. Perhaps, after all, he was only coping with the basic problem faced by every freelance journalist sooner or later, whether he or she

* Cohen's italics.

ends up taking an assignment from a large-circulation periodical or a public relations firm.

As Cohen himself put it: "... I had to earn a living."

Nevertheless, during that same period, Cohen was severely critical of the mainline press for surrendering its independence:

"A hundred years ago," he wrote, "it was possible for the press to be free because then all it needed was a couple of hundred dollars, a man who could handle hand-set type, and an editor who was a reporter, proofreader, advertising man, distributor and sometimes pressman rolled into one.

"Those were the days when William Lyon Mackenzie could edit his own paper or when Joseph Howe could roll his voice like thunder across the pages of his paper in Nova Scotia.

"But capitalism's progress struck the death blow to that kind of newspaper. As industry and commerce made gains, publishing a daily newspaper became a more expensive proposition. Journalism reflected the industrialized age. It became the concern of financiers and money-buccaneers.

"As the newspapers came under their control their character and politics changed. Once it was the task of a newspaper to print the news factually.

"Today most of them 'slant' their news in the interests of their owners. Once the newspaper editor spoke out in the interests of the people, defended their privileges, extended their interests...

"There was a William Lyon MacKenzie to indict the family compact... a Papineau to denounce hierarchical rule. Today it is different.

"The myth of Canada's press is expounded with vigour by the newspapers themselves. But in truth their character contradicts their assertions. With the exceptions of the forthcoming *Daily Tribune* and possibly the Glace Bay *Gazette*, Canadians are obliged to face the fact that daily publications of this country are actually sounding-boards and conveyors of misinformation deliberately designed to delude them, hold them back, exaggerate the unimportant, hide and conceal what is actually happening, spawning an atmosphere of fear and political ignorance behind which Big Business, of which the press is a vital cog, forges ahead unchecked."[34]

There is a good deal of irony in the fact that the man who wrote those lines would one day be chiefly remembered as an employee of the biggest newspaper in the country, the Toronto *Star*. The irony wasn't lost on Cohen, either. "My God, I've been co-opted," he exclaimed, the first year his income exceeded $10,000.

If Cohen could be acerbic in his social criticism, he could also be prophetic, as he illustrated in this 1947 item on the growing influence of the military on American affairs:

"More than a year ago, in an article on this very page, I referred to the alarming growth in the United States of military control over and intervention in, civil affairs," he wrote in his column "Turning Pages."

"With unusual haste, President Truman was summoning army and navy leaders to become ambassadors, undersecretaries, and consuls. This situation, I said then, was entirely incompatible with the theory that the United States was a civil republic, directed and supervised by persons elected from the population itself. The founders of the American state tried to guard against the country ever becoming controlled by officers; for this reason the President was made commander-in-chief of all the armed forces. The assumption was that this would frustrate any effort of military usurpation.

"The state of affairs has become considerably more

serious since I last wrote about it. Today, according to Hanson Baldwin, at least fifteen members of the soldiery occupy what were formerly exclusively civilian positions. The most outstanding is, of course, Marshall, the secretary of state. Placing a general in charge of foreign policy is a practice entirely alien to other democratic countries.

"But this is only the beginning. The army and navy chiefdom have now accorded to themselves unique privileges. They insist on their right to do as they please; the slightest criticism of their actions is branded as treason. For daring to criticise the army's recruiting program one senator was smeared by an 'unidentified' officer as an agent of the Communists!

"Congressmen who denounced the granting of additional moneys to the Navy were impudently castigated for their 'treacherous conduct.'

"Not only is the military itself raised to the level of a Brahmin caste, but militarism is on its way to becoming America's new religion."[35]

Subsequent U.S. history, from the "Cold War" and McCarthy era through to the debacle of the Vietnam war has proven this assessment of the disastrous consequences of the military's involvement with government to be correct. And however commonplace the ideas are today — with the 20/20 hindsight of experience — it took a certain amount of audacity, not to say courage, for a young freelance journalist to express them in the late 1940's, when dissidents on both sides of the border were viewed as a threat.

However, Cohen, who had by this time already begun to make something of a name for himself in Toronto circles because of his theatrical reviews, was also increasingly turning to the importance of art as a counterweight against the rigidity of hardline political dogma and doctrine. In a later column devoted to the American poet Sol Funaroff (who died in 1942), Cohen even took an oblique swipe at the concept, so dear to doctrinaire leftists of the time, that all art should "speak for the people":

"It would be going too far to say that he was a great poet," Cohen wrote, "but great poets are very rare in our age. Industrial rapacity has squeezed their hearts out, flattening their melodies, draining them of their natural exuberance, encrusting their emotions with glacial upholstery, transforming them into intellectual experimenters or dilettante poetasters.

"Funaroff belonged to that privileged class which, realizing that poetry is meant to be read aloud, and not just printed on paper, believed that poetry should speak to the people, as well as for them."[36]

Cohen also tried his own hand at poetry, in a memorial to the dead of the Warsaw ghetto:

Ancestral heroes sired in sorrow
Mothers who did not see tomorrow
Children forced to die so young
Men whose saga but now is sung:
Should it befall that we forget
The fate which unto you was met
And dare to truth turn weak deaf ear,
Surrendering all to craven fear —
Make us recall!

Ghetto deceased, make us recall
How once you ate of wood and gall,
When the Nazi cracked his sullen whip
And snorted through his simian lip,
And when he bade you squirm and kneel
And lick his brutish, bloody heel
Until you rose in thousands strong,
Rebels in arms against the wrong —
Make us recall!

Remind us how, on Pesach day,
Captive Jews declined to pray
And made Warsaw streets run red
With the blood of tyrants dead,
Took up the challenge, met the foe,
Flung away their cloaks of woe,
Choosing instead to die as men
Who never would be slaves again —
Make us recall!

O modest martyrs of unknown name
Sheathed in history's holy flame,
Folk of courage, age and breadth
Undaunted by the face of death,
Inspire us with your sacred light
Make us stronger than the might
Of iron monsters planes and fire
And killers robed in gay attire —
Make us recall!

Now hear my prayer, hear my plea
You humble builders of liberty,
Guide us forever, along the way
To mankind's brighter, better day
But if we to truth turn weak deaf ear
Surrendering to coward's fear,
Should we dismiss or, worse, forget,
Make us recall our matchless debt —
Make us recall![37]

Unfortunately, despite the tragic nature of his subject, Cohen's emotional reach exceeds his technical grasp, and the poem is little more than versifying — and derivative versifying at that;* perhaps realizing it, he seems to have ceased attempts to publish his poetry.

As Cohen-the-critic came into prominence, Cohen-the-political-analyst receded into the background, al-

---

* The influence of John McCrae's "In Flanders Fields" is obvious.

though he was never to entirely disappear. Nineteen years later, in 1966, he was to treat his listeners to this explanation of how his youthful indignation and moral outrage over politics — or more particularly politicians — had mellowed into an attitude of rather whimsical disgust:

"How," he asked, "can I work myself up about a show at the Royal Alex or the Crest or the O'Keefe Centre or wherever, when the cabinet ministers, the ex-cabinet ministers and the other members of parliament are cutting up as they are in the House of Commons, at press conferences, and in off-the-record stories to the press. Was there ever such a spectacle?*

"I know I am supposed to feel high indignation and moral wrath at these events, but overall, everything about them is high comedy ... no, not high comedy, low comedy ... and that is the only way in which they can be regarded.

"I have always denied the proposition that Canadians lack a sense of humour. Maybe we don't realize we are being funny ... but funny we certainly are as the conduct in the House is demonstrating to the world.

"When Mr. Pearson was first made leader of the Liberal Party of Canada, I said in a radio broadcast that Canadians would one day realize how right the American people were in refusing to make the late Adlai Stevenson president... Mr. Stevenson and Mr. Pearson being so much of a kind.

"And for saying that I came in for a great deal of censure. But in that prediction history has vindicated me all the way.

* This was at the time of two celebrated spy-cases, one involving a postal clerk, George Victor Spencer, the other a German call-girl named Gerda Munsinger.

"When I was much younger, I took Canadian politics very seriously. I still do, but nothing on earth will convince me to feel the same way about politicians, beginning with Mr. Pearson and Mr. Diefenbaker.

"They're in the wrong line of work altogether ... and that's why the Canadian political scene today shouldn't be reported by political correspondents, but by drama critics and show business columnists.

"If they have the strength to keep up with it."[38]

And he was to write of Prime Minister Pierre Trudeau, in 1970:

" ... Surely it is exquisitely comic that at a time when we are addicted to the cult of youth, our country and our youth should choose a middle-aged, conservative bachelor millionaire as a symbol of a swinging new day..."[39]

Yet, as we have seen, the youthful Cohen did take his politics extremely seriously from his college days onward, and an element of political criticism and a certain sympathy for socialism continued to play an important part in all his writing.

Two things were to happen to Cohen in 1947 which were to finally settle his mind on becoming a professional theatre critic, rather than continuing as an incipient I.F. Stone. One was his marriage that year to the former Gloria Brontman, and the other was his attendance at a production of Toronto's New Play Society.

Cohen and Gloria Brontman met in October, 1946, when she was assistant editor of *Canadian Woman* and he editor of the English section of the *Wochenblatt*. They were married the following June. Cohen was an intensely private man who doted on his family (two daughters, Phyllis and Susan) and treasured the sense of stability it was to give his life. Of his marriage, Cohen would write to actor Sean Mulcahy, on the eve of the actor's own nuptials:

"I hope your marriage will be at least as felicitous as my own, now entering its 24th year of reasonably conjugal contentment and the absolute certainty that both my wife and I made the right decision."[40]

And of the New Play Society's performance, Cohen was to publicly credit actress Nancy Pyper's magnificent delineation of Juno in Sean O'Casey's *Juno and the Paycock* at the Royal Ontario Museum theatre in 1947 as the motivating factor in his decision to concentrate on theatre criticism:

"That was a fine production of a fine, fine play," Cohen remembered in a 1967 broadcast, "and the best thing about it was Miss Pyper's strong, plain, poetic and magnetically vital characterization of the woman, wife, and mother who holds on even as the only world she knows is collapsing about her.

"I have seen much good — and some great acting since then — I have seen theatre in many lands — but the memory of Miss Pyper as she leaves her home for the last time is as vivid ... as clear ... to me now as when I first saw her give it.

"Indeed, more than anything else, it was her performance that turned me to drama criticism. I was anxious to try and describe her portrayal in words and tell people about her. And so for better or worse Miss Pyper was a major force in the direction my life took."[41]

As he sat with his massive six-foot-plus frame crammed into that seat in the crowded little theatre, and watched, hypnotized, while O'Casey's drama of poverty, death and revolution unfolded before him, twenty-three-old Nathan Cohen was moved to tears.[42]

He may have recalled his own experiences amid the

grime and poverty of Cape Breton's miners and their families; his own attempts to create better conditions, a better, cleaner world, and how they were becoming twisted in the service of doctrinaire political hacks.

He may even have thought about his own illness, which cut short his law career and still sent chilling little tremors to his heart; of the brevity and brutality of much of life, and the need for a man to leave some kind of mark.

And yet, when he emerged from the theatre, still terribly moved, and walked along Bloor Street in the crisp air filled with the sound of streetcars clanking their way under a crisscross canopy of overhead wires, he was also tremendously elated. He had caught a vision, for the first time, really, of the power of the theatre as an art form. Not just as a medium for entertainment — like his university productions — but as a vehicle for beauty and truth which could send him out of the performance aching to share his experience there with others. It was the very stuff of life, presented through the medium of living flesh and intellect, right before his eyes.

He was a writer; this is what he would write about, and to hell with the polemics that didn't seem to change anything, when it came down to that. And if there were flaws in the way a drama was presented, surely pointing them out would only add to the play's purity.

Tentatively, but with increasing firmness after that night, Cohen was to get a grip on what it was that he had really been looking for in the stimulating and frustrating years since he'd left university. He had begun by trying to learn a writer's trade in college and, as a working journalist (despite his brief fling at turning out propaganda), he was turning it into a craft. As a critic, he was to finally find a sense of vocation.

Speaking of Canadian artists of the calibre of Nancy Pyper and New Play Society founder-director Dora

Mavor Moore, Cohen remarked, with reference to his own career:

"We are all in their debt for what they have done to maintain the idea of theatre in Toronto. And I am especially in their debt for what, as artists and as people, they taught me."[43]

For all his boundless optimism about writing professionally on theatre in Canada as he walked home that night in 1947, Cohen already realized that both he and the theatrical community still had a tremendous amount to learn about theatre — and criticism.

3

THE WAY WE WERE

Even after Nathan Cohen had decided that he wanted to become a professional drama critic, he still faced the problem of whether there was enough theatre available in Toronto to provide work for a full-time reviewer. For years, the standing joke in Canadian arts circles had been that while Japanese critics could at least discuss the merits of both Kabuki and Noh theatre, in this country there was simply No Theatre, to speak of. There were, of course, the inevitable British and American touring companies, amateur productions, and a small nucleus of semi-professional actors, writers and directors who performed mostly in radio dramas. But, such sporadic efforts notwithstanding, the seriously inclined critic was forced to face the fact that Canadian theatre — as distinct from "theatre" in Canada — was to all intents and purposes nonexistent.

The history of theatrical performances in Canada,

Cohen reminds us*, can be traced back to 1604, when Marc Lescot produced an open-air pageant called *La Théâtre De Neptune* at Port Royal, in Acadia. In French-Canada, amateurs were staging productions of Corneille's plays in 1651 and, because of censorship, trying and failing to stage Molière's *Tartuffe* by the late 1660's. In English Canada, on the other hand, indigenous amateur theatre was almost totally absent.

Robert Gourlay, in his *A Statistical Account of Upper Canada*, illustrates the dearth of theatrical performances in the 1820's by declaring that Canada was "... too young for regular theatre entertainments and those delicacies and refinements of luxury which are the usual attendants of wealth."[44]

By the mid 1870's Canadians in Toronto, Montreal and other large centres were treated from time to time to the appearance of various British, American and even some Canadian travelling companies, but even the better productions were scarcely appreciated by their audiences:

"We take our amusements sadly, someone has said, and the remark is one that may truly be made of the manner in which the patrons of the drama in Canada enjoy their occasional evenings at the theatre," the writer observed in the December, 1875, issue of *The Canadian Monthly and National Review*.

"But with even the best entertainments provided at our opera houses, their success owes little to the sympathy and appreciation of the audience.

"The houses are cold in their recognition of effort: the audience spiritless and indifferent in showing its acceptance of the play, and utterly lacking in that

---

*For much of the general outline which follows, we are indebted to Cohen's own lecture, *Theatre in Canada: An Expendable Commodity* given at York University, 1970. (Unpublished.)

contagious feeling of pleasure and satisfaction which good acting merits, and is entitled to receive...

"There is little desire to come to the play actuated by an intelligent interest in the drama or from sympathy with its history and traditions, or from the motives of comparing actor with actor, in the rendition of their parts. Only from the lower motives of seeking an easily satisfied pleasure, or to pass an otherwise tedious evenings do we find the bulk of our theatre audience drawn to the house."

Former actor and CBC drama producer Murray D. Edwards, who quotes the above passage in his book *A Stage in Our Past: English Language Theatre in Eastern Canada from the 1790's to 1914* remarks that the writer's observations "have a prophetic ring familiar to anyone concerned with theatre in Canada today."[45]

In discussing the career of actor Denman Thompson, who successfully toured Canada in his production *Joshua Whitcomb* in 1876, Edwards again strikes a theme familiar to those interested in Canadian culture:

"It is aggravating," Edwards writes, "but typical that Thompson, who spent so much time in Canada and who obviously developed his skill as an actor performing for Canadians, should have chosen to develop an American character. However, this was, and still seems to be, the trend. A Canadian performer who achieves a certain stature inevitably seeks wider acclaim. To achieve international importance, he must conquer the theatrical centres of the English-speaking world, and to do this he must develop his material in a manner and style accepted by those centres."[46]

When the commercial theatre did begin to grow in Canada, in the 1880's and 90's, few Canadians were to share in the profits. As is the case with the movie companies of today, the American and — at that time —

British touring companies held a virtual monopoly on Canada's theatres. They sent the shows in, and carted the money out:[47]

"Of the hundreds of touring companies travelling in Canada during this period, few were Canadians," Edwards writes. "Both the lack of interest on the part of Canadians in native talent and the fact that local groups were unable to compete financially with the more established English and American companies accounts for this."[48]

But something else accounts for the lack of success of the Canadian companies as well, as Edwards further records:

"The Canadian touring companies did not prove to be exceptional in any way. They did not establish any significant standards in presentation or in the acting and their choice of plays is disappointing. . . No experiments were made. No play by Ibsen, Shaw, Galsworthy or Pinero was produced by them."[49]

Canadian touring companies failed also to aid in the development of Canadian plays or playwrights, even within the context of the comedy and melodrama favoured as entertainment by Canadian audiences. The innate conservatism of Canadian audiences also seems to have inhibited even experimental productions of playwrights such as Ibsen and Shaw, for example, and Edwards concludes: "The forces against the theatre were many and vocally effective. Unfortunately there were not a sufficient number of sophisticated and well-educated theatre supporters to create a demand for what the bourgeois considered questionable. There were too few people willing to accept the theatre as an art. To most Canadians it was just a pastime; to some an unnecessary evil. . ."[50]

Sadly, this is a conclusion to which one returns time

and time again, up to and including current history. Robert Gourlay's phrase about Canada being a "young" country is still repeated *ad infinitum*, *ad nauseam* today by both its youthful and ageing cultural *Wunderkinds* who spend far too much time being graduate students of their own identity crisis.

In any event, this adolescent carping about the "youthfulness" of Canada — particularly when used as an excuse for clearly second-rate artistic accomplishments — continues to make the country an international intellectual laughing-stock; London *Times* critic Bernard Levin, for one, was quite right in his recent reaction to it. The perennial Canadian cry of "youth," in Levin's view, is based more on rhetoric than reason:

"If I hear the phrase 'We are a young country' once more, I shall scream," Levin told a conference on the arts in Ottawa. "When faced with a work of art and with the responsibility of judging it, I don't want to see its passport. Whether a work of art comes from an old country, a young country or a middle-aged country not only is not, but should not be, our concern."[51]

Unfortunately, in cultural as well as political terms, Canada is — and has always been—a middle-aged country, built on the values of middle-aged conservative men, and those values are continually reflected in its attitude toward its art and artists, and frequently by the artists themselves. The "young" countries today — in the sense that Canadians misuse the word — are to be found within the so-called Third World, notably in black Africa, with its almost Elizabethan sense of energy and political flux.

This is not simply a metaphor. It also applies to attitudes toward the arts. For example, former Toronto *Star* entertainment writer Morris Duff, now a university professor in Lagos, Nigeria, recently described how crowds of ordinary Africans responded to outdoor productions of Shakespeare's *Julius Caesar* and *Macbeth* (both dramas of civil war) with the same sort of spontaneous identification that was displayed by the lower class English crowds in the pit of Shakespeare's day. To them, the plays are not "classic," but contemporary. Such distinctions were rarely lost on Nathan Cohen, who regarded theatre as much more than a form of social "play," but, as we shall see, they were invariably lost on his audiences.

To return to a time when the country was younger in years, if not in attitudes, the touring companies remained the chief — if not the sole — providers of theatre in Canada until after World War I. And although some of the resident stock companies held on until the mid-1930's,[52] the development of the talking picture and the Depression finally led to their demise. In their day, those troupes had been popular, and had frequently provided work for some local Canadian actors; but they left behind no discernible heritage in terms of playwrights and actors who influenced the community, developed an artistic identity of their own, or passed on anything of value to future generations of Canadians.[53]

Following World War I, amateur theatre began to fill in the gaps left by the rapidly vanishing repertory companies, and some of these amateur groups at least attempted to perform plays by Canadian authors. During the 1920's, for instance, a succession of original Canadian plays were presented at the University of Toronto's Hart House, which also printed volumes of full-length and one-act plays by Canadians. The results, however, despite receiving the plaudits of culture-buffs such as Vincent Massey, were far from auspicious.

"The saddest part of this shockingly bad collection,*"

*The volumes are still gathering dust at Toronto's Central Reference Library.

Nathan Cohen suggested in 1970, "is the optimistic introduction by Vincent Massey, so confident that the work had quality, so certain that here at last was Canadian drama coming of age.

"Not one of these plays survives as an actable work, not one has any value even as a literary piece. But the enthusiasm and hopes did not diminish. The illusions persisted. When I was going to high school I was required to study a one-act play called *Drought*, about which all I now remember is that it had something to do with famine, the depression, and a woman going mad in Saskatchewan, and *Brothers in Arms*, a one-act farce by Merrill Denison... Both of course long ago vanished from the repertoire of Canadian drama groups."[54]

Despite the lack of worthwhile indigenous plays, there were a number of Canadians who made money writing for the theatre — including Montreal lawyer W.A. Tremayne who turned out a sizeable number of melodramas for the American stage in the 1890's — although there was very little which was distinctively Canadian in their work.[55]

Even the optimistic Vincent Massey, writing in a 1922 issue of *Queen's Quarterly*, had few illusions about the prospects for future Canadian drama:

"It is as easy to be witty about Canadian drama as about the Canadian Navy*," he commented. "Each at the moment may seem to represent a well-meaning but insignificant effort to complete our national equipment — to suggest a pious aspiration rather than reality."[56]

Massey also exhibited a realistic, if bourgeois grasp of the problems besetting Canadian amateur companies when he added:

* A few castoff former British Navy vessels.

"Amateur theatre suffers from two evils — preciousness in art and instability in finance. If commercial theatre errs in trying to give the public what it wants, amateur theatre makes the frequent mistake of giving its public what it thinks it ought to want — often sublimely confident that food to be wholesome must be unpalatable."[57]

In an essay on nationalism and drama written in 1929, playwright Merrill Denison was amusingly but unmistakably disgusted with the idea that a distinctively Canadian brand of theatre was even possible:

"I find writing about Canadian theatre or drama depressingly like discussing the art of dinghy sailing among the Bedouins," Denison wrote.

"There is so little to be said on the subject save to point out why there in none...

"It is not at all surprising that there should be no Canadian drama.

"One's surprise comes from learning that anyone could have seriously believed there could be a Canadian drama. Let it be noted to the credit of the mass of Canadian citizenry that but a small fraction of its number has ever concerned itself about the matter. It has been a fancy of a very special and narrow group which, for want of a better name, may be called intellectuals..."[58]

In Denison's view, Canadian culture — with the possible exception of Quebec's — was either colonial or American; with the balance shifting toward the American because of a similarity of lifestyle. Denison concluded that until the national intentions of Canada are greatly clarified, the theatre would at best be an artificial graft supported with as great a travail of spirit and purse as a native orange industry:

"But there is this to say about a native theatre: in a

discussion of none other of the arts are the realities of our cultural pretences brought so sharply into focus."*⁵⁹

The amateurs persisted, however, and by 1930, amateur theatre in Canada had entered into what some commentators — notably Betty Lee, author of *Love and Whiskey: The Story of the Dominion Drama Festival* — still refer to as its golden age. Sparked by the efforts of an Englishman with the resoundingly theatrical name of Vere Brabazon Ponsonby — a millionaire margarine manufacturer and fanatical theatre-buff who as the Ninth Earl of Bessborough became Governor General in the early 1930's — the Dominion Drama Festival was born. The DDF, a cross-Canada cavalcade of social-climbers, dilettantes, and genuinely dedicated would-be professionals with nowhere to go in the Great Canadian Cultural Desert, began, in true Stanley Cup style, with its first national "playoffs" in 1933.

Almost immediately, the Festival was recognized as a major social — if not artistic — contribution to Canadian cultural life, but there were also the skeptics, like critic B.K. Sandwell, who on the eve of the first finals wrote in *Saturday Night*:

"It may be doubted whether a Canadian drama can ever be developed on a purely amateur basis.

"The players are all right; plenty of them are just as good as the average on the professional stage. The playwrights might achieve a considerable height of excellence without becoming exclusively dependent on their royalties for a living. But the direction still remains a problem.

"Without it, the other two elements will never get

*In reprinting Denison's essay in 1975, the editors of *Canadian Theatre Review* remark: "Perhaps the greatest tribute CTR can pay to Denison is to point out that his perceptions are still valid nearly half a century later."

anywhere. It must be competent, original, experienced, creative. It must also be continuous over a considerable period of time. Institutions such as Hart House and, in lesser degree, the Ottawa Little Theatre ... can make a large contribution towards this need. Can they do enough? And are they, and is their public, greatly interested in this particular objective? A Canadian drama whose sole impelling motive is a rather self-conscious patriotism is not likely to get very far; and at present that does seem to be the chief preoccupation among both workers and followers in this sphere of our national art."[60]

Whatever else the Dominion Drama Festival was to accomplish, it at least provided a national exposure for an increasing number of Canadians whose aim was the development of an indigenous professional theatre — among them, actor-producer Andrew Allan, who appeared in an award-winning Hart House production of *His Widow's Husband* in 1935, and actor Alan King, whose appearance in a production at the Victoria regional playoff in 1933 prompted him to work his way to Toronto as a guard for the Canadian National Railway, in the hopes of finding professional work.[61]

No matter how successful each annual series of DDF finals became, however, there was still the problem of funding, and the indifference of large and diverse segments of the Canadian public to theatrical events, particularly those controlled by a cultural and social elite. Cultural mandarin Vincent Massey, for example, was in the habit of approaching some of Canada's industrial magnates when funds were short, but even then the reaction was frequently mixed.

In July of 1935, Massey found that he needed $750 to balance the Festival's books. He wrote to Colonel R.S. McLaughlin, asking him to contribute the money, and pointing out that it would mark an embarrassing end to Bessborough's term in Canada if his favourite project wound up in the red. McLaughlin, head of General Motors of Canada, replied:

"It is easy to understand why you and His Excellency are so deeply interested in affairs of this nature ... But how could you even guess that a country boy like myself living way out in the suburbs would be much, if any, interested in an affair of this kind requires some imagination.

"However, if you think I should make a contribution, call on me for anything within reason. Say $100?"[62]

The Festival did, however, scrape through the next four years, until it was eclipsed by the larger drama of the Second World War. After the war, the DDF resumed its operations in 1947 with a great fanfare of publicity but, as Betty Lee suggests, "those last months of 1935 marked the end of the beginning."[63]

Perhaps author and playwright Robertson Davies best summed up the DDF's contribution during those lean years:

"Though the DDF never succeeded in bringing a Canadian drama into being, it kept the whole country aware of what was being done in world theatre. . .

"Thanks to the Dominion Drama Festival, Canada was never without a theatre."[64]

Nevertheless, like all blessings, those of the DDF were not unalloyed. The prevailing atmosphere of amateurism — that of theatre as a social, rather than an artistic, endeavour — was to continue to permeate theatrical circles in Canada long after the Festival's resumption at the end of the war. And an attitude of rivalry — not to say downright hatred — on the part of the upstaged amateurs against the upstart professionals who were beginning to take over the spotlight, was to impede the development of full-time regional theatre across the country.

During the war years, when the DDF lay dormant, events occurred which were to have a more immediate effect on Canadian cultural life than the rather mandarin-oriented Festival was ever to achieve, and those events centred around the exposure of millions of Canadians to the relatively new medium of the Canadian Broadcasting Corporation's radio network — and the work of a young actor, writer, and director, Andrew Allan.

Former CBC luminary Harry J. Boyle described the pivotal nature of Allan's contribution in a 1974 reminiscence:

"In those days Canada was still a series of relatively small cities, towns and hamlets with a majority of people living in rural areas," Boyle recalled.

"It was connected by two railroads and the Canadian Broadcasting Corporation, founded in 1936, which had been thrust into war-reporting before it could really find its feet. In those days Canada had no national drama; American and English touring companies played the principal cities.

"Radio was noted for commentaries, an emerging news service, regional farm service, and propaganda-oriented documentaries or variety shows selling War Savings Bonds — using American headliners.

"In those days too, radio drama owed more to the traditional theatre than anything, and in Canada the only excitement tended to revolve around the appearance of foreign theatrical stars.

"Then suddenly one Sunday night in 1944 the *Stage 1* series went on the air, and the Canadian cultural scene had changed forever."[65]

Allan, a sometimes haughty, remorselessly intellectual man, had gotten into radio writing almost by accident during the Depression. He would sell a one-hour play for as much as $25 and appear in it as an actor for $10 more;[66] and during the 1930's had written and directed Canada's first soap-opera, *The Family Doctor*, starring full-time lawyer and part-time actor Frank Peddie whom he had met at the Dominion Drama Festival.

After a peripatetic start oscillating between Canada and the United Kingdom, Allan settled down in Vancouver in 1940 as a CBC radio producer. In those days, Vancouver was the headquarters for a genuinely fantastic array of talent, most of it centred around CBC radio, which included writers Fletcher Markle and Lister Sinclair and actors Alan Young, Bernard Braden, Alan Pierce, Larry McCance and the inimitable John Drainie — all of whom were to follow Allan to Toronto when he moved there as Supervisor of Drama for the CBC in 1943.

Beginning with a series of half-hour dramas (*Stage '44*), Allan produced a groundbreaking experiment in native Canadian radio-drama which in the following twelve seasons was to air the work of some sixty-eight fledgling Canadian playwrights and become second in CBC listener-interest only to *Hockey Night In Canada*.[67]

Broadcast "live," each program (lengthened to an hour in 1947) generated an unforgettable sense of immediacy and excitement, and for the first time brought Canadian performers — including Alice Hill, Ruth Springford, Tommy Tweed, Jane Mallett, Bud Knapp, Aileen Seaton, Frank Perry, Lloyd Bochner, Lorne Greene and Barry Morse — to the attention of a mass of Canadian listeners who rarely attended — or were rarely given the opportunity to attend — live theatre.

Concomitantly, when the Dominion Drama Festival

staggered, broke but exuberant, back to life in 1947, Allan's radio dramas helped provide an initial training ground for a whole new generation of Canadian actors who, besides some of those already mentioned, included Eric House, Terry Tweed, John Coghill, Amelia Hall, Johnny Wayne, Frank Shuster, Douglas Rain, Chris Wiggins, Sammy Sales, John Vernon, Ted Follows, William Needles, Paul Soles and Leo Ciceri.

Post-war professional theatre groups — notably Toronto's New Play Society, founded in 1946 — were also beginning to form, but were still drawing their members primarily from the relatively small coterie of Canadian radio actors performing in the city.

Although live theatre in the country was still a tenuous thing, Allan's radio dramas reached into the most out-of-the-way and culture-starved areas of Canada from coast to coast; and his regular repertory company of actors who performed them became known nationally as distinctive voices, if not distinctive personalities in the Hollywood sense. Who, once they had heard it, for example, could fail to recognize the vibrant timbre of Lorne Greene or John Scott? Perhaps the most vivid example of the power those broadcasts exerted on so many of us, is contained in a lovely anecdote of Andrew Allan's.

Allan had once remarked vis-à-vis the so-called "Golden Age of Radio" that "No age is called golden until it is long past. Any age is mainly foot-slogging and twenty-five-hour days. To survive you need a good capacity to absorb disappointments." He was tired and despondent after several seasons on in-fighting at the CBC, and ready to walk away from the *Stage* series. On a train trip to Vancouver, his letter of resignation in his pocket, Allan fell into conversation with a pretty girl who introduced herself and rather startlingly told him "You're the reason I'm here."

"We live on a farm, away up north of Edmonton," the girl explained.

"We're just plain people, I guess. We haven't got any books to speak of, or pictures, or music, or anything. But I have a little radio in my room.

"Every Sunday night I go up there to listen to your plays. All week I wait for that time. It's wonderful. It's a whole new world for me. I began to read books because of your plays — all kinds of books I never thought I'd be interested in. And now I'm on my way to Vancouver to stay with my aunt — and in the fall I'm starting at the university. And it's all because of you and your plays. . ."[68]

Allan tore up his letter of resignation, and went on to produce seven more years of the *Stage* series.

Despite the mass success of CBC radio drama, which was bringing an increasing number of Canadian artists aesthetic, if not financial, satisfaction, there was still a good deal of frustration and bitterness on the subject of Canadian theatre. In the face of the mini-Renaissance apparently beginning in 1947, playwright John Coulter, who ten years previously had won a Dominion Drama Festival award for a play about Ireland, could still exclaim:

"Canadian theatre? What is it? If only playwrights, actors and producers north of Niagara would turn their eyes from Broadway and look around them at a place called Canada! There is inviting subject-matter for plays in prairie droughts and crop-failure, in mining disasters, in the poverty of slum dwellers of city streets or country shacks.

"But accurate reporting of misfortune or disaster or accident is not enough to make a play. And, indeed, what is dark and grievous in the actual circumstances of life has no rightful place on the stage till it is transmuted by art into the very different category of tragic experience.

"True comedy can be as serious as tragedy. A hundred grand plays are waiting for Canadians who will write them. But if there were a great Canadian play, would Canadians bother to stage it —any more than they bother now to stage that first Canadian grand opera, Healey Willan's latest and major work, *Deirdre of the Shadows*?

"Cover it up with Canadian dust and let it lie," Coulter wrote bitterly.

"Some day the Americans or English will do it and tell us not to be ashamed and then, having their word for it, we will tardily take the duster and disinter a work once made in Canada."[69]

Even serious criticism of its arts was, more often than not, approached from the standpoint of anthropology, or even botany — as if the artists were members of a bush-dwelling medicine society or had sprung directly from the earth itself, like some strange variety of plant.

Writing in 1946 of painter A.Y. Jackson, the English author and artist Wyndham Lewis — who had a cruel, neglected time of it in Canada — remarks:

"There is gaiety somewhere in Jackson, but it is rationed. His vision is as austere as his subject matter, which is precisely the hard, puritanic land in which he has lived; with no frills, with all its dismal solitary grandeur and bleak beauty, its bad side deliberately selected rather than its chilly relentings."[70]

That this is nonsense (Lewis was visually tone-deaf: Jackson was painting a lovesong, where Lewis evidently expected to find a squaredance) is unimportant, except to the extent that it indicates the intellectual colonialism with which refugees from Europe's fratricidal culture regarded the arts in the physically "brutal" environment of Canada. It was also a lead eagerly embraced by Canadian academic critics, leaving the odd impression that since the country had no other "culture" of its own, the work of its artists could at least be explained in terms of agriculture. As late as 1964, for instance, Neil Compton, of Sir George Williams University, was still going "back to the land" to explain and, one suspects, justify, the underdeveloped nature of Canadian arts:

"Canada's marginal culture," Compton wrote, "occupying a middle ground between British and American, English and French, civilization and wilderness, appears to form the interpretive and critical, rather than the fiercely creative, intelligence. Life in Canada inculcates a respect for the brutal, objective thusness of nature and an awareness (sometimes a wry one) of the validity of opposition to it.

"Canadians tend to become singers, actors, critics, and diplomats rather than composers, dramatists, poets or political geniuses."[71]

Compton might well have tempered this romantic foolishness by adding that for most people, life in Canada also inculcates a respect for the objective thusness of highly-organized urban living, and an awareness (always a wry one) of the validity of opposition to nature limited to short sabbaticals at the cottage spent swatting mosquitoes and complaining about thunderstorms.

In any event, although the physical environment in which the artist exists may indeed have some bearing on the art he creates — if only in a negative way — the concept, inflated out of all proportion to its significance is still a critical cliché, and in its "harsh environment-harsh art" incarnation has little validity even in the worst of circumstances. Anthropologist Peter Farb, for example, points out that the implements used by northern Eskimos are often beautifully made, and that the fact has interesting implications for theories about the beginnings of art.

"In the far north," Farb writes, "where man must face the constant threat of starvation, where life is reduced to the bare essentials — it turns out that one of the essentials is art."[72]

Farb cites an account by the eighteenth-century explorer and trader Samuel Hearne, who came upon an Indian woman who had been fending for herself for months in the desolate tundra and surviving on what game she could kill:

"It is scarcely possible to conceive that a person in her forlorn condition could be so composed as to contrive or execute anything not absolutely essential to her existence," Hearne observed. "Nevertheless, all her clothing besides being calculated for real service, showed great taste, and no little variety of ornament. The materials, though rude, were very curiously wrought, and so judiciously placed as to make the whole of her garb have a very pleasing, though rather romantic appearance."[73]

Critic Northrop Frye, however, uses the term "environment" in a more correct sense, in the Canadian context, when he speaks of it as a result — rather than a cause — of the artistic temperament:

"In defiance of every geographical and economic law, Canada has made itself not simply a nation but an environment," Frye writes.

"It is only now emerging from its beginnings as a shambling, awkward, absurd country, groping and thrusting its way through incredible distances into the West and North, plundered by profiteers, interrupted by European wars, divided by language, bedevilled by climate, yet slowly and inexorably bringing a culture to life."[74]

Frye's account more or less adequately describes the

general cultural climate in the late 1940's, when the long-deferred aspirations of a generation which had survived both depression and war on a massive scale began making themselves felt beyond the traditional boundaries of class and economics. The description too, is particularly apt in terms of theatre where, as Merrill Denison pointed out, the realities of our cultural pretences are brought so sharply into focus; and where newfound enthusiasm was running high.

If the period was never to become a "Golden Age" of Canadian theatre, it was at least the beginning of a full, rich, spring season, and it was into this environment that Nathan Cohen was making his first exploratory forays.

4

BEGINNING AS A CRITIC

Writing reviews for the mass media is one thing, becoming a critic another, and being recognized as a critic of influence is something else again.

Nathan Cohen's rapid transition from the first to the final category has given rise to its own mythology. Novelist Mordecai Richler, for instance, treats us to one version of the myth in his short, satirical novel *The Incomparable Atuk*, in which Cohen appears as the critic "Seymour Bone:"

"Because he liked going to plays and sleeping in late, he decided to become a drama critic, but nobody would hire him," Richler writes. "So Seymour Bone, investing the last of his inheritance, decided to put out a critical journal of his own written entirely by himself and (wife) Ruthy: *The Genius*.

"It did not do well the first year, even as a give-away to actors, writers, and producers. But the second year a miracle happened.

"Within one week, both *Time* and the *London Spectator* decided to do humorous columns about culture in Canada and chose Bone's journal as a logical taking-off point. Very few people in Canada realized that their struggling, no-saying critic was being ridiculed. On the contrary. Most people were impressed.

"'It doesn't matter what we think,' a realistic CBC producer said. 'If the *London Spectator* feels he's worth writing about, we ought to give him an opportunity.'

"'How come *Time* never quotes our drama critic?' a newspaper publisher asked.

"So Seymour Bone, critic, was born.

"He overate so much before attending his first play for the *Standard* that, though he was enjoying himself immensely, he simply had to flee before the end of the first act.

"BONE STOMPS OUT, one newspaper headline boomed over a four column photograph of the critic seated in the second row, his face a map of suffering and distaste. CANADA'S RUDEST DRAMA CRITIC, another headline ran.

"The story was picked up by the Canadian Press and ran across the country. Bone went to the theatre constipated and woke up a national figure.

"But his newly won reputation was also to ruin his pleasure for years to come. For the truth was that Bone was delighted by most plays, especially if they were full of salty jokes or good-looking girls, but he felt if he didn't walk out on every second one, people would say he was going soft.

"So walk out he did, often returning in disguise the next night to surreptitiously enjoy the rest of the play.

"Bone, now a national figure, was immediately offered a CBC television panel show, *Crossed Swords*.

"He blossomed forth as a sort of reverse Liberace. The Rudest, Most Outspoken Entertainer in Canada. He talked about his column on television and wrote about his show in his column. His column was widely read. But as Bone's celebrity increased, even as his insults grew more shrill, he became personally unpopular. Nobody asked him to parties anymore. . ."*[75]

There are those who would like to see as much truth as fiction in Richler's satirical portrait.

Another common misconception which was to build its way into the mythology is that there were simply no critics writing about theatre in Canada before Cohen came on the scene. This is not entirely true. There had been no dearth of critical comment on the development of Canadian theatre over the years, and even when Cohen began to attract attention there were reviewers — one thinks, for example, of the late Rose MacDonald of the Toronto *Telegram* — who at least tried to develop a critical attitude.

It is true, however, that while the "serious" critics of theatre alternated between patriotic drum-beating and self-conscious breast beating when they discussed theatre in Canada, the purely journalistic "critics" were in reality little more than reporters or feature writers who contented themselves, and their editors, with giving a brief synopsis of the plot, a voter-list of the characters, and as many words of encouragement to the local actors as they could muster when they reviewed a play.[77]

Even when they did contain some opinion on the values or degree of competence of the play and players, these reviews remained for the most part limited to the event, with little attempt at putting them within a broader

---

* Cohen's response to Richler's *roman à clef* was a typical combination of criticism and grace: "I may object to Mordecai Richler's treatment of me and the quality of his writing generally in his novel *The Incomparable Atuk*, but I can't object to his right to include me in his cast of characters."[76]

artistic or social context. As the American critic Jack Richardson has remarked: "The most interesting theatre criticism is that which is based not on discrete moments of isolated experience but on cultural foundations that provide a continuity of attitude and a reference for judgement that the ordinary theatre reviewer generally lacks. To possess an intellectual background more varied and extensive than the memory of a dozen or so theatre seasons means, at the very least, that one is fortified against the assaults of spurious novelty that, in our time, have been the most frequent threat to critical sanity."[78]

Cohen's background, while limited by his youth, was varied in education, experience, and a catholicity of interest which was to prove invaluable to the quality of his journalism.

Tentatively at first, and then with increasing fervour, Cohen was to make an attempt to turn the rather superficial task of reviewing — at which he ostensibly earned his pay as a freelancer — into criticism. While still relying on the features and political articles and columns such as we have already considered as the mainstay of his journalism, Cohen began to lay the groundwork for his eventual acceptance as a critic.

Following the positive response to his review of *Ah, Wilderness!*, Cohen continued to contribute a series of reviews and columns on theatre to the publications for which he was writing: the *Wochenblatt*, the *Canadian Jewish Weekly*, the *New Voice* and the *Canadian Tribune*. Here is one, of February 1st, 1947, from the *Wochenblatt*:

"For its second play of the season the New Play Society has selected William Saroyan's *The Time Of Your Life*. The deservedly well-known radio playwright Fletcher Markle produced, directed, and starred.

"The cast was taken largely from the radio world and included such luminaries as John Drainie, Jane Mallett and Lorne Greene.

"Although *The Time Of Your Life* won the Pulitzer Prize and the New York Critic's Circle Award in 1940 the passing years have done it ill.

"Some of the dialogue remains as fresh and lyrical as ever, but the play as a whole already has the musty air of a museum piece. Most of the action takes place in a waterfront honkeytonk where lost, hopeless, dream-enmeshed people come to gain solace from a bottle or by pouring out their hearts to Joe, a wealthy barfly with a spacious soul.

"As directed by Markle, the play has a jitterbug innocence about it.

"The humorous episodes often verge on the cute, and the more serious ones tend to the soap opera level. In this, of course, Markle is not altogether to blame. He shares the fault equally with Saroyan.

"The play is at its best with the deliberately grotesque characters.

"An alcoholic old cowhand (superbly enacted by Alex McKee) tells tall tales with magnificent bravado. A villainous detective (played to the hilt by Sholome Gelber) reminds one of Basil Rathbone at his most sinister.

"There is a pathetic young man (Alfred Scopp) whose sole ambition is to beat the slot machine. In the end everyone gets what he wants except the detective who is killed.

"The stage setting is up to the usual New Play Society level and notwithstanding the smallness of the stage and the abundance of characters the actors do not get in each others' way. Timing was excellent throughout, movement was natural and effortless. If the play bogged down and crawled in the second act it was mainly because Saroyan chose this act to expound his wearisome philosophy at length.

"Among the women, Claire Murray was unquestionably the ablest. She conveyed a nervous, exciting sensitivity to the part of a fading young matron looking for dewy-eyed romance and starlit adventure in the four walls of a barroom. It was a case of making a walk-on bit splendid theatre. On the other hand Jean Cruchet was unimpressive as Kitty Duval, a streetwalker. Too healthy looking, for one thing, she played the entire part in one key without emotional variation or tone.

"We have nothing but praise for John Drainie, Mavor Moore, Peter Mews, Frank Willis, and George Luscombe, all of whom performed flawlessly.

"In the central character of the wealthy barfly Joe, Markle spoke in a monotone and conducted himself like an automaton. His movements were too slow, his gestures highly stylized.

"He, Lorne Greene, and a number of others suffered from a failing common to radio players. In radio, a voice going over a microphone is sufficient.

"On the stage one must act as well as speak."[79]

During this period, of course, local productions of live theatre were given only short runs — in many cases only for two or three days — and although the actors were trying to make a living in radio, it was still essentially an amateur theatrical environment. Even if Cohen's reviews came out normally after the play's run had been completed, their critical candor was at least refreshing and informed.

To take up the slack between productions, Cohen wrote general articles — in fact, opinion pieces — on the state of theatre in Canada and on the dangers, as well as the possibilities, of amateur theatre:

"Plays are not an escape from reality," he wrote on February 13, 1947. "They are an expression of it. In the same manner actors are not persons who get away from it all; they are, whether they know the fact or not, impersonating people as they are, as they would like to be, and quite often as they ought to be.

"The standard for good acting is convincingness. The test is not whether the actor believes he is playing his role well, but whether he convinces the audience that no one could play the part better.

"Amateur actors suffer from 'staritis,' the disease which places billing above performing.

"Good amateur productions cannot be introduced overnight. They require thought and care, selection of theme, training of actors, and understanding of the stage medium.

"There aren't enough one-act plays produced by amateurs. We would like to see more one-acters with imagination, taste, and intelligent preparation.

"Audience interest in the theatre has never been greater. The fact that a second-rate British travelling company like that of Donald Wolfit's can pack a Toronto theatre for two weeks, presenting shoddy and inferior versions of Shakespeare and Ben Jonson is proof positive.

"The two best amateur productions we have seen in Toronto were *Ah, Wilderness!*, performed by the New Play Society, and *Saint Joan*, produced at Hart House Theatre. The poorest was *The Taming of the Shrew*.

"The best example of how an amateur can go wrong was afforded in *Street Scene*, where uniformly poor casting, ragged tempo, and weak direction ruined one of the best contemporary dramas.

"Toronto needs a progressive, socially conscious

theatre group, having a long range perspective, willing to perform before union groups, at meetings, and for small audiences. There are plenty of plays, modern and classic, available. To mention a few of the modern ones, *Deep Are the Roots, On Whitman Avenue, Home of the Brave, All My Sons*; the number of one-act plays is substantial.

"We would like to see some original Canadian plays, not the foolish kind offered by Arthur Stringer, but plays that reflect the Canadian scene with animation and courage, interpreting life in this country, showing the relations of people, plays that find their roots in what is going on and leave their audiences entertained, disturbed, more informed when they go out than when they came in; plays capable of moving people to thought and action."[80]

There are several things about this little essay by a relatively unknown young writer, writing for a small circulation paper in the Jewish press, that make it remarkable; and it contains many of the tendencies that were to contribute to Cohen's quick recognition by a public larger than that of the ethnic press.

First, Cohen is not content to merely review plays as they come along — he feels compelled to write about theatre, and the background and conditions under which plays are being produced. He writes for a reader who is as obviously interested in theatre as he is, with the assumption that the reader has seen the productions to which he refers — but the effect is not one of a writer writing over the head of the person who has not seen them.

Again, he is prepared to define his standards for acting, and in the process take a healthy swipe at starstruck amateurs who are more interested in playing actor than viewing acting as an art. Also, in a discussion of essentially amateur acting in a country generally regarded as a cultural backwater, Cohen has the temerity to single out a British professional company headed by a distinguished actor as an example of second-rate theatre — an attitude which was to quickly make him the bane of foreign touring companies.

In addition, Cohen here utters an early call for socially relevant theatre companies to break out of the straitjacket of purely proscenium stages and theatrically conventional plays of the allegedly commercial variety — a call which incidentally was to be taken up first in the early 1950's by George Luscombe's Workshop Productions, but not to be seriously workable until the late 1960's on any scale.*

Finally, he offers some definite and informed opinion on the type of plays which he feels will be useful and indeed necessary, to help establish the sort of theatre he would like to see come into being. It is, in fact, precisely the sort of little think piece almost guaranteed to be passed around by people interested in a "new" theatre movement — and as much of a mini-manifesto as it is a critique.

Cohen attracted further notice with his February 24, 1947 review of the New Play Society's production of James Bridie's play, *Mr. Bolfry*, which dealt allegorically with a battle between a bigoted minister and the Devil for the souls of three parishioners:

"As is usual in such cases, the Devil's advocate has the best lines, the best situations, and the most likable character," Cohen wrote.

---

*This type of theatre is now producing some excellent results, with plays like Theatre Passe Muraille's *Farm Show*, and Luscombe's *Ten Lost Years*.

"He is thwarted in the end only by the minister's faith, a denouement that may please the clerics, but leaves the audience greatly dissatisfied.

"The play, though hardly the happiest initial choice, was well-directed and mounted, sustained mainly by Mavor Moore's graceful and delightful performance as the supernatural Mr. Bolfry.

"He easily dominated the cast. We saw the play on its opening night; there was an irregularity of tempo which has probably been overcome since. The high level of acting that characterizes the efforts of the New Play Society was evident in full force, except, we thought, in the efforts of Michael Ney, a promising young actor, who was miscast as a Cockney soldier.

"One other weakness was manifest. Since *Mr. Bolfry* is a play where dialogue is all important, the actors must enunciate their lines clearly and distinctly. There were times, however, when whole sentences were blurred and swallowed; the audience had to strain its ears to follow. . ."

However, Cohen ended his review by asserting confidently:

"If any doubts lingered about the important contribution which the New Play Society is making to Canadian theatre they can now be dismissed.

"The Society's productions are of a remarkably high standard, showing imagination, intelligence and good taste. They offer far more to the discriminating theatre-goer than do most other professional plays shown here."[81]

Cohen's final paragraph was almost immediately picked up by the New Play Society, and included in their next publicity brochure, thus considerably aiding his reputation, as his comments were carried alongside those of the *Telegram's* regular reviewer, Rose MacDonald, but at greater length.

Although in this review he was ostensibly writing for a Toronto audience, Cohen is already speaking of a contribution to "Canadian" theatre, rather than simply viewing the efforts of the New Play Society in the light of their influence on the Toronto scene — this too, was to be a salient feature of Cohen's work. From the beginning, he deliberately sought to present the perspective of a national, rather than a local drama critic.*

But though Cohen wanted to encourage the development of a more experimental Canadian theatre, he was still extremely hard to please when it came to the content of new plays, as is evidenced in this criticism of the North American premiere of a verse drama, *This Way to the Tomb*, by Ronald Duncan, with music by Benjamin Britten. Cohen found the New Play Society's production "showed boldness and daring, but it has to be said that the play did not justify the effort."

"Duncan's plot, to stretch the word far, pits faith against reason, with faith emerging triumphant," Cohen explained. "It is a case where the victory of faith is more apparent to the playwright than to the audience.

"The technique employed by Duncan is that of the masque, a medieval form of religious drama, followed by an anti-masque. The first depicts the valour of the monk Antony in resisting all the worldly temptations to sublimate himself with God. There is no action whatsoever and its value depends upon the lines and their meaning. We found the act tedious, the craftsmanship of the poetry being superior to the poetry itself. The second act, or the anti-masque, savagely satirizes the modern world of reason. Mr. Duncan evidently abhors an industrialized society where the emphasis is on materialism instead of mysticism.

* Cohen's scrapbooks from this period also show that he was already receiving regular invitations to review plays throughout Ontario.

"At times the satire sparkles and effervesces, but the playwright's ogre of skepticism collapses from Duncan's prejudice rather than through philosophical defeat.

"For the play's actual direction and production, however, we have only the highest praise. They were on that level which has made the New Play Society a fine and splendid Canadian theatre repertory; professional in the best sense of the word. The spotlighting was ingeniously contrived. In the first act, change of scene is done entirely by shifting of the lights yet the continuity was never once slowed up. The acting was excellent.

"We thought that Pegi Brown, Patricia Arthurs, Barbara Kelley, John Drainie and Gordon Keeble were especially good in small roles.

"As monks, Bud Knapp, Glenn Burns, and Lister Sinclair merit commendation, especially Sinclair. He spoke his lines with a fine appreciation of their rhythm and melody. His musical diction, clear and unforced, was altogether satisfactory."[82]

Here, Cohen was continuing to reverse the trend in Canadian criticism of its own theatrical productions. Normally, in dealing with plays imported from England or the U.S. and produced in Canada, it had more or less been an assumption that the plays themselves were works of quality which suffered at the hands of local theatre companies who lacked the experience or the technical expertise to do them justice. Cohen, on the other hand, took the rather radical view that a company such as the New Play Society, for all its limitations, was in fact far superior to many of the plays it was producing. By concentrating on the limitations of the scripts — written by foreign playwrights who were widely accepted as masters of their craft — Cohen began to subtly suggest that, as Canada could produce theatrical companies which were superior to the plays, it might well begin to produce authors who were superior to the playwrights.

At the same time, Cohen, using the pseudonym "Jack Stayne,"* continued to write film criticism which was enthusiastic — if at times over-optimistic — about the future of film as an art form:

"Sergei Eisenstein's *Ivan the Terrible* is unlike any film hitherto seen on the screen. Nor will you see anything else like it until the second and third parts of the Ivan trilogy reach Canadian theatres," he predicted on April 10th, 1947.

"In this first episode, Eisenstein tells the story of Ivan's coronation, his struggle against the Boyars (early feudal princes) to unify 'armless and legless' Russia, the loss of his wife, his renunciation of the throne and his return to Moscow on the people's request.

"The narrative is historically accurate. In the early part of his reign, Ivan was, by sixteenth century standards, a progressive monarch.

"It was only in the latter years that his epilepsy (already hinted at here) and mental derangement spurred the frightful atrocities and massacres with which his name has ever since been associated.

"In directing this film, Eisenstein has endeavoured to present a true history of medieval Russian life in a medieval fashion. Sight, sound, and image, composition and atmosphere have been coalesced for that purpose. The master artist of the screen, Eisenstein has eclipsed time and space into a single entity, hurdling great stretches of time and brushing aside unimportant personal attributes (just as Shakespeare did in his historical chronicles) reducing great social struggles into conflicts among representative individuals, to exact from the pas-

---

* Cohen frequently had several articles appear by him under different bylines, a common practice for freelancers at the time, and he seems to have reserved "Nat Cohen" for his columns and editorials.

sion, blood and drama of medieval Russia a saga of monumental impressiveness.

"The Eisenstein touch is visible throughout; in the pomp and pageantry of the court, in the sumptuous and majestic coronation scene, in the weird religious rites of the priests, and in mass scenes done with a sense of rhythm, grouping and style that indicates just how great a medium of art the motion picture is.

"Yet the miracle of *Ivan the Terrible* is that the slow-moving tableau style does not bore, nor, what could have been fatal, overpower itself with detail. On the contrary, everything in the film is part of a calculated and contrived pattern whose meaning is unmistakable and whose focal point is the struggle of Ivan to make Russia whole.

"If we were unable to refer at length to the acting or the musical score it is only because of space limitation.

"Sergei Prokofieff's musical score is a masterpiece of tonal image.

"Never before has music been so integral to visual action. *Ivan the Terrible* is final proof of the glory of the screen: the newest of the arts is also the greatest."[83]

Although Cohen correctly emphasized the necessity of integrating image and score in a film, audience perceptions have subsequently altered and oddly enough, the tableau style Cohen lauds in his penultimate paragraph can kill a film today. Audiences have become accustomed to the neurotic visual shorthand of television, with its quick cuts and constant changes of viewpoint. Thus in a film like Stanley Kubrick's *Barry Lyndon*, in which scenes were deliberately orchestrated visually to fit the musical score (the long final scene being, in effect a visual coda), the audience perceives merely a series of beautiful but static pictures, and finds the film a bore. The result today, even in many of the better films, is that the art of the cinema now resembles that of the comic book, rather than the novel, or even the play, where the individual action is by definition conceived of in terms of the single shot.

In following the evolution of the newly-developing live theatre in Toronto, Cohen felt himself increasingly obliged to render not only opinions, or criticism (the two are not always the same), but also advice:

"The New Play Society, dedicated to the building of a native Canadian drama movement, showed courage and audacity in presenting last week the performance of an original play by Lister Sinclair," Cohen wrote on May 8, 1947.

"The performance was graced by fine production values including excellent lighting and the brilliant cast was headed by John Drainie, Glen Burns, Miss Arden Kay, and Budd Knapp, all players of unusual competence.

"If the play was not the success that we, for one, hoped it would be, the reasons lie in the confusion of the theme and the manifest unfamiliarity of Mr. Sinclair with the stage medium. Briefly, the story concerns a professor (Drainie) who invents an annihilating ray and then tries to find someone who will accept responsibility for it.

"By symbolical examples and techniques, Sinclair establishes that the professor himself must accept the responsibility. Here the play ends, and yet clearly here is where it should begin.

"In this day and age the playwright's task is to tell 'ordinary men with guilty consciences' how to shoulder their responsibilities, since they already know that they should. But the audience is confronted with a plot that is all prologue.

"This weakness was emphasized by the manner in which Mr. Sinclair, a well-known radio writer, directed his own play. It is both written and directed in radio style, with scene cutting in upon succeeding scene and with sound effect being used much oftener than necessary. The curious radio belief that what the characters say is more important than the characters themselves and why they say what they do is milked dry. This technique may be good in radio but it falls flat on the stage. This is one reason why Norman Corwin's radio plays have failed abysmally in the living theatre, and is the core of many of Mr. Sinclair's mistakes as well.

"Since, however, this is his first attempt with stage-craft, his errors are largely natural and forgivable. There is no doubt in our mind that he is a talented writer except for a tendency to rely on facile witticism instead of genuine humour. He has a keen gift for satire and some of the dialogue sparkles with effervescent charm. But his first play lacks conviction, continuity and decisiveness. The characters are types, rather than flesh and blood people. And we add this as a postscript. It is certainly not a Canadian play. There is nothing Canadian about it, neither in content, characters nor atmosphere. Perhaps his next effort, by being of more modest pretensions, may also be more successful.

"*The Man in the Blue Moon* completes the regular schedule of Toronto's New Play Society for the current season. Next week it sponsors the famous French-Canadian company *Les Compagnons* in two plays by Molière.

"Under these circumstances it is not amiss for us to venture some observations concerning the Society and its future plans.

"We have already stated that the Society is rendering a notable service to Canadian culture by establishing a permanent theatre with clearcut aims and purposes. Under the direction of Dora Mavor Moore, its founder, it has introduced Toronto to some extremely fine plays. It has featured and encouraged scores of able Canadian actors and actresses who otherwise would have been unable to display their talents.

"Among the women we particularly refer to Pegi Brown, Connie Vernon, Patricia Arthurs, and Clair Murray. Among the men Mavor Moore and Bud Knapp come immediately to mind; a longer list would naturally include John Drainie, Glen Burns, Tom Tweed and Michael Ney. Though many of the players are, in a sense, amateurs, the overall direction has been of such a calibre as to make them realize all of their innate abilities.

"The productions have been lavish when necessary, experimental if called for, ingenious at all times. Working on the back-breaking schedule of one play every two weeks, the Society's record of eleven plays in eight months is dazzling.

"In the spirit of constructive assistance then, we offer certain suggestions.

"It is our opinion that the Society should change its schedule from one play every two weeks to one every three weeks.

"This allows more time for rehearsal, eliminating that necessity for haste which, specifically, marred the production of *The Inspector General*.

"We feel too, that the Society should produce more well-established plays.

"Of the five produced since January, three were never seen in North America before; only one, *Mr. Bolfry*, was really meritorious, and even it was not the happiest of choices. Our view is that the Society would render a greater service by bringing to the stage such plays as *Candida, An Enemy of Society, Awake and Sing*, and, if it could be done, *Lady Windermere's Fan*.

"Then there is that wealth of untapped treasures

consisting of works by Richard Sheridan, John Ford, John Webster, and other celebrated dramatists who are virtually unknown today.

"Their plays deserve a showing. Naturally, we believe that original Canadian plays should be presented, but let them be Canadian plays.

"Finally, and these two are interrelated, the Society should obtain for itself a larger theatre than the Royal Ontario Museum and ought also to embark on a more extensive publicity campaign. The small stage at the museum presents great, and unnecessary, difficulties; all too often, it has stood in the way of an otherwise flawless production. As for the question of publicity, it is sad but true that there are still far too few Torontonians who are aware of the New Play Society and the marvellous work which it has been doing."[84]

Although the commentary and advice was coming from a man scarcely into his twenties, Cohen was being listened to with increasing respect within the essentially small-town atmosphere of theatre in Canada's second largest city.

One thing was obvious — in spite of a writing style that could be unduly ponderous, and at times even curiously ungrammatical, Cohen was a man who took theatre seriously as a motivating force for society as well as an artistic medium, and he insisted that its practitioners, amateur or professional, take it just as seriously. He not only observed and commented on the technical aspects of the productions he reviewed (often merely the refuge of reviewers who questioned their own ability to assess a play), but he also did his homework, and was becoming generally familiar with the social atmosphere in which plays were being produced in the Toronto of the late 1940's.

Yet, when it came to writing about the plays, his descriptive style could still be oddly flat, although this was no doubt partly the fault of the space limitations of print journalism under which he was working. For instance, Cohen had been so moved by Nancy Pyper's performance in *Juno and the Paycock* that it was a major factor in turning toward full-time drama criticism, and he left the theatre "anxious to try and describe her portrayal in words and tell people about her." Nevertheless, when he wrote the review, Cohen, although he passes an opinion on the level of the performance does not describe it, and just mentions her in passing:

"It's no wonder that the Irish priests and patricians screamed for the playwright's head after seeing *Juno and the Paycock*," Cohen wrote in the *Canadian Jewish Weekly*:

"Revolutionary-minded Sean O'Casey, equipped with a deep understanding, pitiless contempt for hypocrisy, and rich, cadenced prose, held a mirror up to the face of Ireland, and what he saw therein was foul.

"In language that excites the emotions and scenes which rivet the spectator to his seat, this great Irishman placed his curse on poverty and called on mankind to shatter the illusions which enslave it.

"O'Casey reminds one of Gorki, with his boundless love for the ordinary folk and his abiding hatred for the conditions and the forces which oppress them. He has the bold sweep and soar of the Elizabethans in the disciplined resiliency of his word rhythms and indifference to minor matters of craftsmanship. He is like Sholem Asch in his capacity to draw the dividing line between humour and tragedy, so basically akin, which is the very stuff of life. In the roundness of his characters he is distinctive. He is a poet of the theatre whose speech runs the gamut of melody and acute sensation, until illusion becomes reality and it is the world off-stage that is make-believe.

"*Juno and the Paycock* has inspired the director, the cast and the crew of the New Play Society to a brilliant level of interpretation. Guided by Mavor Moore, who extracted from them all their native flavour and atmosphere, the events unfold like an Homeric dirge, moving forward inexorably toward their climax.

"A pervasive melancholy prevails reminiscent of the brooding wail of the ancient prophets. My only objection was to certain groupings of the players, but this was unimportant. What counts is that here was great theatre, courageously conceived and splendidly executed.

"In the almost flawless cast, it is impossible to single out any one performer. Nancy Pyper, the mother, rose to great heights in her final moments.

"Ruth Springford, as a lonely widow whose son is killed, moved one to tears. Mona O'Hearn was natural and perceptive as the daughter while Pegi Brown provided comic relief in a role far removed from her Lady Macbeth, but equally convincing.

"In the leading male part Frank Peddie supplied that precise shade of littleness which was required to make him whole. The 'paycock' clings to his illusions to the bitter end, an object of scorn rather than compassion.

"John Drainie, the traitor son, sustained a mood of subdued nervous tension that imperceptibly glided into utter hopelessness. Alex McKee was 'Joxer,' comic yet sinister, a parasite of society credibly delineated.

"The entire production was provocative proof of what a true Canadian theatre can achieve, given popular support. The genius of dramatic art is beginning to flower on a Canadian stage, promising even better things to come."[85]

In many respects, Cohen's review of the play which had moved him so profoundly is still literary criticism, rather than drama criticism *per se*. He spends more time discussing the play than the production and his comparisons (Gorki, Homer, and Asch) are essentially "literary." Yet Cohen, when he specifically discusses the production, does so in terms of criticism, rather than reviewing. He eschews giving a synopsis of the plot, and touches only peripherally on the characteristics of its protagonists and, in the few paragraphs allotted to him, deals with the *impact* of the production on him as a viewer. Even the final paragraph could have emerged as a gratuitous observation — the play is no more "Canadian" than Sinclair's *The Man in the Blue Moon* — yet Cohen's meaning, in terms of the quality of a production achieved by its quasi-professional Canadian cast is unmistakable.

If his own style had its flaws of craftsmanship, it could still be stunningly personal and distinctive, and written with all the energy of a young man preparing to embark on a crusade. But even with his fervour, Cohen was, and remained, an essentially cerebral man who insisted on looking behind the facade of any performance, no matter how much it impressed in itself, to the roots of what the dramatist was trying to say, as well as how effectively it was interpreted. And despite his respect, verging on veneration, for a truly great playwright, the results of this intellectual anthropology could sometimes be surprising. On one occasion, it led Cohen, who was always a champion of freedom in the theatre, to advocate the censorship of Shakespeare, in an article titled *The Shylock Image*:

"Roughly 300 years ago," Cohen wrote on June 19, 1947, "William Shakespeare wrote a comedy entitled *The Merchant of Venice* whose villain is Jewish. Cruel, avaricious, and evil Shylock epitomized the Elizabethan Englishman's contempt of the Jew in appearance, disposition and character.

"There were few Jews in England in Shakespeare's

day. Two centuries before an ardent Roman Catholic king had expelled them all, believing that this would provide him with a passport to heaven. As time passed a few straggled back.

"One of them was a Spanish doctor who became involved in a plot to assassinate Queen Elizabeth. There is no evidence to this day that he was really guilty, but Elizabeth had him publicly hanged.

"Feeling ran high against the Papists and Jews.

"It was just after this episode that *The Merchant of Venice* was written. Shakespeare, who wrote and acted in plays to make a living, knew the value of catering to public prejudice. A play at that time which featured a Jewish villain was bound to attract big crowds.

"That Shylock is a villain is indubitable. He stops at nothing to gain his ends.

"From time to time he shows human emotions, but in general he is moved by diabolical impulses and heartless motives. A few efforts have been made to portray Shylock on the stage sympathetically, but these have failed. Shakespeare meant him to be a villain; the play is so constructed that his villainy becomes all important; no amendments or revisions can change this.

"I make these observations relative to a new play that has just been presented in New York. Entitled *Shylock '47*, both written and directed by Montreal-born Peter Fry, its purpose is to dispel the 'Shylock Image' from Jewish minds. The idea is noble but futile. It is not Jews who must get rid of the Shylock image.

"The Russians, I think, have a better way. Great Shakespeare-lovers though they are, they have abolished this particular play from their textbooks and their stages.

"Their reasoning is entirely sound. The ingredients of the play are anti-Semitic. It might be different if Shylock were a villain who, by accident, happened to be a Jew. But this is not so. Shylock is a villain only because he is a Jew, for no other reason. To the Russians, this slander and pillorying of the Jewish people is simply inadmissible.

"I agree with that view, wholeheartedly. The Shakespeare Shylock is a malevolent and baseless caricature that provides grist to the anti-Semitic mill.

"The Nazis knew, and appreciated this. That is why *The Merchant of Venice* was so popular in Hitler's Germany. There can be no justification for presenting such a play to school children, or for depicting it on the stage. It is a medium for religious and racial bigotry. The world will not suffer if Shylock departs from it, nor will Shakespeare's luminous reputation lose lustre.

"But stop, someone interrupts, you are setting up a dangerous set of standards. Would you abolish all plays, all novels, which contain anti-Semitism?

"Candidly, I would. I know that *The Merchant of Venice* has some eloquent passages. But the bad that is in it more than offsets its puny virtues.

"The same applies to Marlowe's *Jew of Malta* and Dicken's *Oliver Twist*."[86]

Was Cohen over-reacting? He was, after all, a Jew, writing for a Jewish publication, and he was also once again obviously writing about something that was on his mind. He mentions, but does not discuss, Montrealer Peter Fry's play in New York, and there is once again that uncharacteristic and uncritical view of conditions in the U.S.S.R., but what really concerned Cohen was the demonic content in a drama by one of history's great playwrights.

And to a Jew, faced with the incontestible evidence of the hideous — and very real — consequences of anti-Semitism during the war which had transformed "cultured" European soil into a Jewish ossuary, it is understandable that Cohen would feel as he did. In any case, although he was to objectively review succeeding performances of the play, Cohen continued to detest it, and his animus was carried over to similar productions including Lionel Bart's musical-comedy *Oliver*.[87]

He simply felt, and flatly stated, they should never be staged.

The article is notable, however, for something that was to become another characteristic of Cohen's work. Where most of the Toronto journalists writing about the arts, when they were not actually reviewing current shows, operated somewhere in that twilight zone between the gossip column and public relations flackery, Cohen, who began to consistently follow up on Canadians who were becoming successful outside the country, normally tried to tie what they were doing into a larger framework. And when his comments were concerned with the broader cultural spectrum beyond pure theatre in Canada, Cohen also tried to augment his social criticism with practical advice, as when he wrote of the economic problems facing two young Canadian composers:

"John Weinzweig of Toronto and Alexander Brott have, in a comparatively short time, earned eminent reputations for themselves. Weinzweig is generally considered as one of the ablest composers in Canada and his works have been played abroad to critical acclaim.

"It is unfortunate that such men are not given the opportunity to devote their entire time to their art. Canada has not yet reached the stage where serious composers can earn their living by their works alone. They should be given the chance. Men like Weinzweig and Brott are enriching our country's artistic life, while imbuing much of their work with the spirit of their own people. Foundations have been established in other creative media. I suggest that with all propriety the Canadian Jewish Congress may well consider the value of assisting Jewish composers who today, because of economic pressure, must give their creative work secondary importance."[88]

In this small sampling of the hundreds of articles which constitute Cohen's print journalism from 1946 to 1949, the focus has been on his reviews of the productions of the New Play Society, which Cohen himself regarded as probably the most significant development in Canadian post-war theatre. But during this period he was also reviewing all manner of the purely amateur productions which made up the bulk of Canadian-produced shows in Toronto, and in the process beginning to exhibit an amiable but obvious contempt for the work of other journalist-critics — whom he felt exhibited either a lack of background, perspective, or honesty — an attitude which was to make him alternately feared, hated and respected by the objects of his scorn.

In Cohen's case, this was not, as has frequently been suggested, simply a matter of his considerable egotism running amok in a frenzy of self-promotion. He could be lavish in his praise of other critics he respected, and not infrequently went out of his way to help younger critical aspirants find work, but he had little time for those he considered mere hacks who were making a living off the arts, and no time at all for cultural charlatans, critical or otherwise. As he indicated in the following assessment of a highly-praised Hart House production, Cohen viewed a lack of critical candor among his colleagues as a detriment to the artistic growth of the performers being reviewed, rather than a polite omission of unpleasant elements which marred an otherwise enjoyable production:

"Robert Gill's production of *Romeo and Juliet* for Hart House Theatre had much in it to commend. It was unquestionably the result of time, care, patience and thought. Sumptuous costumery and effective lighting blended harmoniously into the deceptively simple decor. The crowd moments were excellent, well arranged and convincing; likewise, the fencing scenes were both spirited and realistic.

"I enjoyed the many little touches: the brawlers abrupt hush when the prince first appears; the drunken pantomime of the revellers; the friar's amused chagrin when Romeo reveals his new love; and the bold use of near darkness throughout the climactic episode in the tomb.

"Yet the play as a whole was uneven; erratic in conception, and at times, wearisome. One never felt that he was experiencing or witnessing intimately a romantic tragedy of love thwarted by family conflict and invisibly hostile powers.

"Nor was there ever conveyed that sense of great passion which must be established, with the lovers first meeting, to make all that follows more than just a handsome spectacle. The leading characters were not sufficiently rounded. Romeo (Murray Davis) was always lovesick and Juliet (Charmion King) forever coy. But Romeo is an impetuous blade who acts first and then thinks, while Juliet overnight becomes a woman trapped in a girl's body, throbbing with all of the sudden strange emotions which besiege her heart and mind.

"So too the nurse (Jean Ross) is a plain-spoken peasant, not merely a convenient comic foil. As portrayed, they all lacked clarity of delineation and seemed ill at ease in their feudal Italian surroundings.

"Most of the cast were wanting in naturalness of movement and appearance. They did not know what to do with their hands nor how to register several degrees of mood at once. This was particularly noticeable in the balcony interlude and in the scene where Juliet is discovered, supposedly dead. Quite reasonably, this uncertainty of conduct was further betrayed in the dialogue, a great part of which is rhymed and metrical.

"Monotone expression slurred over the lyric fragrance and meaning of most of the lines.

"There were other jarring notes. Insufficient attention to detail weakened the final effect. Tybalt, stabbed through the chest, dies on stage with his blouse immaculately clean and not a trace of blood in sight.

"Benvolio, horrified by Mercutio's death, rushes in to tell Romeo; it would have been better for him to cry out Romeo's name first, and then appear. Again, there were several occasions when the windows were drawn to let in the sun and several seconds passed before light flooded the stage.

"While these are minor matters they enhance the production, when they are attended to properly, and linger intrusively in one's memory when they are not.

"To be sure, university students cannot be expected to display that same thoroughness of characterization and technical polish that one demands from professionals. But Mr. Gill, as he proved in last year's *Saint Joan*, is himself a professional, and he has a very competent backstage personnel.

"If Hart House is to regain its standing as Canada's outstanding centre of little theatre, it will have to do considerably better.

"That it can do so I do not doubt: it has the ability, talent and material resources. But it can also do with more critical candor than it has so far received.

"Of course, *Romeo and Juliet* is an extraordinarily difficult play, and the ironic truth is that it requires adults to depict the famous young lovers with the necessary psychological diversity.

"That is all the more reason why the players who acquitted themselves well should be mentioned. I liked David Gardner best as Benvolio and Don Corbett as Escalus and Robert Doree as the friar also performed well. As Juliet's mother, Lillian Schrager almost succeeded. Michael Ney, one of the better university actors, gave his Mercutio dash and sparkle. Perhaps he missed the poetry inherent in the Queen Mab speech, but he nonetheless declaimed it with contagious relish."[89]

This review reveals a number of things about both Nathan Cohen and the attitudes of professional directors such as Robert Gill towards the staging of productions in Toronto at that time.

The first is that Cohen begins his critique on a complimentary note, stressing the points in which the production had merit — which he would normally do in the case of a worthwhile dramatic effort, even if it was something less than totally successful — and also ends it on a similarly laudatory note.

He then moves on to the technical errors of the production (Tybalt's bloodless death scene, the badly handled lighting cues, etc.); and those errors are glaringly amateurish in nature. In fact, it was typical of the almost mystical regard in which actors and producers held the fact that they were indulging in live theatre at all, that audiences were expected to suspend belief in the laws of nature and accept a bloodless stabbing and similar laughable visual gaffes, on the grounds that they were watching art, somewhat in the manner of the operatic tenor who shouts "I am slain," and then proceeds to sing at the top of his lungs for the next quarter of an hour.

Cohen, who voiced many objections to the popular Canadian style of radio acting, where what the characters said was considered more important than how and why they said it, also proceeds to discuss these characters as human beings, rather than literary contrivances, and takes exception to the lack of humanity in the players' portrayal. Obviously, he respected the Hart House Company, and Mr. Gill, and it was because of that respect, that he chose to apply the standards of a critic, rather than a reviewer, to their performance. And while he makes no secret of his enjoyment of the play, neither does he avoid pointing out that a more rounded production could have provided a more vivid experience of theatre for the audience than simply enjoyment. In cases where critics or reviewers let a competent cast away with a less than competent job — and in fact praise them for succumbing to their limitations, rather than urging them to transcend them — Cohen obviously felt the critics were as much at fault as the cast.

In a series of two articles for the *Canadian Jewish Weekly*, Cohen summed up the 1947/48 theatre season he had covered, and found it a rewarding one, both from the standpoint of the productions he had seen and the "more than generous" reader response to his own efforts at evaluating them:

"A critic's primary duty is not to lay down rigid rules and thereby arrive at decisions, but to serve playgoers as a guide and to assist dramatists and performers and producers by constructive suggestions, in raising their standards of achievement," Cohen explained. "This, in essence, is what we have tried to do.

"Our entry book would be less than complete, however, if we did not register a vigorous dissent to the enthusiasm which greeted the recent London-imported version of *Macbeth*. We consider it wanting in tragic excitement and internal security. It resembled a motion picture, glacially impressive in technical accomplishment, but otherwise shallow and even mechanical. Michael Redgrave was ill at ease throughout. Flora Robson was more consistent in her interpretation, handling the always impressive sleep-walking scene with smooth restraint. As a whole, the production only confirmed our previous thesis that, in Shakespearean tragedy, the players are supreme; virtuosity of stagecraft is never a substitute for thespian ineptitude.

"The Toronto musical *Spring Thaw*," Cohen continued, "was something else again. Since the greater part of it was just as good as advance notice claimed, it seems best at once to dispose of its shortcomings. To begin with, it was not really a review, but a collection of skits, solos, and impersonations very thinly linked together. At least two sketches, the Kinsey Report satire and the newsreel parody, were much too long. The latter half of the entertainment did not possess the bounce and exuberance of the original half. It limped and stuttered, probably because of inadequate rehearsal.

"It was unfortunate that some of the members of the cast applied themselves to the devious art of scene stealing.

"The practice distracts audiences far more than it amuses them.

"Having made these points, we can say that the review as an entity was bright, unpretentious, engagingly funny, and sometimes as gay as a pinwheel. It was, moreover, happily free from the smoking-room smut which so frequently clutters up shows of this type. The lyrics were light and catchy, the atmosphere intimate, and the plot nobly inobtrusive.

"A good deal of the material was Canadian in content and setting, showing genuine imagination. Tommy

Tweed's songs on price control and the tactics of strikers were especially good.

"We cannot mention the entire cast, much as we would like to, but Jane Mallett, Connie Vernon, and Margaret Brenton scintillated among the women. Miss Mallett's facially gyratic lecture on etiquette and Miss Vernon's disquisition on modern Canadian music were unequivocally delightful. Miss Brenton, both as a Vancouver farmerette and as heroine of a Victorian melodrama, revealed personal style, good voice, and fine stage presence in abundant measure. Peter Mews led the male contingent, while others who excelled were Bud Knapp, Alfie Scopp, and Eric Christmas. The juvenile lead, Don Harron, could have been better if he had 'mugged' less but his problem was chiefly one of inexperience.

"Mavor Moore again deserves a sentence to himself. Besides composing several of the melodies and their lyrics, he stepped in at a late moment as director and master of ceremonies. Beyond any doubt, *Spring Thaw* was a substantial success and we should like to see it become an annual event.

"Some observations are now in order about the actual state of theatre in Canada today," Cohen concluded. "The most galling fact is that while Canadian theatre flourishes, Canadian drama does not. There is a dearth of Canadian plays. (Canadian plays being, it needs to be said, plays written by Canadians, but not necessarily about Canada.) An anomaly plagues us here.

"Potentially fine dramatists are loath to write for the theatre in Canada, because, to put it crudely, there is no money in it. On the other hand, we cannot expect Canadian drama to advance much further than it already has unless there are native playwrights. A few individuals do exist, however, who are willing to risk their abilities and write for the stage. . ."[90]

The constant search for playwrights of national stature from all parts of the country, rather than just in the Toronto area, was a continuing trait of Cohen's, and it became even more evident as he continued his summary in the next edition of the paper:

"The radio dramatist Lister Sinclair is easily foremost in Canada's array of postwar playwrights. He is distinguished by a singular loveliness of language and brooding wit, but his plays as a whole are deficient in characterization, cloudy in meaning, and promiscuous in technique.

"It is hard to decide whether he is an ecclesiastical medievalist or a classical nihilist. But this much is certain: a man possessing Mr. Sinclair's catholicity of talent and knowledge ought to cope with modern life in his plays, not retreat to less troubled pastures.

"Out West, the leading playmaker is Elsie Park Gowan. Miss Gowan has a decided flair for farce and comedy and believes implicitly in expounding the Canadian way of life. Her ultra-nationalism is hardly tenable in a country whose psychological character is still far from determined.

"About two decades ago, the plays of Merrill Denison were widely hailed as representing the quintessence of Canadianism; today, only suffering students recollect them.

"Unless Miss Gowan is wary the same fate will befall her. The play is the thing, not the country in which the play is located.

"The only other noteworthy new playwright is Mavor Moore. His *Fox of Bay Street*, a serious drama with humorous overtones, is still in script form and subject to revision. Even as it stands, however, it is a stage-wise affair punctuated with some fine stretches of dialogue.

"Moreover, the play wrestles earnestly with and affirmatively with questions which, if they are not inherently Canadian, are most certainly familiar to Canada.

"Mr. Moore's protagonist is a greedy and unprincipled Toronto financier whose repulsiveness is matched only by his determination to stay out in front in the rat race.

"Academicians may enjoy the exercise, but it is futile to detect any special trends in Canadian drama at present or to delegate the latest playwright to particular categories, or to prophecy the future of Canadian drama with any degree of certitude. Too many imponderables are involved. Yet it should be clear that, no matter what else occurs, the Canadian theatre will assume true significance only when Canadian drama ripens into maturity. This condition is of the essence, and it is still remote.

"Nonetheless, there has been exceptional progress in other branches of the theatre since the war's end. English-speaking theatre, we believe, has begun to root itself firmly into the cultural soil. Substantial sections of the public are enthusiastic about living entertainment, justly preferring it to the routine eroticism of the average motion picture. There are other important symptoms: the provincial competitions which culminate in the Dominion Drama Festival, the mushroom growth of summer stock companies and winter dramatic schools, and the establishment of university drama departments.

"These developments should not be minimized. There is no doubt of course that the little theatre will continue to provide the main outlet for this resultant activity, but even here higher standards are being effected.

"In our estimate, the most hopeful event of all is the appearance of what we choose to call the 'legitimate theatre' as it is exemplified in the New Play Society of

Toronto, the Everyman Players of Winnipeg, and, less successfully, the Montreal Repertory Players. These companies are professional in all except the customary meaning of that word. The old-style professional theatre is disappearing from all except the world's largest cities. Subscription membership units and traveling repertories are taking its place.

"This tendency may well prove to be the salvation of the live stage.

"If conditions are hostile to commercial theatre, they are eminently receptive to arrival of the social theatre. No one who saw it at its best will ever forget the Theatre of Action; its dissolution in 1939 was a great pity.

"Canadian culture needs the stimulating effect of groups who are willing to unite technical experimentation with the dramatic exposition of contemporary problems. We are informed that the social theatre has been recognized with some success, and we hope that Toronto, Winnipeg and Vancouver will follow suit.

"Here in Toronto, the 1947-48 season was well above average, and introduced to appreciative playgoers three talented new directors, a score of capable performers, and several plays never before seen on the local stage.

"Of all the productions, our favourite was *Juno and the Paycock*.

"It was a nerve-tingling dramatic experience, highlighted by acting that was individually creative and collectively synchronized. The test of good acting is that the people in front of the footlights should feel as one with the people behind them. In *Juno* the players realized this harmony to the full."[91]

Having built a place for himself as a critic who was being increasingly listened to on the Toronto scene, Cohen here clearly set out to expand his horizons by assessing the effects of the postwar drama scene in

Canada on a national basis, and even at this early stage
in his career, he was deliberately laying the groundwork
for his emergence as Canada's first truly national drama
critic.[92]

This is not particularly surprising, since Cohen had
already adopted a national viewpoint and, even more
significantly, an international perspective, to almost any
of the writing he had done since his first editorials for a
university paper. But it is notable that within the
framework of this national perspective, Cohen rejected
spurious nationalism which concentrated on superficial
Canadian characteristics of geography or nomenclature
and insisted that a genuinely Canadian theatre would
only be possible through the depth and quality of plays
and productions. Despite the overwhelming preponder-
ance of amateurism in Canadian theatre circles, Cohen
correctly recognized that the legitimate theatres then
being established in various centres across the country
were to become the most significant factor in giving birth
to such plays and productions.

In addition, he also showed prescience in arguing that
the social theatre — both in the sense of subscription
membership units and the dramatic exposition of contemporary concerns — was to become a more significant
factor in the development of a Canadian theatre than the
purely commercial companies, who for the most part
drew their material from London or New York.

If, however, Cohen's expectations for the still-
developing professional theatre companies were high, his
impatience with the general level of amateur productions
in Ontario was becoming obvious:

"Theatre-goers who attend amateur productions are
naturally inclined to be lenient in their judgement,"
Cohen wrote in a follow-up on amateur companies for the
Canadian Jewish Weekly. "What they ask for is a reason-

able indication of dramatic competence: they expect the play to be understandably acted, appropriately staged, and clearly related in theme and development.

"What they frequently find is a deliberate mediocrity of conception and execution which discourages enthusiastic support of the little theatre movement."[93]

Of all the Toronto critics, Nathan Cohen had clearly become the man to please, and had become so, surprisingly, while writing for specifically Jewish publications which — while they were in their own way influential — were relatively obscure when compared to the regular press.

His growing reputation was still confined mainly to the Toronto area, but that situation was to suddenly change with the announcement of a new feature on CBC radio. Beginning on Sunday, October 17, 1948, the announcement said, the "popular journalist and critic," Nathan Cohen, would "review all plays being performed in Toronto, with special attention to the local little theatre movement," for radio station CJBC.[94] The original program, *Across the Footlights*, was to give Cohen his first widespread exposure as a critic and its successor, *CJBC Views the Shows*, in his own words, "made my reputation."[95]

It was also to give him his first real exposure to the almost unbelievable hatred that can come a critic's way.

5

FIRST SEASON IN RADIO

In many respects, Nathan Cohen and Canadian radio were made for each other. His broadcasts, delivered in a distinctive nasal voice caught somewhere between a Papal pronouncement and terminal sinusitis, became a very personalized extension of his newspaper writing, so that the listener — who in so many cases still had scant opportunity to attend live theatre himself — not only heard what Cohen had to say *about* a production he had attended, but in a very real way shared in the vicarious experience of actually going to the theatre *with* Cohen.

As Andrew Allan's drama broadcasts had already shown, the widely decentralized Canadian mass audience was hungry for cultural programming, and perhaps because of the experience of thousands of Canadian service personnel overseas during the war, its tastes were becoming more sophisticated. After all, the men and women who had served abroad had gained firsthand experiences of culture outside of the rather narrow and essentially rural confines of their own country, and even though the exposure was gained under wartime conditions, it had left its mark — and if Canadians were less parochial, they were also less impressed by foreign culture.

In addition, the war had left Canada with a greater sense of its own identity and potential and, by 1948, a growing interest in Canadian personalities, artists, and critics, who were becoming familiar to listeners of CBC radio.

Beginning in the late 1940's, radio was in fact to usher in a unique period in Canadian cultural history in which not only the arts, but arts criticism became for a time a subject of widespread general interest and influence in developing national cultural standards.

"It all began in 1947," Cohen later reminisced, "when criticism was scarce in our few journals of opinion, and virtually non-existent except on the most superficial level in our newspapers.

"That year, Clyde Gilmour, in Vancouver, began a fifteen minute program of movie criticism which the CBC carried on its then Trans-Canada network.

"In Toronto, a CBC continuity writer, Gerald Pratley, was able to get a similar program launched for the local and key station of the other CBC network, the Dominion.

"As a result of the reception, another program was begun in Toronto on which I reviewed theatre and ballet.

"The general response made it plain that these programs were serving a useful purpose, were filling a void in the cultural scene.

"In the fall of 1948 the CBC's public affairs department initiated a national magazine of review called *Critically Speaking*. It ran every Sunday for thirty minutes, and was divided into three segments: films, books and one other: broadcasting or some such other art form as ballet or painting or architecture or opera.

"The only regular critic was Mr. Gilmour. The other departments had panels of rotating reviewers.

"Among those I remember with special respect were Chester Duncan, a frequent radio and TV critic from Winnipeg with a wispish, waspish voice and Sally Creighton from Vancouver, a trenchant book critic whose dry, inflectionless voice ... quintessentially Canadian, I always thought ... held me in thrall.

"The heyday of *Critically Speaking* and its regional offshoots in Vancouver, Winnipeg, Toronto and Montreal was between 1940 and 1960.

"By then the quality of criticism was beginning to improve in the newspapers in the larger Canadian cities.

"Within the CBC itself the interest of producers moved from formal opinion programs to reportage, to interviews and on-the-spot reports and conversations.

"Regular coverage of books and broadcasting and films was dropped.

"Reviewers were asked to cut down on the length of their critiques, which were sandwiched between other features.

"By the time the title was changed to *The Arts This Week*, about two years ago, it was obvious that this kind of show was exhausted.

"Whether it really outlived its purpose, or was abused into ineffectuality, is another matter altogether."[96]

When *The Arts This Week* ended in September of 1967, Cohen quite correctly saw it as the "end of an era in CBC broadcast journalism," and of a period "during which CBC radio had been an outlet for criticism of the performing, plastic and literary arts in this country, and was for a time the pace-setter, our leading force, in the establishment of critical value judgements."[97]

If there is a tinge of bitterness in Cohen's assessment of the way in which criticism came to be gradually dismembered and emasculated by the CBC, there was more than a bit of naiveté in his attitude toward the constructive spirit in which he felt criticism should be accepted when he began broadcasting. By November of 1948, he was beginning to feel the backlash, as well as the satisfaction, that went with his role as a critic:

"In the last seven days, a director has described me as a blight on the earth ... two actors offered to cut my throat ... and some woman sent me her play, promising a handsome reward if I get it staged," Cohen told his listeners. "These events aren't typical ... but they do indicate that drama criticism in Canada, as elsewhere, can be a lively art. People associated with the theatre regard us as necessary evils ... and people who go to the theatre are convinced that we have unlimited influence, and can get whatever we want.

"I've been a critic now for two and a half years. During this time I've seen well over three hundred plays; of these only four were written by Canadians. In my innocence I at first presumed that actors welcomed criticism; I soon found out that human nature is just as sensitive here as elsewhere.

"I've noticed this though ... professionals accept suggestions more willingly than amateurs. The trouble is that the Canadian theatre is basically an amateur institution ... with a placid tradition of mediocrity and self-praise ... offering no opportunity to men and women qualified to make the stage a lifetime profession. At least, this was true until recently. Today Canada has two permanent dramatic companies of superior quality: Les Compagnons of Quebec and the New Play Society of Ontario. This last named draws its talent largely from radio ...

"Now a drama critic must do more than just examine play structure and performance ... he must also search for subject values and explain to the audience what the author of a play wants to say and how well he has made his point.

"Here in Canada he has additional duties. The first is to encourage the embryonic legitimate theatre which has to fight against public apathy and amateur resentment. The second is even more important. We have no body of drama ... indeed we have no drama whatsoever. That's natural enough. Ours is a young and culturally divided land without a dynamic and homogeneous past.

"But until we develop competent playwrights of our own, Canadian theatre must remain a minor and rather snobbish form of entertainment. I'm not prepared to say that such playwrights are appearing ... that would be too bald a prediction ... but I do think that the upsurge of belated nationalism is acting as a positive catalyst.

"In a primitive and rudimentary form Canadian drama is beginning to assume an identity of its own ... and to me, nothing could be more satisfying.

"To witness the birth of creative drama is a sensation few are privileged to experience ... and I honestly believe that I will be among the lucky ones."*[98]

Here Cohen was already exceeding the CBC's expectations (indeed perhaps desires) of his announced format of reviewing Toronto plays "with special attention to the local little theatre movement," and even in this brief drama item, he was stepping into his self-appointed role as a national critic of the legitimate theatre, and in effect

---

*The elliptical style which is beginning to appear in Cohen's writing is in fact his own. It is a normal device in writing for broadcast to measure the cadence of sentences to the speaker's breathing patterns. I have retained it to preserve the flavour of the broadcasts, not to make the writer out to be a follower of the style of Céline.

declaring war on the amateurs. Or at least, it appeared that he was doing so to the amateurs; but as he was to explain, if that was how they chose to take it, it was their problem:

"It has been suggested that my criticism of them (amateur groups) is unduly severe," Cohen dutifully noted. "Of course it is . . . by local standards . . . but that's not my fault, and I don't propose to play along with the barbarous custom of turning drama criticism into social page reportage. I want to see the little theatre movement with higher standards than have hitherto been shown. I think the way to get it is by discussing errors and weaknesses as well as the virtues, but not magnifying the latter at the expense of the former.

"Frankly, I like plays . . . and I like to see them well-staged and well-acted . . . and I won't be satisfied with less. I think it was Bernard Shaw who said that if you don't get what you want . . . you'll want what you get.

"That's exactly how I feel about it . . . but exactly."[99]

Cohen also began to take to the barricades to define and defend the role of the critic, for the benefit of his listeners if not the increasingly irate amateur theatre-buffs:

"During the last ten days or so I've been reading books about the perfect society," Cohen noted. "Plato's *Republic*, More's *Utopia*, Butler's *Erewhon* . . . things like that . . . and while all of them pay due respect to the artist, the critic gets a fast and unceremonious brushoff. I'm not surprised. My profession is just naturally unpopular. Nobody loves a critic . . . nobody ever has . . . and likely nobody ever will.

"All the same, the critic plays an important role in the development of creative art. Criticism itself is an art form . . . a contributory one I'll grant you . . . but an art form nonetheless. And in my ideal world I'd make the critic adhere to a definite pattern. Briefly, I'd make him follow a play through... from the original script... through the tedious chores of casting and rehearsing... until finally, he takes in the acted play as a member of the audience. I'd have him do this... because it's the only sensible way in which he can give a production the informed and thorough examination it deserves.

"Of course, this isn't the model state... and critics are obliged to work in a very different fashion. We see a play on opening night... and we're expected to deliver it up to final judgement the next day. That sort of thing is silly... and unfair... especially to the cast and personnel of the show.

"In some instances a critic can get away with it. He'd be wasting his time, say, if he attended more than one performance of *The Drunkard...*"[100]

One wonders if Cohen, whose exposure on CBC radio was beginning to earn him a great deal of emnity as well as respect, didn't turn a bit away from his earlier identification with the actor and artist in the theatre, and increasingly attempt to at least win his non-theatrical audience over to his point of view; and whether this attempt — at least partly — was something of a defence mechanism. Granted, he had always, even in his college and print journalism, tried as well as he could within the limitations of time and space to make the reasons for his opinions clear to his reading public. But now, with a full fifteen minutes of airtime at his disposal, Cohen, in 1948, could not only give his critical judgements, but could also expand on why he made those judgements, not just in terms of the technicalities of production and performance, but also within the context of his own background and temperament. Broadcasting in a manner that could only be termed "biographical," he was to emerge from the microphone as a rounded personality, as well as a critical intelligence.

Once again, this was not simply an exercise in egotism and self-promotion, as has often been suggested. Cohen was — and remained — an individual who was genuinely interested in his own life and his own experience, and he saw no reason why he shouldn't share his fascination with his listeners. He reasoned that the more they knew about him personally, the more they would be able to understand what he was trying to tell them.

An early broadcast for *Across the Footlights* — the CBC radio program which first featured Cohen talking about theatre — was typical of this personalized approach, and also showed that he was ready to do battle with more formidable opponents than disgruntled amateur actors. The broadcast, in which Cohen emerges as something of a cross between W.C. Fields and H.L. Mencken — with perhaps a dash of Samuel Johnson thrown in for good measure — is theatre reviewing only in the nominal sense:

"As trades go, huckstering is old and disreputable," he announced. "In this case though, age doesn't count because its principle is always adaptable to new conditions. Barnum summed it up once by saying that there's a sucker born every minute to be taken advantage of, and that about tells the whole story. It's more or less true too. There are a lot of people waiting to be fleeced and just as many willing to oblige.

"I've known quite a few of these professional hucksters. I met one man, down in Nova Scotia, who sold shares in a gold mine located in Inverness. There was a mine all right — a coal mine — but the provincial government owned it, and the pseudo-owner didn't even know how to spell 'Inverness' correctly. Still, he disposed of three or four hundred shares before the police caught up with him. I met another man in Montreal who manufactured an ointment which restored falling hair, banished arthritis, and could be used as a love potion in an emergency.

"He made this concoction from plain water mixed with colouring fluid, and sold it for three dollars and fifty cents per bottle. But he couldn't speak French, so he left Montreal and went to the United States.

"The last I heard of him he was in Colorado State Penitentiary for selling his cure-all without a license.

"Of course, these two stood very low in the huckstering world.

"They were just above the characters who fix wheels at the carnival or play the shell game. They were swindlers, yes, but small-time swindlers who didn't belong in the same class as the high-pressure commercial advertisers. The latter, even those in Toronto, think and act in terms of millions. To the hucksters, legitimate advertising represents the pinnacle of their profession. It's the safest racket of all, one of the very few in which you can lie with impunity. You see, the law allows the advertising copywriter to be almost as dishonest as he likes. That makes advertising respectable and dignified, altogether beyond reproach.

"For all that, it's only another version of huckstering, cut from the same mildewed cloth. The whole idea of that handsome come-on in the newspaper, of that sparkling comedy half-hour on the air, of that free offer sent to you in the mail, is to make you buy something that you can well do without or to make you yearn for something which can't possibly do you any good. The point is to overcome your sales resistance; every tactic being used to knock you into submission.

"And many people are gullible. Convinced that what

they read is true, they insist on buying only one kind of cigarette. Charmed by the wit of a comedian, they patronize one type of coffee brand exclusively. Misled by that letter in the mailbox, they order the pills which promise to give them eternal youth. Human nature being what it is, I guess we can expect this to continue for quite a while yet. That doesn't bother me so much. What really worries me is the way in which the hucksters have branched out.

"They exert influence everywhere, in the strangest and most unexpected of places; and their aim is always to browbeat people systematically into critical insensibility so that they'll never be able to differentiate between what's good and what's bad; between what's useful and what isn't.

"This is so, of course, about show business, where the press agents are usually of secondary importance. That's because they are frankly liars, trying to get publicity. Here it's the producers and exhibitors who wield the big sticks, and the persons they hate most of all are the critics. If they had their way, they'd do away with critics altogether.

"Failing that, they'd like to turn them into stooges who rehash the official publicity handouts.

"I can give a personal example of how they work. I was once invited to attend a movie premiere. That was on a Wednesday. I went to see the film, didn't like it, and said so in the Thursday issue of the paper. On Friday, the local exhibitor cancelled his advertising. He didn't say anything. He didn't have to. On Saturday the publisher decided not to use any more movie reviews. The theatre advertisement went back in on Monday. It was as easy as that. Indeed, this sort of thing is quite common in movie circles.

"In England, the cinema critic for the British Broadcasting Corporation was violently denounced by an American studio for not recommending certain shows. Shortly after she lost her job. She took the case to court, but the verdict went against her. Even in Canada, motion picture exhibitors have been throwing dirty looks at Clyde Gilmour, who reviews movies on the Trans-Canada CBC network. I am told that a Toronto trade paper is going to attack him for his harmful, uncooperative attitude. Maybe that's already happened, I heard about it a week ago. This much is certain: the men who make movies and the men who distribute them don't like honesty in criticism.

"They stand to lose too much money that way. They fear a forewarned public.

"Now, when a critic is disparaging of a play — to return to the theatre — it isn't because he feels grouchy, or just because he wants to crack wise at some hapless member of the cast who can't answer back.

"Speaking for myself, I'd much rather praise a play than do otherwise. But it isn't that simple. I could hardly acquit my responsibilities sincerely if I said a production was good when, in fact, it wasn't, or that it had no faults when indeed it had many, or that a play was done well when quite the reverse was true. The director and the players may resent it, and I'm sorry, but hypocrisy isn't, and cannot be, my basis for evaluation.

"It seems to me that a critic must unite three qualities in his work: a love and understanding of his medium; an ability to probe for the play's underlying value — (what does the play have to say? How is it said? How well is it said?) — and, finally, a desire to see a play performed as well as possible, never settling for less.

"If it falls short of the standard he has set up, then he

—*113*—

must point out this fact and indicate concretely how, in his opinion — for it's always his opinion — the production could have been improved.

"But this is the day after Christmas, I'm still in a mellow mood, and so I propose to pass over the two plays which I took in last week briefly, very briefly. It would be wasteful to apply serious dramatic canons of judgement to them. Besides, I did review *The Drunkard* just a month or so back, and what I said about it then still goes. The production remains, after a second showing, a juvenile roundelay, unimaginatively staged, mechanically acted and decrepitly mounted. No one can ever accuse Brian Doherty of squandering money on this play. The other item on my list is an adaptation of the Charles Dickens story *A Christmas Carol*. This was presented by the Dickens Fellowship for the pleasure of the Society's members, and they appeared to enjoy it hugely.

"I can only report that the spectacle was stodgy and automatic, and the director made little attempt to bring the Dickens tale to life, imaginatively, in terms of the stage medium.

"With your permission, I'd like to develop this issue of imagination a few steps further. It's a vitally important matter, and one that has not been given nearly enough attention. I believe that the best production is one which, besides interpreting the author honourably and accurately, strives also to attain a telling interplay of sight and sound for the maximum satisfaction of the audience. Do you remember when Michael Redgrave played here last season in *Macbeth*? In it, there was a scene where Banquo's ghost appears in the banquet hall to haunt Macbeth, the man responsible for his murder.

"The traditional style calls for the ghost itself to appear, bathed in blood, while Macbeth stares around in panic, distrusting the evidence of his eyes. Well, that's the way it was done in the Redgrave version, and the effect was strained and unconvincing. The appearance of the ghost itself was the cause. We realized immediately that what we saw was an actor, cleverly made up, but for all of that an actor, solid of flesh. The quality of illusion was irretrievably lost. We knew that we were in a theatre, watching an acted play. But the moment this happened, the spell was broken, and the play became just that and nothing more.

"A few months previously, Mavor Moore directed the same play here with a cast of local players. He tackled the problem of making the ghost's presence seem plausible in a novel and ingenious way. In this production, Banquo never appeared. Macbeth saw him, but we in the audience didn't. Nonetheless, we knew that there was something in the banquet hall frightening Macbeth because of a wind instrument tone which penetrated from the wings, venturing a low, eerie wail that surged and subsided menacingly. The impact was one of visual and auditory sorcery.

"There stood Macbeth, and we experienced with him that same feeling of incomprehensible horror, while at the same time we shared the distress of his wife and the perplexity of his guests.

"Imagination! That was the secret. In this instance, Moore used sound for a specific dramatic purpose. He built the play up to a pitch of unbearable intensity with a technical ruse, and the resultant magnificence of mood proved his approach valid. Moore has, on many occasions, displayed a lively aptitude for heightening the spirit of a play through the unity of gesture and voice. He showed it most brilliantly when he presented Sean O'Casey's wonderful drama *Juno and the Paycock*. I am thinking right now of that scene where Ruth Springford, as the widowed mother of a dead Irish revolutionary mourns for her son. The setting is subdued. The colours of the costumes worn by the others were bleak, indicative of lamentation. The mother wore black cloths, the one sign of gentility among the miserably poor.

"As she began her dirge, she moved slightly from side to side, rocking her body in rhythm with her musically-tired voice. The words that she spoke had about them a poetic cadence of death and apprehension. They were at once a prayer and an incantation. While she spoke the others on the stage gradually stiffened into a position of immobility, and we perceived—in a flash of mental lightning—that there was more here than the tears of a woman who'd lost her only son, who had outlived her husband and child and time itself.

"This was also the soul of Ireland, weeping over its past, despairing of its present, and shrinking from its future.

"It takes remarkable insight and feeling to conjure up such an impression, for it's an impression that can last physically but a moment, while it may linger for years in the spectator's mind.

"Moore, by skilful arrangement of voices, action and ceremony, succeeded admirably. The play was put on here two years ago, but that scene, and the whole play itself, stays with me unforgettably. Among other things, it also proved that Toronto players are capable of greatness when they have the right guidance and the right material. . ."[101]

After a long anecdotal introduction to an attack on mendacious advertising men and their warped mores (one would suspect from Cohen's illustrations of how they attempt to bend the press, that he was himself under some pressure), Cohen simply dismisses the plays he's seen in a few sentences and gets on with what's really on his mind — a discussion of criticism and imaginative values in the theatre.

In passing, it's interesting to note that in this broadcast, Cohen finally manages to come up with an exciting, powerful and intensely moving description of the New Play Society's *Juno and the Paycock*, which had continued to haunt him since he'd seen it two years previously. And it's also of interest that the broadcast's tone of high indignation towards the lies and manipulations of the advertising industry — it was also the time of Frederic Wakeman's critical novel *The Hucksters*, for example — has, to all intents and purposes, disappeared from journalistic criticism today. The demeaning of audience intelligence by nightly television commercials is now so commonplace that it is not thought worth commenting upon. Unless, of course, comment is made to compliment these hype artists on the creativity and cleverness of their output.

Cohen continued to weave his thoughts on specific social mores into his broadcasts, but he was also careful now to include an overview of Canadian culture as a whole, whenever he could fit it in:

"Most of us know Dr. Lorne Pierce as the head of Ryerson Press, and as a sincere patron of the arts in Canada," Cohen remarked in a January, 1949, broadcast. "But before he became a publisher he was equally famous as an educator and had written several books for college consumption."

"I remember one especially well. Called *An Outline of Canadian Literature*, it had much historical information about our various men and women of letters, both French and English. It also outlined certain critical observations which puzzled me a good deal.

"For instance, Dr. Pierce spoke lyrically regarding Isabelle Valancy Crawford, who can best, and most charitably, be described as incompetent.

"He recommended Marjorie Picthall for untold virtues, and pointed to her play *The Woodcarver's Wife* as a classic example of closet tragedy.

"Like Vincent Massey, he was awed by the makeshift plays of Merrill Denison, whom he declared to be the founder of Canadian drama.

"Now why? Why did Dr. Pierce attribute such exaggerated merits to those three people? Why did John Logan and Donald French print a survey which claims that Canada possesses authors comparable to Dickens and Hardy, poets as gifted as Herrick and Keats and Shelley and Manley Hopkins, and playwrights in no wise inferior to Shakespeare and Shaw?

"For that matter, why do S. Morgan-Powell of the Montreal *Star* and William Arthur Deacon of the Toronto *Globe and Mail* still come forward periodically to announce — with a fanfare of trumpets — that Canadian culture has at last come of age?

"I believe I know. I think it's due to their acute desire to gain glory for Canada. Some of our intellectuals long for all mankind to become aware of Canadian genius, such as it is, and to render it honour... If it's true that a nation is remembered only for the contribution it makes to world culture, it's also true that Canada is far behind in the race for recognition. And the men I've mentioned know this, and it rankles. Therefore, they resent our country's youth, its natural bent toward imitation, and its spiritual uncertainty.

"It irks them that French Canada should have a cultural life that is vastly superior. What they overlook, of course, is that French Canada is hundreds of years old, and that its culture has had the time and opportunity to develop among a group of people concentrated in and around Quebec. We, on the other hand, have only begun to feel the wonderful stirrings of true patriotism and kinship. For those of us who speak and think in English terms, life as a national entity started in 1939.

"Well, in their anxiety to prove that Canada is an equal among equals, the Pierces and the Deacons and the others lost patience.

"They decided to invent a mythical culture, a culture that didn't exist.

"They abandoned the principles of constructive criticism in favour of a merry-go-round where true values were secondary. In effect, they tried to reshape the laws of a people's growth to satisfy their own cravings. Mind you, they meant well. They mean well even now when they persist in these fancies. They want to be regarded as members of a mature state, accepted by societies elsewhere. And this passion for international success is not confined to them alone. The day in which we follow even the career of Olympic Skating champion Barbara Ann Scott abroad shows that it's a common Canadian characteristic.

"This desire to belong, as it were — to please others and be part of the gang — is the springboard for action in Morley Callaghan's comedy-drama *To Tell The Truth*. The point is made obliquely and, I suspect, accidentally.

"Its significance gets lost in a scramble of contradictory issues, but if you watch for it, it's there. Callaghan's hero, a boy named George, is discontented and restless with his life in Montreal.

"So he goes to the United States and takes a job for nothing in a hamburger joint where he serves vagrants, amateur philosophers, streetwalkers and other drifters.

Here he meets Dini, the girl whom Joe Taylor owns and won't give up, and the girl whom George loves and wants to win.

"Here too he meets people who like him and call him friend. They hate to see him leave. Among them he finds happiness and security — paradise in a faded poppy field.

"It's this motif, this quest for companionship which, in my opinion makes *To Tell The Truth* a Canadian play. In a way, I suppose, a Canadian play is simply a play written by a Canadian. That's true, in a formal sense, but it isn't the whole truth. For a play to be Canadian it must also bespeak a frame of mind — a way of thinking and acting — peculiar to us alone. This gives it identity and distinguishes it from something written by an American, or a Briton, or a Norwegian. It isn't the setting that's important. What really counts, I suggest, is a mixture of national and personal temperament within the author, and the reflection of that temperament inside the play.

"Mr. Callaghan himself has an interesting history. He is a novelist and short story writer whom the Americans, with their usual lust, have more or less monopolized. There was a time, almost twenty years ago, when his work sparkled with a hint of future greatness. His style was terse and controlled, and his dialogue had the melodic ring of reality.

"He showed an understanding of the feelings of people, and he passed this on, not by explaining the psychology of his characters but by making their behavior talk for them.

"Then something happened. He continued to write, and to write well, but there was no evidence of progress. His fiction took on a vintage hue; his essays became plaintive in tone. Though what he wrote had today for its setting, yet what he said and the way in which he said it belonged to a decade which was recent and dead. It seemed as if he had lost the spark which stimulated his capacities for idiomatic expression and character interpretation. He had entered into a period of crisis, a crisis that befalls every creative writer. During this interval, his powers grow dormant. They either wither and die, or else, all too occasionally, they survive and emerge more vigorously than ever.

"In Callaghan's instance, the signs lead me to hope that he will be among the lucky few. With all of its faults, *To Tell The Truth* — his first play — is consistently entertaining. Originally written in 1939 and since revised — but not revised enough — it's being presented by the New Play Society. You may disagree with its philosophy, as I do, but the chances are that you'll find it interesting throughout.

"It's a play that deserved to be produced, and it's fitting that the New Play Society should produce it. No other organization is doing so much to raise Canadian acting standards and to advance the cause of our national drama. . . .

"With the Callaghan debut, Canadians can now state truthfully that they have uncovered at least three dramatists of ability in the last ten years. In their own way, Lister Sinclair and Robertson Davies also reflect Canadian patterns of living. In the case of Mr. Davies, I comment partially from hearsay because I've only seen his one-act plays.

"I did listen to the radio version of his full-length comedy *Fortune My Foe*, but he's entitled to a fairer hearing than that.

"As for Mr. Sinclair, it has seemed to me for some time now that he is the victim of his skill as a writer for radio. If once he masters the art of the theatre, and guides his talent into composing plays where character and incident inspire the speech, rather than the reverse, it's possible that he'll justify what so many expect of him. But certainly he is a Canadian playwright. He represents another type of intellectual, a university-trained type, which looks for meaning and direction in the realm of universal issues, rather than local ones.

"But perhaps — perhaps the place to look for the answers is right here at home. For it's only when we know how to grapple with the division and perplexity in our own house that we can give our neighbours wise and competent assistance, and be listened to with respect."[102]

Cohen's preoccupation with cultural and artistic values over and above the purely entertainment values of the productions he reviewed was becoming the bane of local drama groups, and it was also apparent that he was more and more regarded as an intimidating, rather than an encouraging figure by them. One local director wrote to Cohen: "I am afraid... to judge from your broadcasts... that you will not enjoy our show. I only hope the evening will not be too boring. No one is more aware than we that the play has little or no literary merit, no theme of any importance. But in our opinion, that does not condemn it as entertainment. If you were to ask us why we produced the play, admitting its many weaknesses, our answer is this: because we discovered last year that the audience of ordinary theatre-goers found the old gags still funny, and the whole thing to them was not thought provoking but terribly good fun."

Cohen included the letter in a broadcast, but did not mention the name of the sender, and even agreed in part with the director's attitudes, but went on to try and explain his own position:

"I don't believe," Cohen answered, "that a show must always be thought-provoking or literary to be entertaining; and it isn't for me to dictate the taste of theatregoers, ordinary or otherwise, although I do reserve the right to question the taste of directors and writers. However, I would like to correct the implication that I prejudge shows — acted plays, that is, not written texts. That's a common accusation against critics, and it simply isn't true. In my own case, I maintain a free and liberal mind until the curtain goes down on the last act, and even for a time after that.

"It's only when I've thought over and examined a play from every angle that I'm willing to volunteer an opinion about it. Reporters, I know, are able to hail shows as 'artistic triumphs' at the drop of a hat. Critics, however, must be more discriminating.

"You see, a critic... by the very nature of his profession... can't afford to be lax in his views. Theatre-goers can, and often are.

"They're anxious to be pleased, and to applaud people as people rather than as actors. When a show doesn't move them as they imagine it ought to, they feel guilty and distressed. That's one of the reasons so many will sit through a degraded commercial spectacle, and defend their tolerance. That too is why they so often submit to the worst intellectual humbug, and pride themselves on their educational insight.

"Not so the critic. In position he stands midway between playmakers and playgoers, acting as a censor of the creative and as a guide to the perplexed. Since he can never hope to satisfy everyone, he can risk the danger of being independent and objective. And as far as performance is concerned, his responsibility, I believe, is that of demanding and encouraging superior standards of techniques from the amateur and professional playmaker on the one hand, while explaining his approach to the playgoer on the other.

"And I think too, that in our insensitive age, the critic

must strive to reawaken in people their dormant appreciation of beauty and genuine feeling, qualities which two world wars and canned culture have made strange to us."[103]

Although Cohen admired and respected the budding professionals in Canadian theatre, he was never awed by them, nor did he go out of his way to avoid applying his stringent canons of criticism to them — even as individuals — when he felt they were lax in their responsibilities towards building a distinctive theatre. In fact, the more eminent the individual, the harder Cohen would bear down on him:

"I want to say something about the University Drama Festival that was held here last Monday and Tuesday. More specifically, I want to talk about the adjudication of the festival, and without mincing any words," Cohen announced on February 6, 1949, during his regular Sunday broadcast.

"I would like to say that I was deeply disappointed by Mr. Andrew Allan's contribution to the program. Mr. Allan, as everyone knows, is the supervisor of drama for the CBC, a noted actor in his own right, and a highly competent stage director.

"He is all this and a good deal more. By virtue of what he has done to assist Canadian writers and actors, he has also become — whether he knows it or not — a major spokesman for the development of a genuine, creative culture.

"Every statement he makes, therefore, is important and worthy of notice.

"Considering this, and considering too that the university is, or should be, the backbone of amateur theatre in this city, I felt that he dismissed his duties at the Festival much too lightly. It wasn't what he said that

Nathan Cohen in a 1947 portrait.

Nathan Cohen and Gloria Brontman in a portrait taken during their engagement.

Nathan Cohen as Dr. Johnson.

On *Fighting Words*, a prize of a complete *Encyclopedia Britannica* was given to any viewer who could stump the panelists as to the source of a quotation used on the show. This photograph is from the mid-fifties.

Nathan Cohen when he was Entertainment Editor of the Toronto *Star*.

THE CRITIC
by HUTCHINGS.

I'M A CRITIC

I DISLIKE MOST EVERYTHING FILMS, TELEVISION THEATRE AND OH SO MANY OTHER THINGS

I'M **VERY** INSULTING AND I'M **VERY** RUDE

NO SHOW HAS A CHANCE ONCE I GET THE OLD PEN WORKING

I DISCOURAGE YOUNG AMBITIOUS TALENTED PEOPLE MY **GOODNESS** I'M EVIL

I'VE BEEN RESPONSIBLE FOR **MORE** UNEMPLOYED ACTORS THAN 50 HOLLYWOODS

PEOPLE LIKE TO BE TOLD THEY'RE LOUSY CRITICISM'S GOOD FOR THE SOUL

MINE THAT IS!

To Nathan Cohen
Best regards
Trevor Hutchings

Cohen surrounded by some of his *Star* colleagues. The headline in the newspaper reveals the photo is from 1967.

In 1967, Cohen received an honorary doctorate from Mount Allison University at Sackville, New Brunswick.

Cohen enjoys a joke with host Al Hamel on CBC's *Nightcap*.

Moderators of various CBC shows. From left to right: Hamish McGeachy, Cohen (with only one glove off), James Bannerman, and J. Frank Willis.

— as far as it went — was inadequate. Rather, it was what he didn't say.

"The earnest, hard working, sincere young men and women at the Festival wanted and needed that very enthusiasm and encouragement Mr. Allan was most fitted to give them. It seems to me that he could well have told them about the importance of theatre to a country, what a great source of pleasure and stimulation it can be, and how it must draw its ideas and beliefs from popular life.

"It seemed to me too that he could well have stressed that, more important even than audiences, are actors and technicians and dramatists who have faith in the dramatic art and its duration, and that a unique responsibility rests with those who have this faith, and are willing to work for its realization. Anybody could have said what Mr. Allan said last Tuesday. No one else could have said, with as much authority and inspiration that which he so signally omitted from his remarks."[104]

Egoes being what they are, this sort of thing was not likely to make Cohen a popular man around the CBC, where Allan was a formidable figure, but Cohen was also making a few friends, as well as influencing a lot of people, by his broadcasts, and he cherished their encouragement. One of them was Maurice Boddington*, a genial journalist and broadcaster then in his early sixties whom Cohen would frequently meet over coffee in the CBC canteen to discuss criticism:

"I first met him in the late 1940's, soon after I began freelance broadcasting for the CBC, and he was one of a handful of encouraging people," Cohen remembered on the occasion of Boddington's death in 1969, at the age of 84. "He talked to me of the changing world of entertain-

---

*To listeners of that era, Boddington is best remembered for *Bod's Scrapbook*, a popular program of gentle and folksy humour on CBC radio for many years.

ment, and of the need for critics who could speak their mind and explain why they thought what they did.

"He was a good soul, Bod, and had a full and rewarding life. That's a good legacy to leave to one's family.[105]

Another of the "handful" of Toronto media personalities who encouraged the trenchant young critic was the redoubtable Gordon Sinclair. In fact:

"It was the attention that Gordon Sinclair paid me, when he was the radio critic of the Toronto *Star*, and I was just a new broadcaster on CJBC in 1948 that really gave my career its first big push," Cohen recalled.

"I used to do a once-a-week fifteen-minute broadcast about theatre in Toronto — and the program was always being shifted to a different time.

"Sinclair reviewed me faithfully, week in and out, and built an audience for me.

"At the same time he kept rapping the CBC for not letting the program stay put so people could be sure when it was on.

"Now the thing was that I didn't know Sinclair. He wasn't doing it ... because I had asked for it — or because I had praised some people in whom he had an interest — but because he liked the program and wanted people to share his discovery and enthusiasm."[106]

Certainly, Cohen's broadcasts were having a peripatetic time of it in 1948 and 1949, to the point where one staff announcer, closing a broadcast with the announcement of yet another change in listening time, was moved to remark: "There seems to be a fear on the part of people who schedule programs that if Mr. Cohen is left in the same period for more than six weeks in succession he may inadvertently build a loyal following.

"As a result of this fear, we notify listeners to *Theatre This Week* that its time has once again been changed.

Beginning next Sunday afternoon Mr. Cohen's criticisms will be heard forty-five minutes earlier."[107]

Whether the broadcasts were shifted because of someone's resentment of Cohen, or simply indicate a typical example of CBC programming is uncertain. Much later, Cohen was in effect to be briefly "blacklisted" by the CBC as a result of pressure from above,* but for the moment his relations with the corporation remained firm, if not always smooth. As did his faith in the theatre, which was by now beginning to take on the aura of a religious conversion, with Cohen acting as an evangelist, as well as a critic:

". . . no matter what happens, the theatre will keep going, you may be sure of that," Cohen said in February of 1949. "But that doesn't mean we can relax. Here in Canada, we have a peculiar situation. Our problem isn't one of saving theatre, but of building it securely. Unlike other countries, we have no dramatic tradition of our own, no body of original Canadian drama, and no great public enthusiasm, not yet anyway, in the art of theatre.

"Our duty then is one of developing a living theatre, planting its roots deeply enough in our cultural soil to make sure it will be healthy, productive and rewarding . . . both to the people who appear in plays and to the people who attend them.

"And I believe this is at last being done. Since 1945, the men and women capable of forming the nucleus of a virile Canadian theatre have begun to appear. They are not amateurs, I want to stress that. They take their theatre seriously, and they are genuine, not hypocritical in their desire to make Canadian theatre a reality. They are actors and directors and technicians who are

*See page 233.

professional, not because they say so themselves, but because the work they do proves it. Intent on raising dramatic standards they aren't discouraged by financial setbacks and they will pay attention to criticism even when they don't like it . . . which, I might add, is usually always. In short, they are theatre-minded every hour of the day, not just a few nights a week, and they earn their living in the dramatic arts as best they can."[108]

In 1949 an impressive array of student-actors were performing regularly at the University of Toronto's Hart House Theatre, re-opened after the war under the direction of Robert Gill, who came to Canada from the U.S. for that purpose.

Included in the number who appeared in those early all-student productions were Kate Reid, Charmion King, Murray and Donald Davis, William Hutt, David Gardner, Ted Follows, Eric House, John Howe, Christopher Taylor, Toby Robins, Donald Harron, Bea Goldberg, Anna Cameron and Henry Kaplan, all of whom became well-known professionals on the Canadian stage.[109] Several of them became involved in what was to be the first, but certainly not the last, direct confrontation between Cohen and a group of actors; an event he was to recall in 1966 with a certain amount of good-natured amusement:

"These people were not content merely to work in the four shows Mr. Gill did each season," Cohen remembered.

"They presented shows of their own. They lived and breathed theatre.

"And in the summer after that year many went along with Mr. Gill to a summer theatre where he was the director.

"They took themselves very seriously, and were

convinced that they already were actors and directors of the first rank.

"In those days I did a fifteen-minute, once-a-week broadcast for the CBC of drama criticism, and one Sunday, a delegation called upon me to protest against what they termed my negative attitude.

"Did I not know, I was asked, that my destructive reviews might drive them out of the theatre?

"No, I did not know, and I did not believe it would drive them out of the theatre. . . . and as the roll call of names makes very obvious, most of them are still with us."[110]

Perhaps it was such a confrontation that prompted Cohen to extend his dialogue with his listeners to include the question, "Is the Drama Critic a Human Being? " as he did on Sunday, March 6, 1949:

"You'd be surprised at the number of people who think he isn't," Cohen began. "Theatre folk, for example, are always denouncing him as a viper, a drooling lunatic, and a poison-dipper in a bottomless pit. According to them, he gets by on spite, ego. . . and nothing else.

"As a matter of fact, the late Leslie Howard used approximately these terms to tick off the New York critics after they objected to his portrayal of *Hamlet*. I can't quote him literally — good taste won't let me — but I'm sure you get the idea. There are dozens who feel the same way. In his new comedy *Light Up The Sky*, Moss Hart lampoons the critics, as persons who hated Mickey Mouse when they were children — if, he adds, they ever were children.

"It's much the same here in Toronto. For me to suggest that a show isn't good entertainment or is badly acted, or needs technical improvement is more than enough to make me a social outcast.

"I remember one hectic week when a director described me as a blight on the earth, and two actors volunteered to cut my throat. Since I began this program last October, I've been accused at least a dozen times in as many talks, of sabotaging Canadian culture. And I've been told more than once that the directors would be just as happy if I missed their shows.

"All right then, a critic isn't popular. We can agree on that. But what is his crime? Why does he stir up so much indignation? The answer is that he commits the unpardonable sin of stating, fairly and truthfully, what he thinks of a play. I know... I know... honesty is supposed to be a great virtue, but that's true only in theory. In practice, honesty is heavily discouraged, and nowhere more so than in the theatre.

"Since drama is based on an illusion, the critic is called on to deceive himself and others by blessing all the plays he sees — certainly the ones he gets free tickets to — and by phrasing his rebukes, such as they may be, in language that will offend no one and contribute nothing.

"If he obliges, he is a good fellow and is referred to favourably.

"No one worries that he is being neither critical nor candid. But if he dares to be selective and conscientious, he is eyed with the same loathing as a defeated candidate the day after an election.

"I need hardly emphasize that drama criticism gets short notice in Canada, and that most so-called drama critics are really feature reporters.

"In a way this is understandable. Like our theatre, theatrical criticism is still in a primitive state.

"It may therefore be presumptuous of me to define the duties of a critic, but that is what I'd like to try to do this afternoon.

"The views that I express are, of course, my own, and some of them are tentative and in a process of reconsideration.

"What then, does a critic do? Well, he does more than merely tell people what the story of the play is and whether it's likely to entertain them. Instead of being an end-all in themselves, these matters are but the foundation upon which the critic develops his opinions.

"Certainly he must have a point of view. As to that, I can sum up my own in a few words. I like it. More than that, I worship it. The theatre, that is. I believe it's the most humanistic of all forms of art, and the most stimulating — emotionally and mentally. For this reason, I believe that every staged play should be as well presented as the talents involved will permit. Anything else will not do. An adequate presentation can never be satisfactory because it doesn't give the playgoer as great a sense of pleasure as he deserves and as, having paid his admission, he has a right to expect.

"Most people want to be entertained at a show. If it does that, they're happy and ask no further questions. But the critic digs deeper. What he wants to know is, why was the show entertaining? In my own case, I look for the answer, in part anyway, in the content and form of the play itself. I want to know what the play says, what its underlying purpose is. I want to discover its human matter and artistic value, to understand the conscious and subconscious mind of the author as revealed by the play. When I find the answers, I pass them on to you so that, when you see the show, you also will be aware of those impulses and intentions and will share a sense of life in the evolution of the play.

"This is essential. The minimum duty of the critic is to explain and interpret a play at least as well as the person who wrote it.

"Obviously, he must know a good deal more about drama than either the ordinary playgoer or playmaker and what he doesn't know he should promptly learn.

"Thus, he must know about the sources of plays. When he talks about *Hamlet* he must also know about the *Ur-Hamlet* of Thomas Kyd and about the original legend. He must know the history of theatre auditoriums, and how they have changed in style over the centuries.

"Again, he must be able to connect a play with the environment in which it was created. A discussion of Ibsen presupposes a knowledge of manners and morals in Europe in the nineteenth century. A criticism of Sean O'Casey involves a study of Southern Ireland before and after it obtained self-government.

"By the same token, a critic must be familiar with aesthetics — the science of fine arts. He should always be on the alert for the beauty that exists within a play. Very often, it's this beauty that raises the drama, like music, to the level of a perfect art.

"So far I've talked about the written play, and there are critics to whom that, by itself, is enough. They maintain that the written and the acted play are one and the same and that a play cannot have dramatic merit unless it has literary excellence. This concept seems to me altogether too narrow. Good literature isn't necessarily good entertainment, and vice-versa.

"In print, Shakespeare is supreme, yes, but on the stage he is as good or as bad as the director and the actors make him out to be.

"What we see isn't his Macbeth, but the Macbeth of Michael Redgrave, not his Cleopatra, but that of Katharine Cornell ... and, I submit, that can be something entirely different. To me, therefore, it is well-nigh impossible to judge the written and acted play in the same fashion.

"For one thing, the written play appeals to the mind and the emotions through the eye alone. You read, and the rest is up to your imagination.

"On the other hand, an acted play appeals to the eye and the ear. It brings the pages in a book to life. Not written words, but actors, voices, scenery, and lighting are the instruments of expression.

"To disregard this is to neglect a cardinal principle of criticism.

"I believe, therefore, that a play can be enjoyable theatrically even though it has no written consequence. On a lower plane, a show can entertain purely by virtue of performance, and can even have an independent art content. By the way, that word performance covers more than just the acting. It takes in the staged version — the actual presentation of the written play to an audience — and it deals with a variety of elements — direction, setting, make-up, properties and so on — considered separately and together.

"It's the job of the critic to evaluate the relative importance of these elements in the completed play and to suggest how they helped or hindered the final result.

"Let me illustrate. You go to a show, like it, and pass the good word on to your friends. If they asked you why you liked the play, chances are that you won't be able to give a precise reply. And there's no reason why you should. This is where the critic steps in with his diagnosis. It may well be that you liked the show because of the way it was directed. You were pleased by the arrangement of line and colour and by the effect of perspective and grouping.

"Coupled with this, the show also had sound and tempo. It was a union of fast scenes and slow scenes that build up in volume and come to abrupt pauses. How about the acting? Did you find it uncertain? The critic may point out that the actors couldn't project their parts or suffered from faulty teamwork. Was the lighting hard on your eyes? Enter the critic to comment on the colour scheme, and possibly the costumes and scenery as well.

"Why the bare stage? Maybe, says the critic, so as to create mood and atmosphere by implication and thus give your fancies wider scope.

"Incidentally, I hope you don't have the idea that I go to a theatre pen and paper in hand and jot down notes while the performance is on.

"Unless it's to immortalize an especially bad line of dialogue, I generally dispense with that procedure. Until the curtain goes down for the last time I am just a member of the audience, nothing more. But once the lights go on my work starts. In my mind, I sort out impressions. I differentiate between the written and the acted play. Perhaps I liked one, but not the other and perhaps I like neither. If amateurs put on a show, I make allowances I could never concede professionals.

"If the performance was marked by perception and inventive staging, I am more likely to be favourable than to one where the atmosphere was mechanical and routine. I take the show apart and then fit the pieces together again. But my ultimate test is simplicity itself. Did I enjoy myself? If I did, then the virtues outweighed the drawbacks, and if I didn't, then the defects were top-heavy. When I have done all this, I am ready to go ahead with criticism proper.

"From what I've said, it follows that a critic speaks mainly on behalf of the average theatregoer. There is a belief that he should be a frontman for the players, one who praises them without reserve (this is to encourage them and spur them on), covers up their omissions, and protects them from popular disapproval. Personally, I think that's all nonsense. Most of our amateur groups are hyper-sensitive to criticism only because they aren't used to it; some still have the village outlook, and regard themselves as a privileged class. Mind you, I do believe the critic owes the theatre enthusiastic and unselfish support, but he is also its conscience, and must fight to keep its standards high and he must oppose every concession to the vulgar and inferior.

"No one knows better than I that a critic rarely wins those battles.

"Nevertheless, by waging them, he renders a useful service. And, for these very reasons, he appears on the scene as the representative of the true theatre public. He tells the people how he reacted to a play, and why.

"He balances one type of play against another, makes comparisons, offers judgements. He seeks out the moral purpose of every play. He discusses technique, as it pertains to story and to performance. He draws to the attention of people qualities that, once they are aware of them, enable them to discriminate between the good and the bad, quicken their appreciation of the dramatic art, and enrich the scope of their knowledge. The public is his master, and it is to them that he is responsible.

"After these remarks, it may seem to you that drama criticism can at times be a grim chore. Well, no job is perfect, and professional theatre-going does have its moments of tedium. Withal, however, it has strong compensations. You see, in its modest way, criticism itself is a form of art, and every play is an adventure into the mysterious, the unique, and the spiritual. Criticism can set up principles and establish new standards. It can throw light on plays, performances, and on life.

"To playgoers, it can give a keener understanding of what they see and hear. To playmakers, it can indicate the vast resources of the dramatic medium.

"And, every once in a while, criticism does become the exploration of a masterpiece — a play that is great both as literature and as entertainment.

"There is no experience like it. The stage crackles with

the flame of genius, and we who watch and listen are oblivious to everything except what is transpiring behind the footlights. When this happens, the critic faces his greatest challenge. He must describe what is indescribable and distill, so that every intelligent person will understand, the meaning and method of this miracle of the theatre.

"In so doing, he has as his aim the awakening in all men of a livelier sympathy for art and a more tangible awareness of the importance of art in our daily lives.

"Tell me, how many others can say that much about their work?"[111]

Lest one get the wrong impression, Cohen spent only a small proportion of the time defending his own position as a critic, and during this period he was reviewing more than one hundred individual performances of both amateur and professional theatre. Nevertheless, there is something oddly touching about his repeated attempts to make himself understood. Like all critics, Cohen, then only twenty-five, was hurt by the fact that while he considered himself a pioneer in promoting genuine culture, he was being accused of "sabotaging it." He was to become accustomed to being regarded with that curious mixture of respect and contempt that Canadians invariably reserve for those who express their opinions in the public media; and though, to a degree, he became inured to it, it always rankled, and never so much as when his point of view was misunderstood, or deliberately misrepresented.

Cohen's discontent with the level of writing on the arts in the daily press was also to make him unpopular with the entertainment writers in Toronto — and elsewhere — most of whom, as Cohen suggested, were simply competent reporters and feature writers who for one reason or another had been assigned to the entertainment beat by their editors, and had little or none of the sophisticated background Cohen demanded of a critic. In fairness, though, it should be pointed out that these writers were working under the superficialities and tight-space requirements of newspapering — and were in fact doing the acceptable job of reportage, rather than criticism, demanded of them by the papers.

Cohen, who had known these limitations himself, constantly fought against them, and saw no reason why a newspaper critic, if he lacked the necessary background, couldn't be bothered to learn it on his own. He literally *demanded* that the standards of journalistic criticism in Canada be improved, and consistently dismissed his colleagues and lambasted the productions they found to be superior theatre:

"Speaking of the low state of modern theatre," he said on April 3, 1949, "I went to see *Brigadoon* the other day.

"My colleagues were pleased to call it an enchanting fantasy.

"That's their privilege. Mine is to describe it as an ambitious fraud. The only original thing about the show is the title. Mind you, the story ... which is about two New Yorkers who stumble on a fabulous Scottish village that comes to life one day every hundred years ... does have possibilities, but the treatment of it is spurious and unimaginative. Considering that Agnes De Mille designed it, the choreography is only passable ... there are no fetching tunes or outstandingly beautiful women (there never are in musical comedy nowadays) ... and the comedy is old hat. I did enjoy a scene where a young woman drapes herself up in a shawl and stumps about the stage in various attitudes symbolizing death ... à la Martha Graham, but I found afterward that I was supposed to take the business seriously. *Brigadoon*, I should explain, is more than Entertainment. Dear me, yes . . . it's Art!

"Trust Americans to vulgarize the word beyond recognition.

"Appraised then, as Art . . . I'm only too happy to discuss it on this basis. *Brigadoon* is very much ado about nothing. The Scottish background is an excuse to haul out some mossback jokes and banter around a few juvenile ideas about faith and reason, and the story ends when the hero, having decided that love is supreme, runs away from New York to join his two hundred and twenty-four-year-old sweetheart and live happily ever after.

"But the real trouble with *Brigadoon* isn't the plot — most librettos for opera are no better. Rather, it's the style. The show moves off at the same time in too many directions. It tries — 'tries' is the word — to be romantic, funny, philosophical, extravagant, melancholy, satiric and tragic.

"There's no balance, no fusion, and the absence of unity makes the entire mixture an unfathomable mess.

"However, let me add . . . even if the elements that compose *Brigadoon* were as good as its admirers make them out to be, the show would still be as bad as I think it already is.

"Of course, even a junkyard can contain jewels . . . and when I made my inventory of *Brigadoon* I did find one or two good things. I liked the sword dance, which was complete in choreography, costume, and musical arrangement, and the masterly footwork of Kenneth LeRoy around the sword took me back to the summers when I used to go to the Gaelic Mods back in Cape Breton.

"This number had a real Scottish flavour. Again, the sets and lighting impressed me as properly lavish, although if I may be allowed this heresy, lavishness seems to have become an end in itself on the modern stage.

"I don't know whether I found anything else of interest in the show.

"The principal players were personable enough, I guess. Nothing was required of them except that they should sing off-tune, and they obliged accordingly.

"In sum, I found the show a hodge-podge and a bore . . . a patched-up affair nervously held together by scotch tape."[112]

So much for the loose-lipped use of the word "Art" to describe trivia, as far as Nathan Cohen was concerned.

Although he could be — or at least appear — cynical and sometimes a trifle pompous when something displeased or distressed him, Cohen could still become boyishly excited when his theatre-going provided him with a fresh adventure, as it did when he went to review his first ballet:

"Let me see now," he began in his characteristic conversational way, one Sunday afternoon in April of 1949. "I'm supposed to tell you something today about the Ballet Russe de Monte Carlo. It won't be easy. Indeed, I know of nothing harder than to put into words the exact quality of a non-literary art form. You can be precise about poetry or prose because you deal with them on their own level — in words — whereas when you talk about music, painting, the dance, and so on, those same words are only a substitute.

"Take musical comedy which can be, and sometimes is, a work of art.

"Whenever I tell what such a show means to me, I'm forced to use terms that don't belong to musical comedy. Thus a rowdy item like *Annie Get Your Gun* seemed to me to have a warmth akin to a noisy, but congenial outdoors party. Conversely, *Brigadoon* reminded me of a flossy colour advertisement about life in a log cabin. When I saw it, I felt that I was being 'sold' a bill of goods.

"Well, that's one problem. Another, of course, is that I don't know very much about classical or academic ballet. . .

"I should have studied ballet as a matter of course, for the simple reason that movement of the body . . . which is esssential in ballet . . . is also vital in the theatre. There's no doubt that the failure of actors to obtain dramatic effects through the use of their bodies has helped to make directors supreme in the theatre. Modern actors have forgotten . . . or have never learned . . . that the human body can get along without speech, and that it's quite able to speak for itself. Profound emotions can be expressed by a single twist of the shoulders, and the use of the face, throat, hands and legs will often tell us more about love and mercy and hatred than a dozen poems.

"But what is ballet? Well, it's not the entire art of the dance, as so many of us laymen used to believe. Dancing, as a form of art, is prehistoric. The branch of it known as ballet is fairly modern. In fact, it had its start in France three hundred years ago . . . and attained its mass popularity only in the last twenty or thirty years.

"We can define it as a means of entertainment . . . intended mainly for the eye . . . that tells a story, or develops a theme, or creates an atmosphere or mood. This is brought about by an orchestration of dancers in costume who perform against a decorated background. The dancers are trained according to rigid rules. They regulate their movements by the tempo and in the spirit of especially written music. The music speaks to the dancers, and the dancers interpret the music to the audience.

"Costume enhances the dramatic atmosphere and scenery . . . although physically apart from the dancers . . . aims to reveal the design and subtleties of the choreography, that is, the arrangement of that part of the ballet that is danced.

"In other words then, ballet is a co-operative art. It is not an independent work like a painting or a play, but a joint production invented by musicians, choreographers, and experts in decor. They work together and the ballet is the outcome of their labours. When they are done, the dancers take over and what they try to do is state, in a convincing and clearly visible manner, the purpose of the ballet. . .

[One] story on Tuesday's program was *The Nutcracker* . . . music by Tchaikovsky, choreography by Ivanov, revised by Madame A. Fedorova.

"Here the plot is thin and the mood tender. The theme is of a happy childhood when life is an eternal round of gaity and when the imagination of the child is still bold, venturous and pure.

"After a Christmas party, the girl Clara has a dream. She sees snowflakes dance, and with a nutcracker come to life, she visits the kingdom of Candy. This is no nuance, what happens is logical. The snowflakes dance because it would be a splendid thing if they could dance . . . therefore in the dream they do. And to a child it is right and inevitable that there should be a world somewhere of peppermint candy and other sweets. Adults have contempt for this kind of fantasy, and I guess, that's the reason why, to the audience and the dancers alike, choreography and music in this number appear to be everything, and the story nothing. The rendition of the Ballet Russe was in this pragmatic vein and the result, if not overwhelming, was beyond question satisfying.

"For myself, I was fascinated by the dance of the toy soldiers in the first scene. This was handled with remarkable precision by Shirley Haines and George Vernak. In the second scene, Nathalie Krassovka as the Snow Queen displayed a good sense of style and stage-craft. Her part required no real emotion, but she exe-cuted her movements with tenuous charm. I like least the third scene . . . it was done too solidly for my taste . . . but here again I must note that the corps de ballet seems mostly to blame. I am told that they were tired — this engagement in Toronto brings to an end a gruelling sea-son — but surely that's no excuse. Slovenliness is no more favourable in dancers than it is in actors. If a show goes on, then the best is the least that can be expected from the cast; the audience is entitled to that.

"But I don't want to end this discussion on a sour note. Let me say then, that I certainly intend to see the com-pany perform again.

"May I make one suggestion. If, like me, you're a novice on ballet, why not do a little reading about it before you go. You will be surprised to find how much more stimulating it is when you know something about its mechanisms and aesthetics.

"You will also find that a useful way to preserve a constructive critical attitude, and I have a suspicion that what ballet nowadays needs more than anything else is audiences who are discriminating rather than partisan."[113]

Cohen's own homework, which he frankly acknow-ledges, shows in the review. The broadcast, cleverly or-ganized behind a conversational facade, illustrates how Cohen was constantly using examples from his own ex-perience to try and develop audiences into people who could distinguish on their own the values of theatrical art forms. In doing so, he expected, and even demanded that the most stylized forms of theatre exhibit a sense of vitality and life to their audiences, so that the allegory of art would become more than an accepted form of pantomime.

In dealing with straight drama, however, Cohen, who was himself rapidly becoming something of an establishment-figure in theatrical circles, always found the concept of social respectability more than slightly suspect (perhaps because of his own quasi-outlaw beginnings as a Marxist journalist), and he frequently used that concept as a jumping-off point for his criticism, as he did in this offering for *Across the Footlights*:

"In our day, actors (besides being glamorous) are also respected members of the community. It wasn't always so. Until quite recently, in fact, an actor was one of the lowest units in the social hierarchy... not a pariah exactly... but not much better than the common variety gangster. He was someone whom all decent folk shunned. Now I wouldn't want to see a reversion to that state of affairs... but I do think that a change in the social climate from warm to slightly chilly might do many actors good. In the process of becoming polite... I'm afraid... the actor has also become inhibited.

"He's learned to pattern himself on a code of behaviour which forbids healthy emotional release on the stage. As a direct result, features of the acting art which were once indispensable are almost completely neglected today.

"For instance... aspirants in the theatre used to be trained in diction and elocution... in dancing... fencing... and body mobility. Not any more.

"Now realism is the rage... and repression the consequences. It's said acting must be natural... and, to achieve this naturalism, dramatic expression must be limited to that zone of the body safely lodged above the throat.

"The modern player conveys understanding, comedy,

horror, pity, and agony ... any sensation you can think of ... by means of facial grimaces ... and very little else. This is probably pleasing to the person who sits in the front row. It's of no use however to the people occupying the upper galleries ... who know the players only as small, distant figures ...

"... It's my opinion that many actors in this city ... the amateur ones especially ... make the error of studying movies to learn about stage movement and character projection.

"Of course, that's wrong. In a movie, for instance, the camera can reveal emotion by registering a close-up of the actor's face ... which will show everything ... even to a tear trickling down his cheek. That could be done in the theatre ... the actor could force tears out of his eyes ... but there's no point to it. In the theatre, it would be necessary to give the same emotion in quite another way ... perhaps by having the actor stand perfectly still.

"Thus the people at the back of the theatre, or the people sitting in the galleries, get the same reaction as those in the more expensive seats.

"Anyway, it's an interesting topic ... and I mention it because one of the local movie houses is trying something of an experiment in this regard. It's presenting a 'live' preview of a forthcoming British mystery film.

"I found this stunt ... and that's all it is, really ... provocative in several ways. I liked the enthusiasm of the audience. They gave the actors a sincere ovation ... and on my way out I heard a number of people say they'd like to see more plays on the stage. They may be fed on a movie diet, but they appreciate too, how much more the stage has to offer. The calibre of the acting was quite good. The three players ... William Hutt, Miss Bea Goldberg and Mel Breen ... were not flustered by the immensity of the auditorium or the good-natured cries from the crowd. They did well in the brief time at their disposal.

"The movie in question is, I gather, one of those hyper-civilized murder stories wherein everyone recites in a well-scrubbed version of the Noel Coward lexicon. At any rate, the cast enacted a scene wherein the jealous husband accuses his wife of infidelity. Just as she denies it, her playboy lover enters and the enraged husband promptly tries to strangle him. You can form your own conclusion from this synopsis.

"Be that as it may, I like this scheme of live previews. Indeed, I like anything which gives Toronto actors more opportunity to act in public and I hope that the practice of presenting trailers in this fashion is maintained. Who knows? The movie firms which swallow up the theatres may yet find themselves bringing back live entertainment in order to attract customers to the boxoffice."[114]

The spectacle of William Hutt, now considered to be one of Canada's leading actors and Melwyn Breen, who was to become a leading television producer, doing an early turn as a living preview in a Toronto movie house and not becoming flustered by "the immensity of the auditorium or the good-natured cries from the crowd," paints its own vivid little picture of the state of Canadian theatre in the late 1940's, as do Cohen's remarks about current acting styles.

Cohen's radio wrap-up of the 1948/49 theatre season gives some further insights into both the state of theatre and his own attitude toward the work he was doing:

"Today marks the end of my first season in radio as a drama critic," Cohen announced. "The fumes of the Dominion Drama Festival have cleared away . . . the summer doldrums are almost upon us . . . and this is the right time to call a halt. It may interest you to know that in the twenty-nine weeks I've been on the air, I attended, altogether, one-hundred and three shows ... ninety-one of them legitimate plays. I cite these figures to prove that, as far as theatre is concerned, Toronto is the heartbeat of Canada.

"We have more companies and see more plays than any other city in the country.

"Bernard Shaw once said that 'to a professional critic, theatre-going is the curse of Adam; the play is the evil he is paid to endure in the sweat of his brow; the sooner it's over, the better.'

"In my own case, I invariably go to a play in a spirit of optimism. I have my periods of depression ... but, as a rule, when the lights dim and the curtain goes up I get a choking sensation in my throat and a sense of quivering anticipation.

"Every playgoer will recognize the symptoms; they are typical of the incurable theatre-lover. To me, a play ... no matter who puts it on, and no matter what it is about ... always has something to offer. The director and the cast may do their best to discourage me, but I stay hopeful to the bitter end.

"In my profession, idealism is both a sedative and a salvation.

"About this program: in it I've had two main aims. First of all, I've tried to share with the average theatregoer ... the person who likes plays and wants to know more about them ... my knowledge of dramatic content and technique ... to pass on to him my own enthusiasm for the theatre, to show why one play is a success, another a failure ... and to champion the cause of theatre as an art.

"Most of us tend to think of theatre as a form of idle entertainment. But it's considerably more. Gordon Craig called it a famous temple, not a cocktail bar, a communion of imagination and action, not a pick-me-up. He meant that true theatre seeks to influence our hearts and minds and to shape, to some degree, our hopes, beliefs, and morals.

"This is indeed so; it explains why theatre remains alive and vital.

"A good play is one that adds understanding and beauty to our lives.

"A great one reveals to us, in a sudden flash, those higher realities of which we are only vaguely aware.

"Flowing out of this, I have suggested to people connected with the theatre that there is a creative and implicit connection between what a play says and the way the meaning of that play is stated in stage terms.

"Naturally, I prefer a play to be both good literature and good theatre, but the fact is that an acted play is a work of art in its own right. For this reason I have emphasized the concept of the play, the approach taken to it by the director, because this concept . . . as revealed in the spoken voice, the settings, the costumes, the appearance, movements and gestures of the actors, the arrangement of persons and objects on the stage . . . is the basis for the style of the play and its cohesion, two qualities that are indispensable to good theatre and that few plays seen here possess.

"The majority of productions that I see are anemic.

"They have no point, no personal feelings, no inventive values.

"They are at best postcard pretty; at worst they are rubbish both as art and entertainment. What I expect from a play, from any play, is that passion and human concern that makes the stage unique. I want it to be itself.

"In pursuit of my desire I have tried always to suggest how presentations could be improved . . . even though, generally, I knew my advice would be disregarded. That's also why I have spent so much time on the issue of technique. There are those who think that talent, in the theatre, is sufficient; I am not one of them. Talent may be good enough for an individual, but it won't solve the problems of an entire production. Here what is required is the co-ordination of several talents into an organic unity.

"That can only be done if talent is supported by craftsmanship and training. Many plays are put on, however, with the actors trusting to blind luck and audience charity.

"What about the past season? What's it been like? I find that, of the eighty-seven plays I discussed on the air, I gave nine unstinting praise, and liked eleven more with reservations. That's twenty, slightly less than a quarter. Pretty bad? Not at all. Quite good.

"Very good, in fact. There are always more weak plays than strong ones and this holds true whether you are speaking of theatre in Toronto or in New York or London. Besides, what make a season memorable are its best shows, the ones that had artistic merit, that were entertaining, stimulating, and positive. Art is measured by the strong links in the chain, a fact we should never forget. Now, a season that brought us, among much else, *Oedipus [Rex]*, *To Tell the Truth*, *You Never Can Tell*, *Julius Caesar*, *Born Yesterday*, *The Sea Gull*, Elizabeth Bergner, Maurice Schwartz, and two drama festivals . . . although neither was really noteworthy . . . cannot be dismissed with a shrug or a sneer. 1948/49 may not have been our finest theatre year, but neither was it by any means the worst. . .

"Since this is my final broadcast, I'd like to list the shows last year that I liked best of all. I want to pay credit again to three university players, Miss Bea Goldberg, John Howe, and Christopher Taylor, for their sin-

cerity and persuasion in the one-act item *Farewell Hope*.
It will be a long time before I forget the seething violence
and emotion that Maurice Schwartz infused into *Shylock
and His Daughter*. As drama this play was crass and
hackneyed; but good direction and magnificent acting
transformed it into a work of art. The meaning of the
play faded fast, but during its running time it created a
powerful illusion. I'd like to mention Mavor Moore for his
direction of two plays, *To Tell the Truth*, and *You Never
Can Tell*. The first, a confused comedy-drama was a success largely due to the work of Mr. Moore.

"He wrought order out of anarchy, beauty out of bewil-
derment, and his style was a striking union of discipline
and apparent discord. A word too for Lloyd Bochner in
this play. As Joe Taylor, he provided a stereotype part
with refreshing individuality; it was a pity that he re-
vamped his role when the show was put on a second time.

"*You Never Can Tell* is, of course, by Shaw . . . a rather
shabby essay on morals . . . but it had the benefit of a
perceptive and witty handling by Mr. Moore, and he had
the help of a first-rate cast.

"The last two plays on my list are comedies . . . but they
are divorced by time, temperament and theme. *The Sea
Gull*, by Anton Chekov, is a brooding and sorrowful
analysis of life in Czarist Russia; it was produced here
last winter by Robert Gill, with an all-university cast. In
thesis and development, *The Sea Gull* is quite unlike
anything in our own drama. Instead of action, there is
inaction, instead of plot, there is mood; the passion lies
under the surface; it is hinted at, it betrays itself by
indirection.

"The people involved live in private worlds of their
own; when one comes in contact with the truth, he flees
from it and retires to the safety of his fantasies.

"I thought Mr. Gill captured in large measure the

irony and sadness of this drama, and while his direction had faults, these were ruled out to some extent by the adult performances he obtained from Kate Reid and Donald Davis as Nina and Doctor Dorn.

"Finally, I want to tell you about another comedy, one that played here only last week, *Born Yesterday*, written by Garson Kanin, with Jean Parker in the lead part. I'd be exaggerating if I said it was a great play but I enjoyed it so much I'm almost tempted to say so. At any rate, *Born Yesterday* is good literature and marvellous theatre. Here is a comedy with a hard, significant core . . . its characters are of true-to-life dimensions . . . the situations are logical and relevant, genuine rather than manufactured . . . and the humour is seasoned and forceful. The play is about democracy in the United States. It is hardboiled but not cynical, and it formulates a faith in liberalism that gives it special meaning in these troubled days; Mr. Kanin not only knows what he believes, he knows how to put it in effective theatre language.

"The presentation here was smooth, handsome; it had pace and purpose, and the direction was first-class in every way. Jean Parker as the mistress of the millionaire junkman was superb. She created a person who grew up before our eyes, both mentally and physically. Sleazy in the first act, she was puzzled in the second, and determined in the third. Her performance had fine detail. As she changed, so did her voice, her manner, even her posture. Throughout, she acted with splendid comic effect.

"Well now, what else? The trouble with last talks is that they leave you with too much to say, and not enough time to say it in. In radio, time is the master. Your ideas are dictated by the clock. I had wanted to say something about the state of Canadian theatre, but I don't know if that's necessary. What can I say? The fact of the matter is that Canadian theatre is here; it's arrived. What worries me is, will it be a theatre of cant and quantity, which is largely the case, or will it be a theatre of quality, which is what I would like it to be. . .

"I know that the theatre can get along without us critics, but I think critics can make a useful contribution, and I would like to believe that I have been of some service. I don't think I've been too severe. I feel, if anything, that I've been too mild. If I have been unable to say a good word about a play, it's because try as I might, I could find no merit in it. Whenever possible though, I have endeavoured to discover virtues and to use them as the springboard for my comments.

"If I have seemed harsh, I think this is due to my use of unfamiliar canons of criticism. But for that I offer no apologies. To me, criticism is more than a stream of words suitable for an actor's scrapbook.

"That's why I frequently found myself on the opposite side of the fence . . . out of step, as it were, with everyone else, and that's why, in the instance of festivals, I preferred to follow my own judgements rather than have them formed for me by visiting critics. But time I think has proved me right in most instances. . .

"And now my time is up. I want to thank the many of you who wrote in and told me your views about these talks. If I have made theatre-going more pleasurable for you . . . and if I have been of help to theatre-people in their problems. . .then I feel I have been of some value."[115]

As indeed, he had been. Already on the road to becoming the most influential and controversial critic in the country, as well as — in the words of a CBC producer — "the most cussed and discussed man" in Toronto,[116] Cohen was having an impact on a whole new generation of Canadian actors, and setting the style for journalistic criticism for years to come.

Actor-director George Luscombe, who began his career in Toronto in those early years, summed Cohen's influence up in its simplest terms: "He was the man responsible for making us take theatre seriously."[117]

6

TOWARD A NATIONAL THEATRE

Although Nathan Cohen had frequently chided other commentators on the arts scene for their premature announcement of the birth of a fully grown Canadian culture, he was himself engaging in some mild hyperbole when he announced late in 1949 that "The fact of the matter is that Canadian theatre is here; it's arrived."

Certainly, Cohen had qualified his enthusiasm over the arrival of a distinctively Canadian brand of theatre by expressing concern about its levels of quality and the ability of audiences and media critics to distinguish between its major and minor accomplishments, and this was to prove a wise and prudent — if not particularly popular — judgement.

For Canadians, who normally think of themselves as a rather stolid lot, are in reality given to uncharacteristic outbursts of enthusiasm when it comes to their real or, as is more frequently the case, imagined, accomplishments in the world of culture, often resulting in a mode of

conduct not unlike that described by the humorist
Stephen Leacock when he wrote of a rider who mounted
his horse "and rode off in all directions." This is more or
less what happened within Canadian professional
theatre in the 1950's and 1960's, in the view of Mavor
Moore:

"The New Play Society, founded in 1946, was the first
of the post-war professional production groups in
Canada. Joined in 1952 by the short-lived Jupiter
Players and in 1953 by the Crest, they promised a renaissance in Toronto theatre," Moore explained.

"This promise was reinforced with the sensational
1953 start of the Stratford Festival and the subsequent
launching of the Canadian Players as a national touring
company.

"But perhaps the expansion was too sudden and too
fast. Perhaps too many key people exhausted themselves
physically and financially in an effort to keep up with it.

"Perhaps the proliferation of smaller professional and
semi-professional companies, all trying to get on the
bandwagon, glutted the market.

"Perhaps too many promising players and directors,
having tasted success, were anxious to try their luck in
London, New York, and Hollywood.

"And perhaps some people tried to spread themselves
too thin by working in stage, radio, television, films and
teaching.

"There was another contributing factor. Amid the excitement of a burgeoning theatre and the wish to be part
of it, some organizations never found or soon lost sight of
a compelling purpose. The New Play Society, despite a
fine record of producing original works, gradually saw its
most serious productions subsidized by its one enormous
commercial success, Spring Thaw, and was gradually
forced into semi-retirement.

"Jupiter Theatre, designed to bring vital contemporary works to the Toronto public, became an actors' theatre and collapsed from their failure to agree. The Crest commenced frankly as an actors' theatre with imported help to provide the polish. The polish was achieved, but at the cost of any consistently meaningful policy — except a kind of desperate striving to discover public demand instead of creating it — and of acquiring a reputation for artiness.

"It is noteworthy that Toronto Workshop Productions, the one recent company that has kept a strong single-minded impetus, has outlasted its predecessors. . .

"The Canadian Players . . . moved from a policy of touring compact versions of the classics to a more daring one; a full season in Toronto presenting a mixed bill with emphasis on new plays. But the theatre they occupied was too small to make ends meet and the new group found itself in financial trouble about the same time as the Crest did, although for different reasons.

"To the public there was not a wide difference between the two organizations — the same actors, directors and designers often worked at both — so to take sides in an effort to raise more money became pointless and even distasteful. . ."[118]

Perhaps the results were inevitable. Canada was, and to a large extent remains, a coat-tail culture, taking its economic as well as artistic cues alternately from *La Mère* France, Mother England, and eventually Uncle Sam. And the offspring of any such union is bound to be more than a bit of a bastard child — if not stillborn.

If a too-eager desire for expansion was to result in the dashing of those original theatrical hopes within the Toronto theatre community, it wasn't because of a lack of warnings by Nathan Cohen. His broadcasts during the opening months of the new 1949/50 theatre season continued to elaborate on the themes of dramatic quality and the need for critically observant audiences and, as well, he was becoming increasingly critical of the dangers of a Canadian theatre which modelled itself on the example of the American stage. And once again, this premature theatrical nationalism was to bring Cohen as much opprobrium as approbation, causing him to remark:

"I have been asked if I have a grudge against Americans, and if that's why my reviews of their shows are usually negative. To coin a phrase, I bear no man ill will... and if my comments about a play are unfavourable, it's because I can find nothing in it to praise.

"In any case, the American theatre today is a graveyard... a happy hunting ground over which lie scattered the bones of many a promising talent.

"You see, art and entertainment are inseparable... but the Americans refuse to believe it. They keep trying to cut the ties that bind the two together. The speculators who run American theatre want us to believe that the wasteland they have created is an oasis... but the truth is that it's no more than an island of desolation."[119]

Cohen was to continue to develop this theme of commercial control of an artistic medium, linking it to the relationship between audience, critic, and the arts, in subsequent broadcasts. He discussed the gradually weakening position of the playwright in the American theatre in the light of the career of Phillip Barry, author of *The Philadelphia Story*, a play then enjoying a revival in Toronto:

"The point I want to make about *The Philadelphia Story* is that it's repetitive. It deals with matters that Mr. Barry had amply disposed of in *Holiday, Paris Bound* and *The Animal Kingdom*. Why then the rehash? It wasn't that the author had nothing else to talk about. He proved quite different in a whole series of plays. They were not good plays, but, in the use to which they put the high comic style and in their perception, they were definitely in the tradition of true theatre, and made it clear that Mr. Barry had talents well worth cultivating.

"The critics, however, took another view. They acknowledged that he was more than a carpenter of clever situations . . . but they claimed the theatre was no place to clarify one's ideas or to acquire new ones, and they rebuked him for daring to measure up to his responsibility as a writer of drama. The audience, of course, took its cue from the critics . . . and Mr. Barry had no alternative. Try to improve though he did, he had to keep turning out carbon copies of *Paris Bound* and his prestige as a playwright accordingly dwindled and shrank.

"The death of Mr. Barry coincides with the end of the first half of the century, a period in which American drama has been widely publicized and acclaimed. There is even a popular belief that, from 1919 to 1939, the American drama enjoyed its golden age and was rich in technical, experimental and creative achievement. I suggest to you that these years were threadbare in quality, and that the one memorable thing about them is the way in which a mass of potential talent was abused and wasted.

"And yet, this act of spiritual self-destruction is not surprising.

"Theatre in the United States has always been immediate. It proceeds from the blind accident of talent itself . . . nothing else. It has no social base, no broad human inspiration, no moral and ethical foundation.

"What counts is the glitter of personality. A play is like a fireworks display. One moment, the sky is ablaze with light and colour; the next all is dark and formless. Each day is a new day, the drama absorbs nothing from yesterday, and leaves nothing for tomorrow. Players are typecast, and plays with imaginative content are shunned or vulgarized. Opinions are amusing, but convictions are frightening. Prejudice is proper, but passion is prohibited. The theatre connects itself to nothing; it's a vast warehouse of disconnected and evanescent memories.

"England has its Old Vic, Ireland the Abbey Theatre, France its Comédie–Française, Russia its Moscow Art Theatre, and postwar, dismembered Germany has its many city and state theatres . . . not because people over there are more gifted than the Americans . . . but because to them the theatre means something; it's more than a form of fleeting entertainment.

"Canadians have much to learn from the fate of drama in the United States . . . and the main lesson is that unless we take our embryo drama away from the speculators and draftsmen and critics, unless we give it back to the actor, the writer, and the discriminating audience . . . we'll wake up one bright Christmas morning to find out that our theatre has neither a present nor a future. It doesn't have to happen. . . . it most certainly can be prevented . . . but the responsibility for that lies on our own shoulders, and the time to realize that fact is now, right now."[120]

The lesson couldn't have been clearer, nor, as we have seen from Mavor Moore's summary of what happened to the Toronto companies which began with such bright promise, could it have been more clearly ignored.

When Cohen spoke of theatre, he was thinking of a theatre of quality — which would produce a body of work which added to the sum total of human theatrical endeavour. Yet in the still semi-amateur, highly personality-oriented world of Canadian theatre, the example of U.S. theatre (and, it should be mentioned, the lure of Hollywood) was one of commercial success and

Croesus-like riches, compared to the makeshift resources available at home. The American commercial theatre appeared to Cohen as a vast artistic and aesthetic wasteland, but to Canadian theatre people, its shifting sands resembled grains of pure gold. The result, as Cohen predicted, and Moore has pointed out, was that while the theatre and entertainment industry was to grow in Canada, it was to do so in the spirit of a boom-town mentality, and without that overriding sense of purpose and consistent artistic policy which is essential to the development of a meaningful national theatre.

Scarcely before it had time to begin, the union Cohen envisioned between the actor, the playwright, and the audience — which is at the heart of genuine theatrical communication — was being disrupted: the critic, often in cahoots with the professional entrepreneur — who had his own idea of the "enriching" potential of theatre — was becoming the arbiter of taste, rather than its interpreter, in the popular media.

In protesting against these developments, which he could clearly see coming, Cohen was also venturing further afield than the limited boundaries of a half-realized Canadian theatre, for the critics of whom he was in turn critical were, in many cases, the American critics — a fact which, since his broadcasts could be heard below the border, was soon to gain him some attention in the U.S. The New York critics, for example, who were almost universally regarded as the toughest and most stringent in the world, were characterized by Cohen during this period as being, on the whole, "a gullible and tender-hearted crew"[121] and he remained skeptical about them throughout his career.

Always the freelancer, Cohen continued during the early 1950's to broadcast on a number of CBC radio programs not directly related to theatre, doing such items as features on *Forgotten Pioneers*, a history of Jewish immigration to Canada; biographies of Canadian characters such as Norman McLeod, an early settler in Cape Breton; and reviews of books, radio programming, and Canadian art for programs such as *Monday Magazine, Books and Shows, Speaking As a Listener, Critically Speaking*, and others on the CBC International Service. His broadcasts for the latter, incidentially, also helped create an interest in Cohen's particular brand of iconoclasm outside of Canada.[122]

However, as Cohen himself freely acknowledged, it was his reviews on the program *CJBC Views The Shows* that made his reputation, and the quality — let alone the sheer quantity — of those broadcasts was to make him a household word in Toronto, a national personality, and help lay the groundwork for his international recognition.

Cohen's own contributions aside, there were a number of other factors which further explain why he became popular, not the least of which is that he was simply the right kind of man appearing at the right time. With CBC radio building a mass audience across the country, and in a manner which was highly conscious of its cultural mandate, the figure of the critic-as-character, in the sense of a highly distinctive personality, was already a popular one in broadcast circles.

Other broadcasters on the arts, in addition to those radio critics already mentioned, had assumed the position of old — if sometimes a trifle odd — friends to regular listeners, including such distinctive types as the late James Bannerman and J. B. "Hamish" McGeachy. Radio commentators in those days could be a colourful lot, and the northern air was literally filled with the accents of what sounded to native Canadian ears like the plummy tones of English remittance men who had at last found a haven in the New World, and Bannerman, the witty but somewhat stodgy-sounding host of *CBC Wednesday Night* (a conglomerate of cultural and dramatic programming) certainly filled the bill.

Broadcaster Max Ferguson — who was himself to become a legend on CBC programming after he grumbled out of the wilds of CBC Halifax and emerged as CBC Toronto's Old Rawhide in 1949—has given us a charming picture of Bannerman:

"It always amazes me when someone occasionally asks, "What's this Bannerman like... kind of stuffy?" Ferguson remarks in his autobiography, *And Now ... Here's Max*.

"I invariably answer by recounting what I know of the man's incredible background — a professional boxer, naval officer, race car driver, a guide-cum-gigolo for hire by wealthy ladies who wished to see Europe, a man who can guess your weight to the pound, having learned the art while traveling and living with gypsies... Bannerman to my way of thinking, embodies the most fascinating blend of the scholarly academic and the earthy stevedore.

"His coherent and always stimulating speech is a remarkable mixture of Coward and Rabelais..."[123]

McGeachy, a regular panelist on both *Now I Ask You*, an amusing intellectual quiz program on the style of the BBC's *My Word* and Cohen's own *Fighting Words* was "first and foremost a newspaperman. He belongs to a vanishing species, the newspaper essayist," as Cohen described him in 1966. [124]

It was natural that Cohen, who rightly regarded his own background as somewhat unorthodox, would be drawn to these men, who were older in years, but in many ways contemporary in attitudes, and who were men of experience as well as men of letters. A system which could find room for both a Bannerman and a McGeachy could certainly find room, he probably felt, for a Cohen.

Cohen was to remember Bannerman as "a personal and cultural essayist: working in the medium of radio rather than in print;" terms of reference which could also have been applied to himself, but, in Bannerman's case: "He was a commentator not a critic. He understood the distinction and never overlapped."

Commenting on how Bannerman's urbane and witty commentaries had been progressively cut from their original fifteen minutes to a superficial five by CBC programmers, Cohen, said:

"CBC radio may have lost faith in itself but Bannerman never lost faith in it; he retained it right on, until he could broadcast no more."*[125]

And of course, the amount of time allowed a critic in those halcyon days of broadcasting was another factor contributing to the popularity of Cohen, as well as the others. Although Cohen was to complain that there was "never enough time" to talk about all the things that were on his mind, by today's standards the time period allotted was enormous. In comparison, the amount of time and space given to the commentator in radio or television now is a miniscule snippet, and that of the

---

*Always a sentimental man, Cohen was deeply moved by Bannerman's death, which occurred only a year before his own. Men like Bannerman and McGeachy were his contemporaries in broadcasting, if not age, and he was hurt by the lack or recognition accorded to their contributions to Canadian culture. In a letter to a friend, Cohen wrote:

"Bannerman was a national asset, and while he received obituary notices it struck me as further evidence of our cultural shallowness that his death received no serious notice — indeed, no notice at all — in the editorial page columns and television and radio columns of the country." (Letter to Mrs. Cynthia Aikenhead of Calgary, December 16, 1970)

newspaper or magazine columnist extremely limited, affording them the opportunity to comment only on the immediate event, with rarely an opportunity to put their criticism into the wide-ranging context that characterizes Cohen's copy of the 1950's.

In fact, while it's true that — as one prominent journalist recently put it — an editor cannot simply bark, "'Get me another Nathan Cohen,' any more than theatre director Jean Roberts can bark, 'Get me another Bertholt Brecht' for a playwright,"[126] it may be equally true to suggest that the editor would barely know what to do with such a critic if he found one. Certainly, the man would be unlikely to be given the forum then available to Cohen.

One of the factors in the success of such broadcasters as Cohen, Bannerman or McGeachy has to do with the ring of authority and sincerity of the human voice coming over the radio, as opposed to the cold objectivity of the printed word, which can be picked up, glanced at, and discarded if the attention strays. True, the radio can always be turned off, but once the ear and the mind become drawn into a *conversation* — which is how Cohen's essays on theatre *sounded* to the listener — it is difficult to turn oneself off.

Although in written form the essay takes shape as a monologue, in the mind of the listener the voice transmutes it into part of a *dialogue* in which the inner ruminations of the listener become another voice.

Also, there was still the novelty aspect of radio itself, in which the listener's imagination created a character to go with the voice and personality to which they had become attracted; thus the listener established a relationship with that character by in effect giving birth to a part of it, rather than being faced with the unimaginative, purely take-it-or-leave-it image presented on the television screen.

In the days before Canadian radio became a flattened surface of audible wallpaper and raucous tonal sentimentality, the nature of its extended conversations, instead of being the newsy bombardment of information prevalent today, caused listeners to become an integral part of the programming. The extended time-frame available to the radio critic in the 1940's and 1950's more or less automatically drew his audience into a relationship to his ideas and personality, and the content of his programs was by its very nature aimed directly at the mind and imagination of the listener, unlike say, the primarily visual offerings of television (even of so-called talk shows). The listener was literally forced to think about, rather than simply react to the images formed in his mind by the words he was hearing, and audience participation in the experience was just that — participation — rather than the essentially static experience of viewing.

However, as the techniques of radio broadcasting adopted their own auditory version of the quick cuts of the visual mediums of film and television — for example, today an hour-long radio program will normally be made up of hundreds of little items pieced together by a tape editor from a mass of different sources rather than a few familiar voices — the person on the receiving end of the radio set became a listener rather than a participant in the sense already described: selecting from the bits and pieces which catch his attention, rather than joining in, in a flow of consistent ideas.

The effect has been a decline in the mass-audience participation in the act of criticism as it was envisioned by Cohen, and a concomitant loss of interest and critical audience perception of what the critic is hurriedly trying to say. The commentator on the arts in today's electronic media projects his information into a vacuum as far as the audience is concerned. It is his *opinions*, rather than their basis, which get all the emphasis and attention. The result is a less critical, but infinitely more malleable audience for the media themselves — as Cohen himself realized when he commented in 1967:

"One of the strange things to happen to CBC radio in recent years has been the elimination of programs of criticism of the performing arts, especially of radio and TV.

"Programs about the performing arts there are in abundance ... but mostly they are commentaries, or promotions, or simply reports.

"Programs which entail the passing of value judgements, however, seem to have faded away.

"The closest thing to one which still pertains on a network basis is the Sunday morning show *The Arts This Week, National Edition*, but even here analytical comment is at a premium, and you are not offered the kind of serious and thoughtful criticism the listener used to get as a matter of course on, say, *Critically Speaking*.

"One of the reasons a program of such criticism is needed is that the newspapers do such a bad job of it. But another reason is that radio and TV in Canada, especially in the CBC, need the kind of monitoring that will keep program planners and producers on their toes, and mindful of their obligations.[127]

As Andrew Allan perhaps all-too-prophetically had also pointed out: "Broadcasting is one of Canada's principal means of survival: it had better not be shrugged off."[128]

If the critic was to fall into evil days in the future, with the Bannermans, McGeachys and Cohens becoming, in effect, as scarce on the airwaves as the buffalo on the plains, in 1950 he was at his zenith and, as in the case of

Cohen, many, if not most, of the critiques in which his listeners joined were exercises in social as well as artistic criticism.

"Not so long ago, right up to the end of the war in fact, Canadian theatre operated in a vacuum of imitation and self-deceit," Cohen announced in January of 1950.

"It was a little theatre . . . fed on the hits of the past Broadway year . . . and it made no contribution to the art of theatre or to its literature.

"Yet it kept the mechanism of theatre going, and reminded people that a live theatre did exist. It helped to bridge the way for the commercial . . . the professional . . . theatre that is now taking form and that will produce the inventive actors, proficient craftsmen, and skilled playwrights on whom the living drama depends.

"The three plays I am about to discuss were written for, and produced by, professional companies. Two of them, *Fortune My Foe* by Robertson Davies and *Who's Who* by Mavor Moore, are not really plays at all, but essays of social criticism in play form. The third, Harry Boyle's *The Inheritance*, is pure narrative, designed only to entertain. All three deal with the Canadian scene as it is now . . . or was, in the immediate past.

"As Robertson Davies sees it, Canada is a nightmare to people of good taste and culture. His place of action is a hangout near Kingston, where professors and newspapermen get together . . . drink whisky from teacups . . . and bare their souls. His hero, Heyward, is an educator at Queens who wants to get a job in the United States because he needs the money, would like the prestige (he calls it 'honour'), and believes this will impress the girl he loves . . . Vanessa . . . a cryptic young woman with an odd assortment of friends. Heyward's mind is fired . . . until some experts on child recreation insult a refugee puppetmaker who had hoped to put on a show for the children.

"The refugee is not discouraged. Someday, Canada will find a place for him and his art.

"Heyward now decides that he too must remain here ... even though it damns him to poverty and means he can never hope to marry Vanessa.

"He remarks: 'Everybody says Canada is a hard country to govern, but nobody mentions that for some people it's a hard country to live in. Still, if we all run away, it will never be any better ... Let Canada do what she will with us, we must stay.'

"Mr. Davies' technique is to pound his arguments home with a battering ram, to draw inconsistent conclusions ... statism, for instance is bad, but the government should subsidize artists ... and to repeat, whenever the action flags, that a civilized human being needs the disposition of a martyr to stay in this cold, hostile country. When he deals with incidental matters ... when the tramp Buckety tells how he used to sell dirty pictures, or Heyward traces the evolution of a pun ... Mr. Davies reveals a rough comedy talent ... but in a general way his play is defensive in structure and feeble in characterization. There is plenty of satire ... but it is topheavy with abuse, impatient with Canadians for their interest in the material things of life ... and the entire play is very immature, very sad.

"Of course, what's wrong is that Mr. Davies is flogging a dead horse.

"The Canada he attacks no longer exists. We reached our majority in 1939 ... and the war set into motion creative impulses of art and patriotism that have turned this country from a household of belligerent boarders into a unified family. The period of change was short; the degree of change considerable... but one can hardly commend Mr. Davies for his failure to realize that the change has taken place.

"What bothers Mavor Moore is the dilemma of the Canadian intellectual... faced with a destiny which appears to have no use for him.

"I can best define *Who's Who* as a play of intention. That is, the story and theme are planned to move on two levels. On the first, Mr. Moore makes use of an old, but always good, trick. When the curtain goes up, the survivors of Robert Murray, an advertising executive, banter unflattering remarks about the dead man. This goes on for several minutes... and then a man runs up from the audience, ordering the actors to quit. It appears he knew the man whose life inspires the play... and what's happening on the stage is a lie... a slander.

"When the author (the intellectual) defends himself... the director, players and heckler turn on him... and insist on showing how his subject matter should have been handled. On the second level... and this appears only after it's over... *Who's Who* is an earnest plea for a workable code of liberalism. Mr. Moore's intentions are honourable... but his proposals undistinguished. They are vague generalities. This absence of clarity makes the last act labourious going... and, after the first scene, the play-within-a-play and audience participation device wears thin and threatens to snap... even though it never does... quite.

"Then too, the deliberate obliteration of character and crisis... without which no play is a play... makes it fundamentally a variety show, or a vaudeville. Yet with all its failings, *Who's Who* seems to me unquestionably the most important play so far produced by a Canadian writer. At least three scenes... the interview with the reporter, the advertising sequence in the last act, and the war effort speech... are satire at its best and show a keen perception of human nature. They stand on their own as imaginative writing; are genuine literature. Finally, the play is superior entertainment, with surprises that startle and amuse the playgoer and keep him wondering what will happen next.

"In these jaded, skeptical days, that's an achievement not to be despised.

"Harry Boyle's play is an affectionate souvenir of Ontario farm life, right after the First World War, that touches briefly on the struggle for authority between the older and the younger generations. *The Inheritance* is the story of a stubborn man who prefers the horse to the tractor and who, with the best of motives, tries to impose his will on his grown-up children.

"His older son, married, with children of his own... has the status of a favourite hired hand... and his younger son* when he marries is forced to move into the house, instead of getting a farm of his own.

"It takes a runaway horse, which injures him and the news that his granddaughter must go through a shotgun marriage, to make Alec MacDonald realize the error of his ways... but once he does, he makes hasty amends... and the family unit is apparently held intact.

"Now, although *The Inheritance* is ordinary in dialogue, incident and action, it caused a remarkable commotion here after its premiere. Why?

"... You know that for years the favourite national pastime has been answering the question 'What is a Canadian? How do you distinguish him?' and so on.

"Mr. Boyle does not set out to answer any of these

---

*Don Harron, who played the younger son, claims he was to use the character and accent he developed in *The Inheritance* as the prototype for his now famous Charlie Farquharson routine, which he introduced in the 1952 *Spring Thaw*. (Interview with Don Harron, Global TV's *Be My Guest*, August 30, 1976.)

matters ... but he does know rural Ontario and the people who live there ... and that knowledge is manifest all the way through the play. Look at some of his characters ... the old man ... hard working, deeply moral but not a bigot, proud that his land is debt free; or the younger son ... machine conscious, impatient and so unruly ... articulate only when he's had a social drink and obnoxious when he's had several ... or the school teacher daughter-in-law, very conscious of her education but no snob. These people are real. We know them. They are part of us ... the kind of people who remind us of ... ourselves ... friendly but somewhat reserved ... annoyed by the new but prepared eventually to adjust to it ... deeply affected by religious principles we are somewhat ashamed to admit ... fundamentally tolerant in moments of personal crisis ... firm in debate but ready to listen to the other side.

"So Mr. Boyle, if he doesn't answer the question point blank ... at least does tell us what some average Canadians are like ... and the amazing thing about them is that they are average, and are Canadian ... and this gives his play a charm and authenticity that compensates for the awkward construction and drab plot.

"*The Inheritance* is good entertainment. That it's crude at the edges and sentimental at the core is true, but it has too, in ample measure, a fluent and refreshing modesty.

"I've an idea that Mr. Boyle's play will become a staple of Canadian drama in the coming years ... and who knows? After a while it may be as much of a fixture on the Canadian scene as bad jokes about MacKenzie King and newspaper photos of Mayor Houde of Montreal in his ... shirtsleeves."[129]

Once again, Cohen's tendency toward hyperbole in discussing matters of Canadian culture got the better of his judgement, and we find him doing precisely what he criticized so many of his predecessors for doing — announcing that the country had, in effect, come of age. Yet, like fledgling Canadian "playwrights of intent" whose work he discussed, Cohen's intentions were good, and in the light of the enthusiasm existing at the time, his conclusions about the potential for Canadian theatrical and overall cultural development were far from unfounded; anymore than was his enthusiasm for the genuine virtues of Mr. Boyle's play about rural Ontario.

If the first rich spring season of Canadian drama was to all-too-soon turn into an indian summer, it was not the fault of the men who were trying to create it; and Cohen continued to hammer away at what he felt was an audience-over-appreciation of theatrical clichés which needed to be discarded. Thus, in his desire to promote the values of criticism, as well as those of the arts, Cohen founded a small magazine called *The Critic*, in 1950.

A lively little six- to ten-page journal, it included theatrical reviews and editorials on the arts by Cohen, book reviews by Robert Weaver, film critiques by Gerald Pratley and a running coverage of art, ballet, music, radio and television by a variety of knowledgable contributors.* Cohen was to continue publishing the magazine, much of which he wrote himself, until the latter part of 1953, when he realized he could no longer afford to subsidize it.[131]

*Copies of the magazine also offer up some interesting material for nostalgia collectors in the way of its advertisements, including an announcement that the Lorne Greene Academy of Radio Arts, 447 Jarvis Street, is opening a "foreign language department"; Francis G. Peddie, Barrister and Solicitor can be located — presumably for consultation on legal matters, or acting assignments — at 17 Queen St. East; and actor William Needles is available for "private tuition in speech and drama" at 136 Lytton Boulevard, in Toronto.[130]

With an even larger forum available to him than his radio broadcasts — in the sense of the amount of space available for discussion — Cohen attempted, in *The Critic*, a more rigorous examination of the Canadian cultural scene. A debate between Cohen and Mavor Moore on the subject of Canadian theatre in September of 1950 is typical of the magazine's universe of discourse, with Cohen firing the opening salvos:

"Even the best among us are not infallible," Cohen began. "Making an inventory of the Canadian theatre in the August issue of *The Canadian Forum*, Mavor Moore finds the shelves stacked high with quality merchandise but the stores empty for a conspicuous lack of purchasers. 'I know of no country,' he writes, 'where the dramatic arts are in such low estate as in Canada; and if we take into consideration the population of Canada, and its importance in the modern world, any other nation's relative philistinism pales into obscurity.'

"The trouble is caused by the animosity of the Canadian public.

"Engrossed in the management of material affairs, disdainful of the creations of the human mind, the (I presume, for he does not define) dominant elements of our English-speaking society have only contempt and condescension for the dramatic arts, regarding anyone who ventures into this realm with serious intentions as a lightweight or queer, or both.

"This attitude is the cause of all our theatrical difficulties, for whatever inadequacies exist in production (Moore has it that only spectacle shows are seriously insufficient), for the inability of many individuals to further their dramatic desires, and for the financial precariousness of the entire Canadian theatrical movement.

"He wraps up his indictment in a flat, all-inclusive sentence: '*It is not the Canadian artist who is not good* *enough; it is the Canadian public which is not good enough for the artist.'**

"This being the case, what can be done to rouse the Canadian public from its sloth? Moore answers: 'What is necessary is a long and wide re-education of the Canadian public away from the barrenness of a life based on running nowhere fast, to a realization of the importance and necessity of creative art. Indeed, this educational process is already underway. There will be many casualties in the coming period but, the way things look now, in about ten years the Canadian theatre is likely to be established on a sound, secure basis.'

"Taken in their entirety, Moore's ideas are not exactly novel.

"Largely, they comprise a restatement of the views Robertson Davies advanced about the arts and humanities in Canada in *Fortune My Foe*.

"Coming from Davies, who appears determined to prove that whatever Canadians try to do on their own must necessarily be inferior to what has already been done in other countries, the heaping of censure on the Canadian public occasions no surprise. But from Mavor Moore, who probably knows more than anyone else just how much progress our native theatre has made since Canadians became aware of themselves as a nation — which is to say since 1939 — this kind of indiscriminate maligning causes perplexity and dismay.

"His own experience should tell him that the Canadian public is more than eager to appreciate and support the efforts of its dramatic artists. The plays Mavor Moore has directed for the New Play Society have been the best patronized in that company's whole history. His comedy *Who's Who* drew more people into the museum theatre

*In the following articles, all italics are those of Cohen and Moore.

that any other of the original plays the NPS presented. (This writer, congenitally averse to superlatives, has not hesitated to describe him as the man who, by his work and influence, has done the most to raise Canadian theatre to a level of artistic excellence, our best régisseur, the only person to whom the word 'genius' can honestly be applied.)

"Others can also attest to the enthusiasm and patience of the Canadian public. The anxiety with which the plays of Coulter, Boyle, Callaghan and Allan are awaited shows that the Toronto playgoing public is ready to support Canadian drama; more than that, this public is disposed to show native playwrights a boundless tolerance. If people did not register the same box-office zeal for some of these shows that they did when Moore's play was performed, they were exercising a proper discretion, and the privilege of any audience. Nor were they by any means wrong in their judgement.

"Where else but Toronto would such unmitigated claptrap as *Narrow Passage* have been allowed to run an entire week? And if *The Inheritance* did not do as well as the NPS and the critics would have preferred, the facts show that so much else was going on that same week it is doubtful that any local presentation would have done better.

"But the Toronto public is not only anxious to give playwrights a chance; it shows the same partiality to the NPS itself. The figures contain the proof. In the first year of operation, an NPS show ran two nights; in the second year three; in the third year seven.

"The NPS was able to expand in this fashion because of a steadily-growing audience procured through the meritorious production of established dramas, experimental plays, and originals.

"Sometimes this audience presevered when the NPS reneged on its own standards. Audiences in Toronto unkind, bigoted, patronizing? Not at all. As the history of the NPS demonstrates they are loyal and, when need be, indulgent.

"The whole matter speaks for itself. Moore should know this, just as he should also know that if, prior to 1946, the Canadian public showed no great interest in local theatre it was because there was no theatre to show any interest in. It is all very well to say people should appreciate art.

"For them to do so however, they must first have it proved to them that it is art, and hence adds value and meaning to their way of life. It is all very well to say that the arts are, or were, scorned in Canada.

"But the statement will not stand inspection. The truth is that, until a few years ago, the only thing that characterized our arts was a hollow adequacy, taxidermal competence, and nothing more.

"There was nothing in the arts for the public to come to grips with; our artists were either dilettantes, who plied a precious ignorance disguised as intellectual mystery, or else flyweight hacks.

"When the situation changed, and the arts in Canada started to throb with life and energy, then the temper of the public also changed and indeed ran ahead. This is proved, not just by the way Toronto took to the NPS, but by the significant growth of summer stock in Ontario and of winter repertory companies across the country, by the continued post-war prosperity of CBC radio drama, and by the upswing of layman interest in painting, ballet, and opera.

"The moment the artists came out of their chrysalises the public was on hand to welcome them. When Moore decries the ingratitude and apathy of the Canadian public, he is, in effect, refuting the facts of his own experience.

"Somehow, I find it hard to believe that he is unaware of these things.

"Moore is no abstractionist. He has his finger on the pulse. His arraignment of the public makes one wonder how much of it was a spontaneous expression of protest, and how much of it was calculated to prod the public into greater manifestations of support for the Canadian theatre.

"If the latter were his intention, what a pity he should have chosen the *Forum* to air his views! Its readers, by and large, belong to the select circle which Moore knows is almost painfully alert to its responsibilities to the creative arts.

"Moore's reasoning about the public and the Canadian theatre does not, however, seem to me half so imprudent or half so perilous as does his evaluation of the quality of the Canadian theatre we are now enjoying.

"From his observations, one infers that there can be found, in Toronto at any rate, an almost inexhaustible supply of artisans and creators whose lust for expression is thwarted by public hostility and indifference. The situation in reality is quite different.

"Certainly, we have in Toronto several accomplished professional actors; but they are not nearly so rife in numbers as Moore would suggest.

"Most of the talent in Toronto is rudimentary, tentative and inexperienced. A few years with the NPS and some shows at Hart House Theatre, doing summer stock two–three years in a row, this constitutes the sum total of these people's training; it is quite insufficient. Talent is accident. Talent without craftsmanship is like playing a Bach fugue on a penny flute. What we have in Toronto at best is a reasonable supply of *potential* professionals. The test is simplicity itself. How many could make the change from lead playing in Toronto to lead playing in Broadway or the West End, *and do so successfully*?

"While possibly Moore himself, or Robert and Margot Christie, or Lloyd Bochner, or (despite the wretched work she did last year) Pegi Brown, or Frank Peddie could make the transition without too much agony, the remainder would be quite out of their depth. I do not say that they would never be able to make the leap, or even that they are inferior to many of those who haunt the streets of New York and London today seeking dramatic opportunity.

"My point is simply that technically the overwhelming majority of our local actors are still not out of the diaper stage, and it would be mischievous to pretend otherwise.

"Besides, Moore does not tell us what he means by that word 'artist.'

"I have gone ahead on the presumption that he is talking about actors.

"But though players are certainly the most important of stage artists, the ones through whom the playwright makes his contact with the audience, the ones who communicate what he has to say, there are other theatre artists who also must be considered — directors, designers, electricians, makeup men, costumers, etc. As to them, our resources are niggardly, and highly unsatisfactory. Indeed, the shortage of *competent* directors is one of the most serious problems Toronto theatre faces. I can think of no more than three who are reasonably proficient, and of only one — Mavor Moore — who understands that an acted play must have its own art content, separate and apart from that contained within the written play.

"Since Mavor Moore believes firmly in the humanities,

he sees the theatre in its broad perspective, not as a commodity but as an influence, not as a glamorous means of employment, but as a superior social force. Fairly early in his essay, he writes: 'I believe the creations of the human mind to be as important as the conduct of human affairs. In fact I wonder to what end the latter are carried on at all, if not to make the former possible.'

"This is a fine sentiment, aptly phrased, and I concur in it wholeheartedly. But just how much understanding do the workers in Canadian theatre have of it? How many of them have done anything to *demonstrate* the importance of their art?

"Or, putting it another way, how much drama was the Toronto public offered in the past year that indicated the grandeur, the excitement, the humour, the wonderousness of the human mind in the process of creation and illumination? Not much. I recall only one, *Heartbreak House*, which was dramatically and theatrically alive!

"In the other few instances where plays of genuine quality were presented, the production of them was scarcely designed to arouse in the spectator-auditor any unique sensations. It was fine, of course, to see *King Lear* done. Here is a play of stunning impact as literature. How many, seeing it, felt that they were sharing in or being witness to soul-stirring events, heard the thunder roar across the moors, saw a man tumble from the supreme heights to the bottomless depths, knew themselves present at the exposure of a man's innermost soul and being? It is a rhetorical question since, if you look at the thing coldly, the dimensions of this greatest of all Christian epics were reduced to the scale of a masculine *Over the Hill*.

"This is not New York or London. Since the competitive side of theatre exists here only in slight form, there can be no valid excuse for our not being offered, in addition to new plays by Canadians, the best in contemporary and classic drama.

"Yet except for the spasmodic Shaw or Shakespeare, usually presented after the same play has been done on Broadway and is hence considered *de rigueur*, fare thrust on playgoers is almost entirely indigestible.

"A living Canadian theatre should include in its repertoire as a matter of course such works as: *The Master Builder, Cyrano de Bergerac, The Lower Depths, Miss Julie, Crimes and Crimes, Naked, Six Characters in Search of an Author, Blood Wedding, The Plough and The Stars, Purple Dust, The Weavers, The Flies, Ion, The Archanians*.

"Theatregoers should be permitted some familiarity too with such pieces as: *The Second Man, Biography, Summer and Smoke, Bury the Dead, A Bill of Divorcement, The Front Page, Minnie and Mrs. Williams*.

"It should not be uncommon too in a living theatre to see done the great Restoration classics, the plays of Goethe and Schiller and Brecht of Germany, the plays of Molière and Racine and Corneille and Obey and Claudel of France.

"For an artist to wish to educate the public is commendable; it is always good to hear an artist admit that he is also an educationalist. But the artist must not neglect his own spiritual upbringing. Let him demonstrate first of all that the theatre is an art form which people need and should want. Let him do so and, (again I use the NPS as an example) the theatre-going public will gladly beat a path to his doorstep.

"In an article I wrote in 1948, I observed that by 1950, by 1952 at the outside, professional theatre would be a reality in Canada. Events show this prediction was not exaggerated. To be sure, the kind of professional theatre taking shape in this country is not of the same kind as can be found in such metropolitan centres as New York (population eight million) or London (population nine million), but surely no one ever anticipated that it would be. (After all, our largest English city — Toronto — has, including the suburbs, a population of just over a million.) What has been proved, however, is that Toronto, for instance, is capable of supporting at least two permanent companies on an annual basis.

"Indeed, it did so last year. If the companies fared less well than they had hoped to, or than was economically safe for them, matters of management must be taken into account. In any event the fact is that a certain number of Canadians have at last begun to make a living from the theatre, and that the nucleus of a professional theatre has already been formed.

"This side of the question of Canadian theatre is being solved through summer stock, winter repertory, and touring companies.

"It will not be solved completely for many years yet, and the number of artists gainfully employed is never going to cause the Dominion Bureau of Income Tax any grief, but the hump has been passed, and this is the basic thing.

"The improved situation is not, it should be clearly stated, a freak development. It has come about because we now have a fairly solid, if small, body of actors who, with all their faults, are not a source of constant embarrassment on the stage, enterprising producers who are not afraid to speculate, and who have proved that businessmen can be induced to invest money in the theatre, and because of the development of a literate, discerning, expanding audience (composed partially of Canadians, and partly of British and European immigrants) which knows or is prepared to believe in theatre as an art worthy of support, but which wants more for its money than merely inept, bedraggled, versions of what can be obtained, more comfortably and ably, at the movies, on radio, or from television.

"Absorbed in the building of theatre, we must give more attention to the kind of theatre our labours are producing. We are in the unique position in Canada of being able to shape and guide, consciously, its form and function.

"This is a rare opportunity; it should be seized with both hands.

"If we go about it in the right way, we will develop a dynamic art medium which is thoroughly integrated into the fabric of our community life. We will prove that theatre can offer people something they can get nowhere else; a unique stimulation, pleasure, exaltation, and collective harmony.

"We will do this if, besides striving to put professional theatre on a commercially secure foundation, we work concomitantly to give it a true artistic quality of expression. Subject matter should be as important as the style of presentation. Not one without the other, but the two together, rendered indivisible; that is the proper goal."[132]

Mavor Moore could hardly help being flattered by Cohen's article — which had, among other things, referred to him as a genius — but at the same time, he continued to feel that Cohen was overestimating the interest, and particularly the theatrical awareness, of Canadian audiences, and was moved to reply in kind:

"I was, if anything, a little generous; many Toronto citizens who regularly turn out in droves to see visiting theatrical celebrities from abroad stay away in droves when anything Canadian comes up. This leaves a small band indeed which we may excuse from the lecture. I know the band is growing, but it's still small.

"You imply pretty strongly that I am ungrateful to this

same small band for the recognition, increasingly concrete, which it has given me personally, and the groups
with which I have worked. I'm enormously sorry that this
impression was created by my *Forum* article and it certainly is not true. . .

"But I think you drastically overevaluate both the size
and the influence of those who call themselves theatregoers; and if proof were needed, you supply it with a list
of plays which the 'living Canadian theatre' should include in its repertoire *as a matter of course.*'

"I am willing to bet that of the twenty-one you mention
— not more than one, *Cyrano de Bergerac*, would be
recognized without prompting by the next fifty passers-
by you meet going down Yonge Street."[133]

What can one say of such an exchange, except perhaps
to mourn quietly that some twenty-seven years later its
equivalent is still tiredly taking place in Canadian arts
circles? The country slips, slides and gropes its way over
its uncertain cultural footing, always grasping at
another precarious root of its branch-plant heritage in
the hope that it will find its feet, so that even today a
critic can once again ask: "Is Canadian drama anything
more than generally mediocre or fitfully interesting? An
answer would depend, no doubt, on one's expectations of
a genre that has only recently begun to develop a bicultural mythology for this country."[134]

7

BRANCHING OUT: THE CRITIC *AND* FIGHTING WORDS

In the follow-the-leader manner of journalism, something becomes news when it is being widely discussed in general — as well as suddenly thrust before the public by specific events — and by 1951 culture, as well as theatre, was increasingly becoming news in the Canadian press.

To most Canadians, who thought of it at all, theatre was the Dominion Drama Festival, causing Cohen to remark that: "... in terms of interest, press and radio coverage, and the like, it seems to me that each year the Dominion Drama Festival assumes more importance in the vital Canadian scene. It will be gratifying if, in addition, as the years go by, the DDF achieves the same significance in the vital Canadian theatre."[135]

But if Cohen was unhappy with the media's coverage of theatre in the country, he was downright disgusted with the media's handling of cultural affairs. For if theatre to the media was in 1951 the Dominion Drama Festival, "culture" was the Massey Report on the arts; and Cohen found both the report and the coverage given to it by the media lacking in substance. In his continually developing role as a critic of the media as well as the arts, he used a front-page editorial in *The Critic* to outline his displeasure:*

"Only one of the three newspapers in Toronto treated the report of the Royal Commission on National Development in the Arts, Letters and Sciences as an event of some importance," Cohen pointed out.

"The *Globe and Mail* gave it prominent front page attention, and an entire inside page was devoted to a digest of the report's findings in radio, films, theatre, publishing, architecture, art, ballet, etc.

"The *Star*, which has always preened itself as a patron of the arts in Canada, confined its first page story to an item with the loaded heading: MASSEY REPORT IS SEEN/APPEAL TO HIGHBROWS/PRO-BRITISH, ANTI-U.S.

The second of the six paragraphs in this piece sneeringly began: 'Of the five commissioners, not one can be said to represent the common man...'

"Near the back of the same issue, close to the two pages of comic strips, the *Star* carried two more stories — one a resumé of the report's recommendations on education, the other an 'interpretation' of the Commission's views on radio and television. No one could possibly grasp, from this biased accounting, the magnitude of the Commission's project, or the very earnest attempt the report makes to answer the desire of a growing number of Canadians for a guide to a distinctive way of living, founded on a community of interest extending beyond the problems of economic compatibility and the accident of artificial geographic unity.

* In the following article, all italics are Cohen's.

"Almost as one, the Canadian newspapers truncated, minimized and garbled the report's actual contents. Very few emulated the objective tone of the *Globe and Mail.* Rather, they concentrated on the Commission's fears that Canada is becoming an American cultural (and by implication economic) colony, and disproportionately emphasized the Commission's suggestion that television, like radio, should be subject to state control.

"Readers were given the impression that the document was put together by 'cultural snobs' and 'longhairs' eager to foist their 'highbrow' ideas on the Canadian public. If we are to take the anti-Massey Report propagandizing seriously, the adult Canadian is thoroughly incapable of mature thought and perception, and has no wish to understand and more comprehensively experience the world he lives in. He is, on the contrary, an unthinking slug, responsive only to the most elementary, preferably the most vulgar, forms of sensory and intellectual stimulation. The 'impractical' intellectuals, in contrast, respect the individual Canadian's intelligence, and do not treat him as mentally incompetent.

". . . Considered in its entirety, the Massey Report is by no means as complete a picture of the Canadian cultural scene as it should be. It's handling of certain fundamental questions is wholly inadequate; many of its proposals are ambiguous, a few are meaningless.

"While something like a score of organizations from Quebec made submissions to the Commission (the provincial government would have nothing to do with it) the report has remarkably little to say about the particular problems of French Canada. Nor is there anything really concrete said about bringing our English and French speaking cultural elements into closer and more positive proximity, although the absence of any true social and intellectual reciprocity between our two main national groupings is a heavy stumbling block to Canadian cultural expression.

"True, a working relationship does exist between French and English speaking Canadians, but in terms of mutual respect and exchange of values the cleavage is as profound as ever. A sensible step between bridging this schism would be to make the teaching of French and English obligatory in all schools, from the primary grades upward. (The autonomy provinces have in education has proved to be a distressingly retarding influence.)

"A second step towards English and French Canadian homogenity would be to introduce in our schools textbooks re-evaluating the Canadian past in the light of our actual history. Canadian ignorance of the Canadian tradition is appalling. (The Commission cites a far from unusual example: only seven of thirty-four students in an eighth-grade classroom knew July 1 was Dominion Day.) We have only the most perfunctory knowledge of the 1837 Revolution, or its significance in our fight for self-determination and responsible government. The Durham Report could be a Caballa Scroll for all we know or care about it. How many know more about William Lyon MacKenzie than that he was MacKenzie King's ancestor, or are familiar with Sir Joseph Howe, whose fight for freedom of the press is a bright chapter in our heritage?

"How many realize that French Canada has a lengthy and honourable record of political liberalism, and — an interesting point, notably for those who believe that French Canadians would deny other minorities the rights they ask for themselves — was the first region anywhere in the British Empire to grant its Jewish inhabitants full equality of citizenship?

"We have some faint inkling of current trends in French Canada, but allowing for *Maria Chapdelaine* and the scribblings of William Henry Drummond, we are completely illiterate about French Canada's accomplishments in such fields as exploration, the arts, and emancipated social thinking.

"One could give endless examples.

"It is precisely because we have no active awareness of our history that such a potentially significant event as the entry of Newfoundland into the Canadian community could be effected without causing even a ripple of excitement. A consciousness of Canada's beginnings would go far to making English and French Canadians useful, complementary members of the same household today.

"The Commission is not very satisfying either in what it has to say about the fostering of theatre and publishing. Correctly rejecting the notion that the establishment of a national theatre in Ottawa will place Canadian drama on a sound foundation, the report intimates that our theatre will make good progress if adequate grants are given to such institutions as the Dominion Drama Festival. This is absurd.

"What Canada needs most are theatres, buildings where shows can be presented. Their lack is the wall which the Canadian theatre movement cannot breach. It is intolerable that, in a city of a million residents, our commercial companies should have to play in inadequately built school halls or auditoriums designed for lecturing. A practical recommendation here would be the establishment, in the larger communities, of state-subsidized theatres, available at fair rentals, for the performance of plays and ballets.

"The Commission is equally foggy about fostering the publication of Canadian books, magazines and periodicals. It deplores that Canadians prefer, numerically and comparatively, American imports to native offerings.

"But as long as American reading matter is more easily accessible and is manifestly superior in appearance, this is inevitable.

"The remedy is a protective tariff that will prevent American publications from swamping our book counters, libraries and newsstands.

"Of course, one reason Canadians are fairly apathetic to Canadian publications like *Maclean's, Chatelaine, New Liberty* etc. is — let us be frank — that they are to a great extent lustreless, synthetic imitations of American models, containing little that is truly Canadian in content and feeling.

"The question of protective tariffs is very vexatious, since a full, free exchange of cultural media among countries is always desirable. Nevertheless, the preference given American publishers at the expense of our own should certainly be curbed.

"But with all the shortcomings, the failure to realize the desperate need of the CBC for a greater budget, the timid amount of authority it would allow a Canadian arts council, the report represents a milestone in our history and is, actually, *a Canadian declaration of social self-sufficiency and cultural independence*.

"It is a bitter anomaly that Canada, which is considered to be near — if not at — the apex of western civilization, is also one of the most culturally backward states in the world. *'If modern nations were marshalled in the order of importance which they assign* [to culture],' the commissioners morosely note, *'Canada ... would be near the end of the procession.'*

"The facts speak for themselves. With a population of fourteen million, we have no national library, only a handful of concert halls, only two commercial theatres (used mainly for the showing of American plays, musicals etc.). Our museums are unprepossessing in appearance, meagrely staffed and supplied; most of our universities are fighting a frantic battle for self-preservation; the few civic orchestras we do have make annual petitions for public support to eke out an existence.

"We lack decent journals of critical commentary. As we know only too well, most Canadian playwrights, painters, composers, actors, can only make a living by working as teachers or in fields other than those they really care for, pursuing their true vocations only in moments of leisure.

"Hundreds every year quit their homes, emigrating to the United States and England where the opportunities are more favourable.

"Some of the reasons for this unhappy situation are discussed above.

"Let us note other causes. One truth is that it is only lately that our artists have started to find meaningful Canadian themes for their work, and also to develop standards of craftsmanship. A second factor is that the public-at-large is not convinced of the necessity for spiritual nourishment.

"Because the arts in Canada have (especially prior to 1939) functioned largely in a vacuum, or seem like pale satellites of dazzling American constellations, there is still a widespread tendency to view them as luxuries not intrinsically related to truly successful living.

"Another hindrance, a very great one, is the exorbitant, feebly-resisted cultural pressure drawing us into the orbit of the state to our south.

"As neighbours of this rich and prodigously productive land, sharing interests produced by language identification, we have allowed the Americans to condition our tastes, standards and values. We read what Americans write at the rate of two of theirs to one of ours, our film fare is almost exclusively American manufactured, there are very few Canadian radio broadcasts that have any-thing like the large Canadian listenership enjoyed by programs piped in from New York.

"The Massey Report says that our reliance on American institutions and our *'lazy, even abject imitation of them, has caused an uncritical acceptance of (alien) ideas and assumptions.'*

"Even our educational techniques and texts are pre-dominantly American in inspiration.

"Such undue influence by one country of another is deplorable under any circumstances. Considering the sterility, negativism and decadence rampant in Ameri-can intellectual circles today, plus the neuroticism, in-stability and *herrenvolk* theorization pouring out in an endless gush from the American mass media of com-munication, the continuation of this unequal relation-ship becomes a menace to our national well-being and integrity.

"Opponents of the Commission's findings have been quick to brand it as anti-American. This is untrue. The report is neither anti-American nor pro-British (al-though it uses the British experience in state regulation of radio and television to ridicule the thesis that govern-ment financing and control stifles free artistic expres-sion).

"*The report is pro-Canadian. It's driving impulse is the fostering of a national culture*, worthy of our status in the international family and our own industrial and intellec-tual potential, embodying all that is best from other lands and peoples, shaped and recast to satisfy the high-est and best Canadian urgings and aspirations — a cul-ture that has deep roots in our own soil and brings our vineyards to a rich and remunerative flowering.

"How is this to come about? The Commission makes three main recommendations.

"One of them — to us the most important — concerns the expenditure of some thirty million dollars for university assistance. Placing such emphasis on the role of the universities in the Canadian scheme of things is far-sighted and practical. As the centres of advanced learning, our universities should be the foci, to an appreciable degree, of cultural cultivation, study and creative expression. But of course moneys given to the universities should not be restricted just to the purpose of getting better equipment, bigger libraries, and abler teachers (paid adequate salaries). Aid must be extended so that all students qualified to do so, but without financial means, can also go to college. As a result of soaring costs, a student's ability to pay fees is becoming more important than his abilities and skills. University education should be made available to all whose academic requirements are sufficient. An extensive system of university scholarship grants is an urgent requirement in Canada.

"The Commission also recommends that a portion of the thirty million dollars should be set aside for the financing of the arts, this to be administered by a Council for the Arts, Letters, Humanities, and Social Sciences, with powers similar to those of the National Research Council.

"Finally, the report proposes the expenditure of some fifty million dollars for the establishment of a new National Gallery; a National Library and historical and scientific museums. This would certainly be a wise investment, if only for the sake of national pride.

"The CBC long ago recognized that national pride is of the essence in laying the basis for a national culture. By making this proposition the foundation for much of its programming (together with some healthy cynicism about false national pride), the CBC has been a catalytic force in the forging of a Canadian consciousness. And, in its way, too, the National Film Board is an equally alert contributor to linking the regions of Canada into a connected chain.

"Now that the five-hundred-and-seventeen-page, two-hundred-thousand-word report has been tabled, the important thing is that it should not be allowed to gather dust. Rather, it should become a rallying banner for endorsation and action by all interested individuals, groups and institutions.

"Also, our political parties — particularly the CCF, which has long advocated extra nourishment for the arts, and which in Saskatchewan has pioneered in recognizing the government's obligation to foster social and cultural resources — should take the initiative in prompting the federal authorities to immediately enact the legislation called for by the report.

"The Massey Commission has provided us with a comprehensive picture of the state of Canadian culture. The steps it urges us to take are few, and some are certainly short, but they do lead in the right direction."[136]

Here we have Cohen the arts-media-social-critic at his best and, depending on one's point of view, his editorial on the Massey Report, read today, tells us much about how far — or little — we have progressed culturally in the twenty-six years since it was written.

In the editorial, Cohen pursues, with remarkable consistency, positions and attitudes which he had been developing from his college writings onward: a critique of the press and media for its superficiality and bias; a defence of the intelligence of the Canadian public against the yahoo image presented in the press; a polemic against divisive regionalism and the lack of knowledge of Canadian history; a remarkable defence of the history of libertarian traditions in Quebec — and the whole salted with constructive suggestions on the educational, cultural and social problems discussed — or ignored — by the report.*

Cohen continued to labour over the long-standing problems of Canadian cultural autonomy in *The Critic*. He was also broadcasting regularly on matters more exclusively theatrical, and while he could still summon up a good deal of enthusiasm for a new star on the theatrical horizon, he was becoming impatient and less kind toward bad performances and pretentiousness.

"A ballerina who has danced lead roles for the Ballet Club, Sadler's Wells, and the Metropolitan Ballet, and who is, as well, a promising choreographer, Celia Franca arrived in Canada a few months ago to investigate the feasibility of organizing a permanent, professional ballet company," Cohen said in June of 1951.

"She is not the first immigrant from the British Isles, or Europe, to come here in the train of Sadler's Wells with such an idea in mind, but she is the first to be invited here for that purpose, the first too to bring with her a tradition and a theory that might prove adaptable to Canadian soil.

"Meanwhile, her decision to make Toronto her main base of activity has caused annoyance in certain circles. All Canada may be berserk about ballet; but not many Canadians favour Toronto as a national ballet centre.

"As the aggrieved outcries from the Winnipeg newspapers and the veteran Winnipeg Ballet demonstrate, our national anthem is not 'God Save The King,' but 'We All Hate Toronto.'

*Parenthetically, if Cohen's suggestion about the teaching of Canada's two official languages in primary grades across the country had been implemented in the 1950's, the possibility is that today we might have the nucleus of a bilingual country rather than a costly and ineffectual language laboratory for middle-aged civil servants, and an issue which literally threatens to dismember the country on linguistic grounds.

"At any rate, it's no easy task she's taken on. By now, having inspected the various candidates and selected some for training, she is aware that while those who would study with her are legion, those with the benefit of a good preparatory technique and the right physical discipline are few.

"And, after her performance last Thursday at the prom, she would be very vain and naive not to understand that Torontonian audiences please too easily.

"At the end of the rainbow of indiscriminate enthusiasm lie vulgarization and superficiality — dangers that Miss Franca will have to fight resolutely if her company is ever to become first-rate...

"In a purely selfish way, let me say how grateful I was that Miss Franca did appear the other night. The occasion gave me one of the few chances I have had all season to make a critical comparison, and comparison, as you know, is the basis of all criticism.

"Without the opportunity to consider productions of some similarity in theme, text and style, and without the opportunity to differentiate between them and productions of another type, a critic of such art media as drama and ballet would work in a vacuum, neither upholding standards, nor revising them, nor creating them.

"A critic may be endowed with all the necessary qualifications ... a passionate interest in the art he is dealing with, a recognition of the unity of form and content, an awareness of the relationship of inventive expression and social reality and need, a loyalty to values validated by time, a skepticism of artistic dogma, an open and inquisitive mind ... but they will avail him nothing unless he can put them to the test of practice.

"There was not much chance to do that this year.

"I state the situation gently and charitably when I say that of the fifty-odd shows I attended since September,

1950, only six merited attention with regard to matter and subject, and no more than two... two... even achieved competence in style of presentation.

"In the absence of any activity of real significance, I found myself obliged to dispense entirely with theatrical criticism and to concentrate on a discussion of the written plays.

"Now, since the written play, that is the play as literature, is fundamentally more important than the acted play, the play as theatre, this procedure would not have been a hardship except, of course, that so few plays of any literary merit were presented.

"For the most, then, I spent the season discussing shoddy plays, and explaining, often repetitiously because the plays were so often repetitious in content, why there is no justification for doing such plays, and why there was no genuine satisfaction to be had when they were done well.

"Do I sound depressed? Well, I feel depressed.

"Frankly, I cannot abide to see so magnificent a medium of human expression as the drama wasted and pillaged.

"For claptrap like *Mrs. Moonlight,* or jazzed-up journalism like *The Silver Chord* or *Thunder Rock* to be enacted while O'Casey's *The Silver Tassie* and *Oak Leaf and Lavender* go unheard and unseen... for us to be deprived of the great dramatic offerings of a dozen European countries while we are subjected to the commercial American inanities that infest the play catalogue around here is to me the most outrageous kind of blasphemy.

"The truth, I suppose, is that I am full of anger against the forces that stand in the way of our developing a dramatic movement of substance and virility.

"It rankles me that Toronto should be studded with movie-houses playing third re-runs of third-rate films while groups with dramatic aspirations must die because they have no place in which to rehearse and perform.

"I marvel at the myopia of those big business institutions which, pursuing the will-of-the-wisp of public approval, squander money on foolish advertisements of wildlife and advice on how to handle tourists, but are blind to all petitions for the erection of a theatre for live drama.

"How do you fathom the workings of a charitable foundation that gives a generous grant to a little theatre organization like the Dominion Drama Festival, but turns a deaf ear to commercial, non-profit organizations which sponsor the presentation of original Canadian plays and of the classics?

"Of course, not all the trouble with theatre in Toronto comes from without. There are stultifying pressures within too. I know of scores of men and women in this city who assert that drama is the main passion in their life . . . who say they want to act, produce, write, direct plays . . . but who confine themselves mainly to talk, and allow what little theatre life we have to be taken over, by default, by amateur organizations that view real drama and professional theatre with a hatred that verges on the psychopathic.

"I am not unmindful, believe me, of the dilemma of those who would like to make the theatre a full-time career and find so many obstacles in their way . . . but too many of these folk are insincere in their protestations; they will do nothing on their own; they want their livelihoods to be handed to them on a silver platter.

"This is no way to build a theatre, no way to win an audience, no way to build a firm foundation for the temple of drama to rest upon.

"If you cannot perform in a theatre with a proscenium arch, why then you play arena style, or in school halls, or in barns or in attics, or where enough space has been cleared away so as to give the actors elbow room.

"You need only three things to present a show: a play, a cast, and an audience. Given a play worth doing, done well, the audience will excuse the rest. The result of such a presentation will be something less than perfect, but it will be much more stimulating than no show at all, and no shows of value at all pretty well describes what happened in Toronto this year because of the obsession about playing in regular theatres or not at all . . . that, and the nonsense that no one will act unless he gets paid for it.

"If your interest in theatre is at all sincere, you will want to be in the play, and make a living some other way. That's not easy, but if the thing really means something to you, it's worth making some sacrifices for.

"And if you want these efforts to bear fruit, as assuredly they can, make sure that good plays are put on. The theatre is too precious to be desecrated. Don't make the mistake of those who, in the delusion that the public must be educated, debauch the drama, insult the playgoer, and piddle away their talents, and those who come in contact with them, until no possible hope of salvation remains.

"What we need in Toronto in the realm of drama are a few tenacious persons of high standards and firm convictions, imbued with a knowledge of what they want and a determination to succeed, no matter how adverse the conditions.

"Do we have any such supermen? There was one, but that person is now anxious to pass on the same burning ideals to someone younger. Are there any others? If there are, it's time for them to overcome their shyness and come out of hiding. There is urgent need of them.

"Of course, even if Canadian theatre was in a state of oriental luxury . . . if all the summer stock companies were suddenly to find their theatres in Toronto, and were to run all winter . . . if everyone who wants to make a living as an actor or a director was at long last able to do so . . . the basic need would not be met.

"The basic need is the writing and staging of Canadian plays . . . preferably with Canadian themes and settings . . . but at least by Canadians.

"The acted play is a fleeting phenomenon; performed, it vanishes and remains only in the memory of those who saw it. But the written play is permanent . . . and if it has poetic truth and human insight, it becomes part of a people's way of life — its culture.

"We have other playwrights besides Robertson Davies whose dramas deserve to be put on and seen. Joseph Schull is one, Lister Sinclair another, John Coulter a third.

"We need to have as many plays by Canadians put on as possible. Some of them will be bad, but that is the risk you always take. The playwrights will learn from their mistakes and, given the right encouragement, will try again.

"Some of the plays will be good; by having them produced the playwrights will be encouraged to write better ones.

"The playwright, the crucial member of the drama, is the most neglected in this country. As long as he is blocked, stifled, and not allowed to be productive, the Canadian theatre will be insignificant.

"The day he is recognized as the life blood of a real drama, and his plays are enacted, on that day the Canadian theatre will come of age."[137]

Cohen's broadcast, partly a review of Celia Franca's performance and potential as he saw it, partly a lecture on critical standards, and largely a plea for dedication, effort, and even sacrifice on behalf of the development of a national drama is delivered in the tone of a disappointed lover, who sees his goddess in danger of becoming a slattern — if not a prostitute — before his eyes.

Cohen is not merely carping. In a strange and touching fashion, (". . . the written play is permanent . . . and if it has poetic truth and human insight, it becomes a part of a people's way of life — its culture") he is, out of his love for theatre, crying out for understanding, even help.

The broadcast is, in its own way, an amazing and revealing performance from a critic, and although Cohen will regain his composure, even his enthusiasm, it is as though he has already begun to see his beautiful — but none the less remorseless — dream of Canadian theatrical perfection start to fade, and a note of harshness, even cruelty and contempt, begins to appear in his writing. By December of 1951, Nathan Cohen, who had always gone out of his way to find something good to say about a play, could harshly dismiss a Toronto production as being simply "put together with a pair of rusty pliers dug out of a mound of discarded fertilizer."[138] Clearly, the velvet glove had been removed and an iron fist exposed.

Perhaps, if Oscar Wilde is correct in suggesting that each man kills the thing he loves, the reverse is also true: the things we love exact a ruthless attrition of our affections as well.

Springtime had turned to fall.

Cohen's disillusionment with the state of American drama was now virtually complete, as he made plain in a series of five radio talks for CBC in 1951 on the history of the American theatre since the First World War. The talks, which began under the title *Afternoon of Decay*, and ended with *The Light That Failed*, were a summary of the ideas Cohen had been developing as to the causes of the decline of theatre in America; the same social and economic sources which he now saw threatening to the development of a Canadian theatre as well:

"Drama as an art is dead in the United States," Cohen declared in the final broadcast of the series, "murdered by the social and economic climate in which it sought to gain life, and also by the surrender of sovereignty by the playwrights, first to the scene designer, then to the businessman.

"Any change of this situation within the framework of the commodity theatre is impossible; it can be affected only from the outside.

"Finally, the dramatic movement will only regain breath and life when playwrights with positive social ideals, a firm understanding of the manner of their art and a profound understanding of human psychology make themselves heard. . ."[139]

Cohen, now well established as a critic with five years experience behind him and recognized as editor and publisher of *The Critic* as well as the CBC's weekly drama reviewer, repeatedly used such special broadcasts, as well as his printed articles and regular airtime, as a means of improving the critical standards of his audience, rather than merely consolidating his own reputation.

He had taken pains to explain how frequently he was forced to dispense entirely with theatrical criticism and simply discuss the written play, because of the inferior quality of so many productions, and how even then he was left to discuss the plots of shoddy, inferior plays. Surely, Cohen argued eloquently, it is impossible to build a living theatre out of second-rate, imitative productions of plays which are already third-rate theatre to begin with. Even a first-rate play, worthy of critical appraisal, can contain its flaws, Cohen pointed out, and it is necessary for audiences to be able to recognize these flaws —

and *why* they are flaws — for them to obtain the maximum satisfaction and enlightenment the theatre has to offer.

Cohen's assessment of Arthur Miller's *Death of a Salesman* is an excellent example of the classical canons of criticism which he applied to plays which he felt deserved them, and of how he communicated them to his listeners:

"Full-grown and humane as many of the sequences are, *Death of a Salesman* is not the masterpiece New York reviewers acclaimed it to be in 1949, nor does it contain the profundity and splendor assorted columnists of the McCullough newspapers professed to find in it during the performance here last week," Cohen explained in September of 1951.

"True, the principal and some of the tributary themes give off waves of compassion, tenderness, despair, irony, and indignation, but we should differentiate between content and the communication of that content.

"Anyone who does so objectively must conclude that the potency of *Death of a Salesman* is heavily diluted by clumsy injections of contrived incident, notably in causing Biff's realization of his father's shame from finding Willie with a prostitute, or again in the business of the sons deserting Willie, obviously wandering in mind, in the restaurant.

"Language-wise, the play substitutes the journalistic devices of brevity and repetition for the emotional concentration and intensification true drama needs. Finally, the play from start to finish is enveloped in a miasma of self-pity, and maudlin resignation, or futility, about the present state and future prospect of the human race.

"In defence of Willie, Linda says to her sons: 'I don't say he's a great man... His name was never in the papers. He's not the finest character that ever lived. But he's a human being . . . and he's not to be allowed to fall into his grave like an old dog. Attention, attention must finally be paid to such a person.'

"Abstractly, Linda boldly affirms man's personal dignity, the right of each of us to an honourable and free life. But Willie Loman is not the best example of a man who merits that right. A failure by his own criteria, he never did well even with the particular frame of his own reference, always exaggerating the number of sales he made, the quantity of his friends, the amount of money he earned, or the upbringing he's given his sons.

"The one thing he fights for is the maintenance of the delusion of his own importance. The root of Willie's trouble . . . at least of the Willie Loman of *Death of a Salesman* . . . is not really the social system, or old age, or disappointment in his children; it's his own character.

"A man like Willie could never carry out any ambition he set for himself. He could never see the truth about himself or his world, or act rationally and courageously to change himself and his environment.

"He is not only blind, but a congenital weakling to boot, and I think it significant too, that though Miller clearly implies that Willie and his children could save themselves despite all his distress, it never dawns on Willie to question the social values of his world, while his sons learn nothing decisive from his misfortune.

"Willie Loman does not move us. Since we can identify ourselves loosely with his difficulties, we are touched by his predicament; shaken by his fate.

"For all of that, he never arouses our admiration, or the hope that somehow he will win through because he should win through; nor do we experience in his fall any feeling of disaster or deep regret.

"A man defeated by the tug of circumstances alone has our commiseration; an elemental appreciation of human dignity and self-respect commands that response. A man however who challenges adversity and exercises his free, independent will against nature and environment for the fulfillment of positive, valid objectives — a man like that commands our love, our wonder.

"Defeat and death in his case come to us as a profound loss. . .

"It would be worthwhile to see *Death of a Salesman* performed by a competent director and talented cast. It would still not reach exalted heights; but at any rate we would see acted out and brought to life the elements of sorrow and reality and truth, which, for all their warp and strain, are to be found in this play. With all my reservations, I would still rate *Death of a Salesman* as the most adult and reputable play to come from the United States in the last decade."[140]

It is interesting to compare Cohen's evaluation of the play with that of the American critic John Mason Brown who wrote, when *Death of a Salesman* was first presented in 1949: "Mr. Miller's play is a tragedy modern and personal not classic and heroic. Its central figure is a little man sentenced to discover his smallness rather than a big man undone by his greatness."[141]

In retrospect, it is Cohen's view which contains the greater insight into the effectiveness — or lack of it — of Willie Loman (and indeed a number of Miller's other characters) as a dramatic entity.*

---

* As Cohen quite rightly pointed out, Loman is not simply a little man destined to discover his smallness — he dies with as much illusion as he lived, thinking about the benefits his insurance money will bring to the family — but a character whose intrinsic faults and failings rob him of the aspect of true tragedy which should be inherent in the play. A little man who exhibits genuine strength of character, ideals and lifestyle, and is defeated by social circumstance, can still be an heroic figure without ever needing to approach greatness. Indeed, this *is* the modern and personal tragedy of our times.

Miller insists on investing his working-class characters with gigantic and frequently implausible melodramatic flaws of character and conduct which

And, just as Cohen was distressed by the treatment frequently accorded the ordinary man by artists, he was outraged by those who attempted to blame the ordinary theatregoer for a refusal to accept mediocre theatre:

"Perhaps you read that article in a Toronto newspaper yesterday citing the poor business done here by *Darkness at Noon* as proof that local playgoers are indifferent to superior drama," Cohen remarked on November 11, 1951.

"It proclaimed 'Those of us who attend the Royal Alexandra each week are fast losing faith in the standards Torontonians demand in theatre.'

"This is pretty alarming, but I don't think there is any real reason for such dismay. If, as implied, the patronage of the shows offered at the Royal Alex is the barometer of drama appreciation, then the citizens of Toronto yield first place to no one and for the last ten seasons have done their utmost to make the theatre management jump with joy.

"This year, the Sadler's Wells Theatre Ballet was a sellout, and the returns were remunerative, though perhaps not exceptional, on *Mr. Roberts, Death of a Salesman*, and *Oklahoma*. In any case Torontonians are not the only ones to cast a midnight pall over *Darkness at Noon*. The show has also been inhospitably welcomed at American centres it's played so far.

"For myself, I would rather regard the incident as indicating that playgoers are again starting to make

---

destroy the audience's identification with them, and rob his plays of genuinely tragic impact. This sort of thing is a puzzling and perplexing element in the makeup of a dramatist of the power and sensitivity of Miller; a half-buried form of intellectual superiority and hubris toward the very people with whom he purports to sympathize. It may be related to Miller's own increasing intellectual and social removal from a working-class background. It is noteworthy, for example, that Miller did not or could not stop a fifteen-minute short from being tacked onto the movie version of his *Death of a Salesman*, a short which extolled the virtues of a salesman's contribution to the American Way of Life.

independent judgements. Indeed, the decision of so many people to stay away from *Darkness at Noon*, probably based on the advice of the majority of people who saw it, would prove to me that the theatre-going public here does demand standards in theatre — better ones at any rate than those deemed desirable by members of the Fourth Estate who slavishly take their cues from the gullible gods of Gotham, except of course when the latter unfavourably review a Canadian-written play.

"Not since World War Two has the modern stage had to tolerate so completely a case of dramatic destitution as this *Darkness at Noon*, adapted by Sidney Kingsley from the Arthur Koestler novel.

"As you know, in times of war, hot or cold, it becomes fashionable to fabricate propaganda tracts establishing the unassailable superiority of 'our way of life' over that of the enemy. These take the form of either a laudation of the wonders inherent in the democratic society, or else an inventory of the horrors associated with the totalitarian behemoth.

"*Darkness at Noon* is of the latter variety, portraying life in the Soviet Union as one of unspeakable brutishness and degradation, and thus parenthetically causing life in America to shine more luminously than ever.

"An editorial platitude, the play has been further fixed-out with intricate scenic accessories and copious intellectual hugger-mugger in the hopes that audiences will imagine the whole thing to constitute drama of dazzling discernment and depth. . ."[142]

As was generally his policy when he was dissatisfied with imported productions, Cohen added insult to injury by following his evisceration of *Darkness at Noon* with praise for an unknown Canadian play — in this case Joseph Schull's *Shadow of a Tree*, which had won a London Litttle Theatre prize.

*

Regardless of his fears for the future of Canadian theatre, however, the early 1950's were a time in which Cohen moved to consolidate the widespread reputation he had already made for himself as a critic. Although he had few illusions about the difficulties of writing for theatre, Cohen made a stab at playwriting himself with what he described as "a comedy of inaction" called *Blue Is For Mourning*, about a union town in Cape Breton which is in the throes of a strike. Given his penchant for attacking his fellow critics and his remorseless demands for perfection on the part of playwrights and actors, it's small wonder that the play received short shrift when it was produced in Toronto.

Toronto *Star* reviewer Jack Karr almost in parody of the Cohen style, wrote: "Seldom, it seems to us, has any play worked so hard to make a point, only to discover, at the final curtain, that there was actually very little point to be made in the first place;" and the gentlemanly Herbert Whittaker of the *Globe and Mail* found the play "difficult to accept as a dramatic entity."[143]

It was Cohen's last attempt at playwriting, and from that point onward he did not make the mistake of stepping out of his role as a critic. He appears to have taken the criticism graciously enough, and there was perhaps even a sense of relief in his final acceptance of the fact that his was, ultimately, a critical and interpretive talent.

On the other hand, Cohen was never content to hide behind his role as a critic, and he welcomed controversy. In December of 1952, Cohen added lustre to his reputation for controversy and debate by becoming the host of the radio program *Fighting Words*.[144] The format of *Fighting Words* was Mavor Moore's. He was CBC TVs chief producer at the time. The title was the invention of

Stuart Griffiths, the CBC-TV program director. Griffiths and Moore appointed Harvey Hart to direct the program and, at their suggestion, Hart hired Cohen as moderator.

As the show's title implied, its format depended on vigorous and stimulating debate. A quotation, sent in by a member of the listening audience, was read to a panel selected by Cohen and the panelists were required to identify its author. Having done so, they then engaged in a freewheeling debate about the validity of the quotation, often humorously, and frequently with high-spirited animosity. If a radical could be found to fit the quotation and be matched against a conservative opponent, Cohen would invariably find him. As he once explained to a friend: "We are getting all the subversives, right and left, and giving them a forum. It fascinates me to see how isolated they are on both sides and what extraordinary difficulty they have in communicating.

"The great goal of technology in the twentieth century, I now realize, is the abolition of reason through communication. I am doing my little bit ... to buck the trend."[145]

Once again, this so-called unabashedly highbrow program proved that there was a large-scale CBC audience for such programming, and the show became so popular that several attempts by the Corporation to drop it from their schedule had to be abandoned in the face of widespread audience protests.[146]

Fighting Words, which ran continuously on radio until 1962, made its debut on the new medium of CBC television in 1953 where Cohen, a large, imposing figure who looked far older than his twenty-nine years, created a formidable impression as its Johnsonian moderator. Despite the ups and downs of his relationship with the CBC, the televised version of *Fighting Words* also ran until

1962. Cohen revived the program on Hamilton's private TV station, CHCH in 1970, but had to give it up after a year due to ill health.[147]

Because of his radio and subsequent television appearances, Cohen was becoming a public figure and, to a certain extent, he began to cater to his image as the irascible enemy of sham in the theatre and society. He augmented the impact of his massive frame by invariably carrying a walking stick. (When once asked by an acquaintance if he "really needed his canes," Cohen replied, "No, they're pure affectation.");[148] and his appearance at a theatre could cause quite a little stir of interest in itself.

For although Cohen delivered his work over a microphone or in print, his real working environment was the back or middle rows of a darkened theatre. Relaxed but attentive, he would keep his eyes on the stage as though he was on the verge of discovering something great that was sooner or later bound to happen there, and he rarely betrayed irritation at what was happening before him. If he became too disgusted, he quietly left the theatre.

During intermission he would stand alone, looking massive and detached, puffing imperiously on a cigarette and avoiding any attempts at chitchat about the performance. On occasion, the hooded glow of a pen light would flicker in the darkness, as he began jotting down notes, and at that point, whether they had seen him before or not, theatregoers who caught the flicker of that bobbing, muted light, would nudge each other and whisper "Nathan Cohen. . ."

"I belong to that school of critics which doesn't believe in taking notes at a show," Cohen said, in 1967.

"Although I don't consider myself a representative playgoer I go to the theatre as a member of the audience and I don't start functioning as a critic until the show is over and I am on my way to the typewriter.

"My theory quite simply is that by this time I certainly know what I thought of the show and my job as a critic really begins when I try to analyse why I responded to the show as I did... what the play has to offer... what in fact the production offered... and the extent to which they corresponded and contributed to my satisfaction or dissatisfaction.

"In doing things this way, I find I very seldom omit anything of consequence from my review, that I touch on all the main matters of the presentation and say, though perhaps in a slightly different way, what I would say if I had a week or a month to think it over...

"In the days when I paid my way into the theatre I would not hesitate to get up and go if I felt I wasn't getting my money's worth. But sometimes the show you're watching is of such a nature that the stage action disturbs your concentration and you can't ignore it... or entails so many serious artistic goofs that you feel honour-bound to make a record of them, since otherwise you can't remember them all.

"When that happens, I deviate from my rule, and make notes, starting with the margins and white spaces in my program, and then on the backs of sheets of paper which I find in my pants pocket, and I continue until my pen runs out of ink or I run out of envelopes, memos, or anything else I have used on which to scribble my notes in the dark."[149]

Cohen's critiques could be personally devastating, particularly to visiting Hollywood actors who had taken to the road in the 1950's. As a result, he was frequently accused of hating actors, but on the contrary, he respected, even adulated, what he considered good acting.

"We may forget the play, the scenery, the theme, the

occasion," Cohen said in 1952, "but the good actor grips our consciousness, and never entirely let's go... the actor is the theatre... and the gratitude we owe him can never be sufficiently acknowledged."[150]

Advance reputation, in many instances, was not enough to earn an actor Cohen's praise. Imagine the distinguished actor Charles Laughton, then at the zenith of a career in theatre and films, awakening blowsily on a Sunday morning in Toronto to hear the following commentary on his performance of an evening of dramatic readings with which he was touring North America in 1953. Cohen first spoke of how Laughton, had he not forsaken the European stage for Hollywood films, would have probably continued to develop in the tradition of the great classical actors. But then, Cohen continued:

"He appears among us as a lost and baffled soul, a displaced person whose one-man shows and presentations of unactable plays and epic poems offer him a refuge but never a home.

"Prevented a natural growth, his abilities have hardened into eccentricities. He is an unbalanced mixture of the inane and the sublime... who frequently makes us cringe with his affectations and extravagances... and who occasionally entrances us with the richness and rightness of his artistry.

"The music of speech makes him drunk... He begins each piece as an artist, and concludes invariably as an entertainer."[151]

As to Cohen's contention that Laughton might have developed into one of the truly great actors of modern times, there was a genuine note of sadness in his conclusion that "Now, neither we... nor he... will ever know..."

If Cohen was becoming more jugular in his comments — he described a performance by Hollywood actor Arthur

Treacher, for example, by commenting: "He at times took on the illusion of something not unlike a human being"[152] — and scathing in his wit (an eventual pitfall for all critics), he remained at least outwardly unperturbed by equally violent counterattacks against him.

By the fall of 1953, Cohen's interests had extended to the new medium of television, as well as theatre, and in typical fashion he combined his television criticism with social criticism almost from the outset. Writing in *The Critic*, Cohen took exception to the CBC's methods of promoting the emergence of Canada as a "Great Nation":

"Henry Luce was wrong, and Wilfred Laurier right. This is the Canadian, not the American, century. The special CBLT program, *The Giant and the Dawn* permits no other conclusion," Cohen stated.

"For a moment, I feared the title might be describing the history of the guest M.C., Bernard Braden, over especially from London for the occasion.

"He was given a remarkably pompous introduction. But certainly no one begrudges Mr. Braden his success, and anyway he tied the pieces of the show together with relaxed skill, plausibly fitting his personality to the tone of the performance.

"No doubt the combination of live-film production, running an hour, probably persuaded viewers to buy more Savings Bonds.

"Undoubtedly it conveyed at least a partial sense of Canada's booming condition. If this was everything producer Sidney Newman, the director, Murray Cherkover, and the writer, George Salverson, sought, then on the whole they succeeded.

"The program had some stirring moments; well-edited film clips of oil gushing up into the skies, sprayers of black gold, an RCAF expedition combing endless bushland for a wrecked plane and an on-location report about the use of the Cobalt Bomb to combat cancer, with Percy Saltzman knowingly interviewing hospital officials. Of entertainment in the variety sense there was none, though George Feyer contributed a good cartoon sequence (stroking the pictures to a music and lyric accompaniment) and there was a good comedy bit with Frank Peppiatt as a man who comes into a store to buy a tie and Eric Christmas as a dolorous clerk who sees (does this make him a dolt?) depression (bust) following prosperity (boom).

"Bernard Johnson, the ballad singer, was good, but Louis Applebaum contributed a disappointingly clichéd musical score.

"The bewildering mechanics of television were used with great efficiency and speed. The cameras performed their duties as to the manner born, and the scene of a cancer patient being treated by a Cobalt Bomb was immensely dramatic. There was no particular audio trouble, never a CBC strong feature, and the device of Braden watching the show with us through a monitor was followed through logically.

"Beyond that — well, what did *The Giant and The Dawn* hope to do?

"Was it selling Canada?

"It tried too hard, adopting the American principle of self-glorification but without the American confidence of speaking divine truth. And there were curious omissions in the text. What stranger visiting Canada might have guessed that ours is a French as well as English-speaking country? That it has other industries besides oil? That it has a past as well as a future?

"Obviously, everything cannot be covered in sixty minutes. But it illustrates a weakness (inferiority complex masquerading as braggadocio) that in showing our industrial growth we should point to the one thing that we have, known to Americans, that in proclaiming our cultural advances the fact that Americans flocked to the Stratford Shakespearean Festival was the *sine qua non* of success. It was a way of saying — here is what the Americans admire about us, and if they are impressed then so should we be.

"The first half of the show, faltering in pace once because of an obviously rigged talk between Braden and a Massey-Harris man who sold Savings Bonds, was much stronger than the second half, which dealt with the Canadian people. A country is not only land and production, it is also people.

"Hackneyed, but true. And how were the Canadian people depicted?

"By means of a quite ludicrous homily showing that we in Canada rise with barely any effort above all obstacles of race and religion and national origin. The evidence? A Czechoslovak, in the country for twenty years, and carpingly critical of young Canadians for their bad manners and lack of cultural interests finds that his daughter has an Anglo-Saxon boyfriend. He lectures the said boyfriend on young peoples' delinquencies. But his all-understanding wife solves the difficulty in a flash. 'You don't like it here? Well, let's go back to Europe. Switzerland would be nice.' Husband is aghast. What, give up home, friends, business? He likes it here.

"Well then. Immediately, he is enlightened, and using Canadian-cum-American colloquialisms and grunts eggs hero on to formal proposal to his daughter. Credit Joseph Furst, as father, for not gagging too heavily on this tasteless diet of vitamins. But Beth Lockerbie was unflatteringly photographed as his wife.

"And anyway, suppose the boy's parents were the objectors? Suppose the girl were Catholic and the boy Protestant? Or Gentile and Jew? And doesn't Mr. Salverson know what happened at Dresden?

"And hasn't he heard of discrimination in British Columbia against Japanese Canadians? The bland assurance that this painful question of racial and ethnic equality can be disposed of in the space of a Lever Brothers soap opera reflects the intelligence of the planners of the show, and scorns the intelligence of the viewers.

"Still, TV production has come a long way in Toronto in the past year, and when the show was conceived and projected in video terms, the results were professional by any standards. But why all the references to Savings Bonds? These pleas were, in a sense, a rebuttal to the theme that in this expanding and prosperous land, security was available to all, and adventure, and ease of mind. Anyway, on such programs, advertising in the formal sense should be held to an absolute minimum. That's the best kind of promotion of all.

"And whoever dreamed up the brief radio 'plugs' for Canada Savings Bonds should be sent back to kindergarten. Their bad taste and lack of imagination are almost past belief."[153]

As he continued to review theatre, Cohen's apparently declining faith in the Canadian theatre movement was at least momentarily restored in mid-1953, with the emergence of the Stratford Shakespearean Festival in a giant circus tent housed in a small Ontario town. Although there were those who would later claim that Cohen hated the Festival and, by inference, made it one of his prime targets,[154] his initial reviews were euphoric.

After announcing that "The Canadian Stratford Festival is here to stay"[155] he went on to describe it as "a cultural event of the greatest magnitude for

Canadians"[156] and concluded that "The Festival at Stratford, on second inspection as at the first meeting, is an event of vibrant theatricality. It marks the beginning of an exciting and vastly hopeful chapter in our theatre life"[157] and "a milestone in our theatrical history."[158]

He was also especially enthusiastic about the initial efforts of a new professional company in Toronto, the Crest Theatre, and remarked that "the launching of this new company with its own playhouse is an auspicious event in our theatre and community life,"[159] as well as having good words to say for the Crest's founders, Murray and Donald Davis, whose work he had admired at Hart House.

"This was the year when the Canadian theatre achieved public recognition," Cohen trumpeted. "And to this biased observer that's a development to be shouted jubilantly from the rooftops!"[160]

Cohen was also optimistic and excited about the progress of the National Ballet, under the guiding hand of Celia Franca. The company, he said, "shows great improvement in all phases of its work. It is already a very great credit to our national cultural life. There is no doubt whatever in my mind that it has the shape, the bone and muscle, of a great ballet company, still in the formative process, but very much aware of its destiny."[161]

Yet for the first time Cohen was to express a note of disillusionment with the Canadian public, not too different in tone than that sounded by Mavor Moore in his article in the *Canadian Forum*, and for which Cohen had taken the actor/producer to task four years earlier; but the critic developed the case much further:

"When His Excellency Vincent Massey speaks out about the arts in Canada, he must be listened to with respect," Cohen said in March of 1954.

"His office demands it, and besides, no one else among

us has worked with a keener apostolic zeal to irrigate a vast cultural wasteland. One of our few public men who truly appreciates the intellect, he has given generously of his time, ability and income to help many laudable causes. Without his aid, for example, the Stratford Shakespearean Festival would never have survived a desperate financial crisis last year. Mr. Massey has never wavered in his faith that the arts would someday come into their own in this country, and lately his tone has become distinctly buoyant. Canada — he told an audience in Fort William the other day — has grown up in fact, and is prepared now to regard the arts as national activities, along with mining, farming, forestry, manufacturing, and, he might have added . . . hockey.

"Nor is the Governor General alone in his opinion. Other men and other voices echo, though more guardedly, his optimism. The sixtieth anniversary issue of the *Queen's University Quarterly* also presents a basically sunshine view. The editor, Malcolm Ross, whose curious notion is that literature is a lively art, says that the time for apology is past, and critics are no longer tempted to 'puff' poor things into masterpieces they are not.

"Aflush with the evidence provided by four contributors, he expresses the hope that 'the myth of Canadian philistinism is on its death-bed,' and adds 'While we have no cause for complacency, we can at least say with honest conviction that Canadians are writing good books and good music and are beginning to create good theatre and good ballet.'

"But is Canadian philistinism a myth, and is professor Ross himself innocent of complacency, and of fostering it? An honest conviction is a feeble substitute for a sound critical evaluation.

"The sources of Mr. Massey's enthusiasm are not hard

to find. The interest in the report of the commission which he headed and the rapturous response to the Stratford Festival must loom very large in his mind.

"No doubt the lively hostility of English-speaking Canadians to the arts has abated, and they are now less inclined to treat the artist as an unwelcome and suspect alien. But it doesn't follow that their attitude has changed to one of active sympathy, or that there's an irresistible groundswell of desire for the arts to become a vital expression of our national identity. In Canada, the arts matter only to a tiny minority. They continue to be . . . the arts, that is . . . a rickety part of a shaky superstructure, maintained by a dedicated few, and recognized, mostly with passivity, by a somewhat larger group eager to prove that they are not entirely absorbed in material pursuits.

"I mean, of course, the modern philistines, who aren't ignorant in the Matthew Arnold sense, but whose values have been decided for them by fashionable experts, and have been so thoroughly and systematically exposed to mediocrity that they can't possibly distinguish between the genuine image and the debased imitations and indeed find the latter easier to accept.

"Professor Ross puts his faith in evolutionary improvement and inevitable progress. In the fashion of the Victorian Utopians and the French quack, Émile Coué, he feeds the illusion that every day and in every way our arts are getting better and better.

"And if you want them, there's no dearth of statistics to bolster that idea. Ten years ago the theatre register was a blank. Now we have four professional organizations and a flourishing summer stock movement.

"Twenty years ago we had no ballet companies. Now two. More books are being published, more pictures

painted, more composers are having their works performed. Sixty years ago, remarks Mr. Ross, we tended to
blow up shoddy stuff into masterpieces.

"Now we modestly point to good works, which stand on
their own.

"Let's follow through on this philosophy of salvation
through quantity. Assuming Canada's continued industrial and population growth and a proportionate increase
in artistic effort, then eventually — in another, oh say,
generation or two — we can expect the automatic production of great works.

"Meantime, we must prepare for the coming of this
Periclean Age, when an admiring world will pay us hom-
age and attest that we are at least the cultural equals of
other peoples.

"There is, mind you, something very attractive in this
logic, or rather in its motivating premise. In theory, the
more activity there is, the more the amount of talent
involved and the larger the audience, then the greater
the likelihood there is of creative achievement.

"It's a by-product of the doctrine of universal education. However, art is not a mechanical process, and does
not march upward and onward in a steady, unbroken
line. If it did, then older and more highly developed
countries like Canada would be able to claim a positively
staggering assembly-like procession of Shakespeares and
Beethovens and Miltons and Keatses and Sibeliuses and
O'Caseys.

"Actually, the creative spark may catch fire at any
moment in a people's history . . . it was so during the first
Elizabethan era for the British, when Czarist power was
at its peak in Russia, when the Americans were still a
pioneer nation and just prior to and right after the winning of their independence for the Irish.

"On the other hand, the flame is very weak today in the

Netherlands, and attempts in other lands to produce fine art by fiat have quite conspicuously failed. Even our own experience belies the proposition. The one literary genius we have, minor but authentic, Frederick Grove, came on the scene without warning and departed without acknowledgement. To this day he hasn't received the credit due him.

"No, the creative artist — and by that I mean the playwright, and not the actor, the composer and not the musician, the choreographer and not the dancer, the creator and not his interpreter — cannot be plucked from air or artificially gestated. Historical forces and his own heaven-sent gift will decide the moment of his appearance.

"If we are going to take the position that, by providing the outlets and the concern, our culture is bound to bloom and world-renowned geniuses to materialize, then we will have to endure a recurrent cycle of unnatural expectancy, gross exaggeration of slim talents, and frustrating disillusionment. As a matter of fact, the pressures against the arts ever becoming creative in English-speaking Canada are quite formidable: our whole way of life shows that. We are psychologically married to the principles of caution and conciliation. Extremism and originality form no part of our character. We agree not to disagree, and are disturbed when friction does occur. We mistrust the impulsive and the non-conformist. We commit ourselves to the second best and the second rate because that seems the safe, the moderate way.

"And though we deny it, we take a certain pride in our lack of colourful leaders, our solemn and plodding state rituals, our beef and potato manners.

"We know all about the fable of the tortoise and the hare.

"It's not true, of course, that English-speaking Canadians are dull individually, but as a group they give that impression. Working in this negative atmosphere, the artist must wage a never-ending struggle not to be overpowered by it.

"He must be ever on the alert against strains endeavouring to make him over in a stultifying mold. He must find the strength and capacity for rebellion within himself to hold fast to his principles, for while the creative spring is inborn, without the right to use it, it will rust and run down.

"In the main, few of our artists have been able to stand up against this menace of spiritual debilitation.

"Indeed, we have no cause for complacency. Culture is a question of quality not numbers, and while things are generally better than they were in the lively arts, we still have very little to be pleased with.

"Naturally, our cultural activities must be encouraged and expanded, and encouraged to expand. We cannot live without them, and we can count on some to understand their real purpose; to object to mere production slickness, to remind us of ideals and standards, and to create a tradition which will be meaningful both in width and depth.

"But we will not get a national culture and lasting art until we develop artists with a clear or significant vision of Canada and Canadian life, and the stamina, the will power to express and keep on expressing it."[162]

As is the case with so much of Cohen's early work, this broadcast, given twenty-three years ago, contains a number of points which are as valid as they were when he originally made them. He referred to the modern philistines, people who are not ignorant in the sense of being uninformed, but who have allowed their values to be decided for them "by fashionable experts." They have been so thoroughly and systematically exposed to mediocrity that they can't possibly distinguish between the genuine image and the debased imitations "and indeed find the latter easier to accept," Cohen said.

Cohen was not alone in his concern about the dangers of the new philistinism. In an article on Canadian culture also published in 1954, Hilda Neatby quoted a character in Robertson Davies' play, *Fortune My Foe*: "The educated like my work, and the uneducated like it. As for the half-educated — well, we can only pray for them in Canada as elsewhere."

"It is the half-educated," Ms. Neatby continued, "that are hostile to the creative artist for they tend to be happiest with the mediocre. Not only have they confused quality with quantity; they tend to blur the terms 'creative work' and 'self-expression' in such a fashion that all self-expression somehow rates as creative work — or something just as good."[163]

Much of the fault for this deplorable situation can be laid directly at the feet of the mass media — which, whatever the shortcomings of the educational system, are the primary source of continuing education for the majority of the public.*

One of Cohen's conclusions during that 1954 broadcast has about it the terrible ring of prophecy with regard to the present state of Canadian culture:

"If we are going to take the position that, by providing

---

* Writing in the New York *Times*, art critic Hilton Kramer has eloquently discussed the situation with reference to the televised version of Kenneth Clark's *The Romantic Rebellion*, and although his observations are made in the context of painting, they are equally valid with regard to the other arts as well, and are worth repeating:

"It is of course, as a historian and connoisseur of legendary credentials that Lord Clark comes before the public in this new series, even more than in *Civilization*," Kramer writes, "for the subject here is organized on art-historical lines. The question then naturally arises: apart from his unreliable ideas about the general drift of cultural history, what does he have to tell us about the paintings and sculptures and other works of art under inspection in the outlets and concern, our culture is bound to bloom and world-renowned geniuses to materialize, then we will have to endure a recurrent cycle of unnatural expectancy, gross exaggeration of slim talents, and frustrating disillusionment."

Perhaps only the tattered survivors of the exciting mini-Renaissance in the Canadian arts of the early 1940's and 1950's; of the New Play Society, Jupiter Theatre, The Canadian Players, The Crest Theatre and the CBC Stage repertory (whose melancholy roll-call has already been dealt with by Mavor Moore), and the early Stratford Festival companies, can really understand what that statement means in the 1970's.

Newer critics, who now speak as enthusiastically as their predecessors of a genre of Canadian drama "that has only recently begun to develop a bicultural mythology for this country," and of Nathan Cohen dying "just as the flame" of a Canadian theatre movement "was being lit"[165] in the 1970's, would do well to familiarize themselves with the cultural climate of that earlier era.

One can concede that it is natural enough for Canadians who are concerned with, or make their living from, the arts, to constantly think in terms of developing a readymade cultural mythology for the country, but one need not respect them for it.

Cohen quite rightly saw that culture may be apprehended corporately, but it is never created corporate-

---

The Romantic Rebellion? The awful, amazing answer is: very little...

"A good deal of the blame for this sort of thing, which distorts far more than it illuminates, must be placed not only on the producer and director of the series, Colin Clark, but on the dynamics of the film medium itself. The video camera is an impatient consumer of pictorial images.

"Its primary obligation is to dramatize. It must always be on the move, and when it does not move fast enough to keep us 'interested,' the editor in the cutting room can be counted on to accelerate the pace. We are never allowed to *think*, as we do normally in looking at an actual painting..."[164]

ly, and its evolution is motivated only by individuals; individuals who may even be considered half-mad by the society in which they are struggling to come into being. When the country has produced a sufficient number of artists whose work, in Cohen's phrase, "becomes part of a people's way of life," or to put it another way, part of the enrichment of the lives of *people*, regardless of country, then, and only then, will their work deserve respect.

Wanting to do so, or trying to do so, laudable as it is, is simply not enough; and Cohen was increasingly to insist that Canadian artists quit drooling and whimpering about their lack of recognition in their own country, and face the fact that while they may not be getting the recognition they expect — it may be the recognition they deserve, given the continental cultural standards to which they have so largely chosen to contribute.

Because of the failure of media critics to develop critical audiences, the public now blandly accepts what it is given on a superficial level and rejects more difficult fare. The easy-way-out has, in effect, become the only-way-out; the quick, slick, way to success for a critic or a performer — and the results, in both aesthetic and cultural terms, have been disastrous.

8

STRATFORD, THE CBC AND THE STAR

When Tyrone Guthrie came to Canada to direct the initial season of the Stratford Festival in 1953, he felt that he brought a winning strategy to create a Canadian theatrical identity: Shakespearean drama.

"I think it is only out of this that there will evolve a distinctive style of Canadian theatre," Guthrie remarked after the first season.

"People may go on writing and producing realistic comedies of Canadian life; but these I believe will remain mere copies of a naturalistic theatre which is essentially the product of nineteenth-century culture in Europe, and is already bygone.

"Any distinctive national style, whether of acting, producing, writing or criticising plays will be founded on the study of the classics. It will only be, in my view, by evolving a distinctively Canadian comment on the classics that any satisfactory native dramatic style will be achieved. Such comment will occur not only in criticism but in performance, since all performance is equally a comment upon, as well as a re-creation of, the work performed.

"Without some classical background actors, authors and audiences will only flounder about, with no fixed stars to steer by, at the mercy of every violent current of popular opinion, blown this way and that by loud-mouthed know-alls who propagate the doctrines which they believe to be fashionable and therefore profitable. . .

"There are not, in my view," Guthrie added, "any actors working in Canada whose mere name on the bills provides for the public some guarantee of status, some indication that the goings-on will be worth the price.

"Similarly in the departments of direction and design, and in the workshops, Canada has not provided the opportunity for Canadians to get the sort of experience which would qualify them to undertake these tasks — yet."[166]

So much for existing Canadian standards of theatre, criticism and production expertise, in the opinion of Mr. Guthrie. Accurate as Guthrie's assessment was in some respects, it saw only half the problem — that of professional standards of production and acting — and neglected the idea that a national theatre cannot develop when the raw materials are plays from another time and place. Cohen correctly recognized that such a theatre must develop its own plays.

Although Cohen had himself greeted the opening Stratford season with delight, the normal run of critical acclaim was more clearly represented by Robertson Davies, who said of the opening production: "It was a fully-rounded artistic creation, and auditors of every condition yielded to its enchantment.

"Let those who reserve the adjective 'great' for performances which take place in capital cities describe this one by what term they please — we know what we saw and felt at Stratford."[167]

Now in Cohen's lexicon, this sort of effusion was barely within the acceptable canons of criticism, but Mr. Davies — who had definitely not been listening to Cohen's broadcasts; or had not been paying attention if he did tune in — made it clear by the end of the second Stratford season that he had developed his own standards:

"What is criticism?" Davies asked. "Is it chiefly fault-finding? Who cares now if Mr. X was irritatingly uncertain of his lines at a particular performance, or if a pistol failed to explode in a certain night? Are these trivialities to be remembered now?

"My own view is that the critic should be of the temperament which a devout wit ascribed to Almighty God — easy to please, but hard to satisfy. . .

"There is room surely, for a critic who would rather praise than blame, when praise may be honestly rendered."[168]

After observing Nathan Cohen's own struggle to develop and maintain critical standards, and explain them to his audiences, what can one possibly say to that?

Cohen himself was easy to please, provided that actors paid attention to "trivialities" such as knowing their lines and delivering them with some semblance of a relationship to the character whom audiences paid to see, but he was hardly satisfied with the plummy-voiced, posturing amateur-night atmosphere of many subsequent Stratford productions:

"According to the press releases the second Stratford Festival is a financial success, but artistically it has been altogether a disappointment, well below the quality of last year's presentations and tainted by an opportunism that could very well be its undoing," Cohen said in 1954.

"This opportunism is the danger; it is a danger against which Mr. Guthrie warned, although he himself succumbed to it; it is a danger against which the people who administer the Festival must always be vigilant.

"For certainly, if the policy initiated this year continues, then a great project will degenerate into just another summer theatre venture, with special overtones of snobbery.

"Perhaps what is needed is a bold idea, a special resolve, a project of exceptional excitement and appeal. As for myself, I know what I'd like to see in Stratford in the next few years. I'd like to see the world's finest actors brought to Stratford in the world's finest plays... Sir John Gielgud as Brutus in *Julius Caesar*, Orson Welles in Marlowe's *Faustus*, Charles Laughton in *King Lear*, with Charles Chaplin as the fool, the supreme jester in the world's supreme jester's role, Gérard Philipe in Molière's *Don Juan*, or Corneille's *El Cid* ... a festival of international artists in a theatre where the playwright and the actor can be kings.

"Does that sound fantastic, too ambitious? Well, maybe, but so was the idea of the Stratford Festival when it was first proposed."[169]

By the end of the 1955 season, even Robertson Davies was forced to mention in passing that there had been "some falling off in performance as the Festival progressed,"[170] but he still preferred to expend his critical energies on applauding what he considered to be the high points of the performance.

However, looking back on that period from the more secure perspective of thirteen years, director Michael Langham gives us a clearer view of what was in fact happening at, and to, the Stratford Festival:

"1955 was the Festival's third season. It was still re-

garded as an adventurous novelty bursting with possibilities for the flowering of untapped Canadian talent
— an artistic manifestation at last of national maturity
— and both press and public were right behind it.

"All this despite the fact that the acting company that
year was very uneven in skill and quite diverse in approach.

"Much talent existed, but with very few exceptions
(mostly non-Canadian) it was raw and confused in expression.

"Some were bent on an introspective American style;
some favoured the empty rhetorical manner which at
that time was the current coin at the Old Vic; some were
no more than gauche and eager amateurs; a very, very
few were of a distinct and maturing quality."[171]

Mr. Langham is partially correct in his evaluation of
the widespread response, but not all of the press had
fallen into line right behind the Stratford Festival, in
1955. Off to the left, marching to the deafening beat of
his own drummer, there was Nathan Cohen:

"The fears Mr. Guthrie evoked at first have hardened
into certainty.

"The plain truth is that a wanton tampering with the
play, a mischievous and irresponsible disdain for the
language and spirit of any text he lays his hands on, is
cardinal to Mr. Guthrie's form of expression.

"He is the heart of any show he directs, its only real
star.

"In effect, he takes from a drama those melodramatic
and/or farcical qualities, those opportunities for large
group scenes, and makes them the core and excuse of his
presentation. Poetry and human passion concern him not
at all. That is why the abler actors at Stratford have
failed to improve on their craft; he really has nothing to

teach them. That too is why he called back, for a second and third season, a great many inept actors.

"As long as they look right, and move well, he is satisfied. That is why also Mr. Guthrie is most effective with second-rate plays.

"He belongs to that school which regards the drama itself as raw material, to be reshaped according to the director's whim and preference. No wonder he is partial to Thornton Wilder among modern playwrights, and that it is with Shakespeare's lesser dramas and the Grade-B Elizabethans that he made his reputation.

". . . by and large the Canadian critics are too deeply committed to engage in criticism . . . [of the Festival].

"The important thing about Stratford surely, what distinguishes it from all the other Shakespearean festivals, is that we have here a stage merciless to mediocrity, and which by its very form, poses an irresistible challenge to people with classical training and scope. It should be put at their disposal. The Canadian theatre and theatre public ought to see performers like Gielgud and Olivier and Redgrave and Evans and Ferrer, working with directors of the calibre of Michael St. Denis and Orson Welles and Charles Laughton. The point, if you like, is that there is no such thing as a Canadian style of doing Shakespeare, and won't be for a long time. Until it does happen, the wise and profitable course is to make Stratford an international home for the creative theatre talents of other countries, a place where they can delight, shock and blast themselves and us into new awareness of the dramatic impulse, and from whose exertions our people will draw nourishment and inspiration.

"Socially, the Festival is now entrenched. It has become something to go to, to see. Artistically, unless it adopts some such policy as the one I have indicated, it is hell-bent for sterility."[172]

"The real Festival achievement," Cohen remarked, "has been to persuade its public that they need not take Shakespeare seriously. To take him seriously is to relate yourself to his plays, for what they have to say, and to readjust your knowledge of the human condition according to their insight."[173]

To Guthrie and Davies and their successors a play was an excuse for theatrically spectacular business and histrionic virtuosity; for intricate or ingenious puppet-master displays of actor-movement and visual effects, rather than a living dialogue between playwright and audience, interpreted by living human beings capable of accurately depicting elements of the human condition chosen by the dramatist to illustrate his point — whether humorous or serious.

To them a play was "play"; to Cohen the life of a play was — or should be — as valid (within its theatrical framework) as the life of the audience who watched it. He had experienced this strange, electrifying rapport between actors, playwright and audience himself early in his career as a critic, and having done so, he could not, would not, settle for less, when the material warranted it. Cohen recognized that in live theatre, the spectator is a participant in a process which is new to both actor and audience each time the actor steps onto the stage. Thus despite such devices as the proscenium arch and directoral blocking, each live performance contains a sense of dual-adventure for both audience and performer that is totally absent from other dramatic media.

While the film and even videotape viewer can have his sensibilities alternately stroked, stimulated, and even assaulted, those sensibilities can never be as thoroughly startled or elevated as they can be by the circumstances which immediately and unexpectedly accompany the act of discovery (insight of inflection or the physical truth of a situation or action apprehended by an actor for the first time) which can and does happen in live performance. Simply put, one *sees* a film, but one *experiences* live theatre, although this basic fact is frequently forgotten, even by actors and directors, who become preoccupied with their own efforts to put on a play.

Cohen's reaction to the Stratford Festival, which he realized was suddenly changing the face of Canadian culture as well as just drama, but not for the better, was to attack it as a premature status-symbol which threatened the future of indigenous theatre in the country far more than it encouraged it.

The Stratford Festival was not the only danger. By late 1954 television had become an even more serious threat, as Cohen saw it, to the development of Canadian culture. And television, although it had consolidated Cohen's reputation as a critic, also ultimately became the final nail in the coffin of a distinctively Canadian theatre as envisioned by Cohen.

The talented, but slender resources of the nucleus of a distinctive theatre were already stretched to the limit; television stretched them to the breaking point. Individual performers and producers did go on to greater things, mostly below the U.S. border. The sense of purpose and the almost communal interests of the theatre companies in creating a distinctive Canadian theatre were dissipated. In fact, despite periodic and laudable individual reincarnations of this spirit in the 1950's and 1960's, it was, for all practical purposes, destroyed.

Regional theatres across the country, although they were to experience an upsurge during the 1960's, also lost their unity of purpose.

Radio, which had been the lifeline in building up a mass audience for Canadian drama and performers faded into insignificance and its casualty lists became tragic and impressive. Harry J. Boyle, for example, explains what happened to the admirable Andrew Allan, who was responsible for so much of that early enthusiasm:

"Andrew was almost fifty when television came to Canada. It was a period of rush and confusion. There were brave words about the new medium being conceived in the same principled manner as national radio broadcasting, but the overwhelming presence of an American system under the influence of merchandising was hard to resist.

"There was a common fallacy that to participate properly in television everyone had to be ritually baptized by studio experience — although, strangely enough, most of the executives promulgating this policy managed to escape it.

"Andrew found himself expected to go through the same mill as the twenty-one-year-old fresh out of college. He also found that television was hostile to his principle of translating the writer as faithfully as possible. In television the writer, with rare exceptions, was to be expendable.

"So Andrew became a television casualty. Perhaps if he had been employed as a counsellor, a source of ideas, rather than as a participant in the abrasive struggle of production, Canadian television drama might have achieved the significance that it had reached in radio. But Andrew left the CBC, disappointed. . .

"The competitive nature of any relatively small world of activities, such as broadcasting, heightens the sense of failure. Andrew, like so many others who came on abrupt changes in their personal lives, found release and bondage in the violet hours of drinking."[174]

Frustrated in his occasional work as a journeyman actor and drama adjudicator, Allan had "reached the despairing stage of sleeping in hotel lobbies." With the help of friends, Allan recovered and worked as a radio essayist, until his death in 1974, but it was a sad finish to a distinguished career.[175]

Cohen, after seven years of regular broadcasting for the Corporation, found himself in trouble during 1954 and, as he described it, aid came to him once again from that totally unexpected source, Gordon Sinclair, who had come to his defense when he began broadcasting:

"I found out about Sinclair's goodness and toughness on another occasion ... in 1954 ... when, because I had inadvertently stepped on the toes of a cabinet minister in Ottawa, I was yanked off all radio and TV work for the CBC.

"A couple of people went vigorously to my defence, not just by protesting that action taken against me, but by finding me other work.

"I didn't know until well afterward that they had gone to Sinclair for advice, and he was the one who had told them what to do.

"I also didn't know, until much later, that he had tried to get me a job on a newspaper. It didn't work out, but it was not for want of his trying."[176]

The specific details of Cohen's brief blacklisting are obscure,* but with the change in emphasis from radio to

* The blacklisting came about after a flag debate on *Fighting Words*. Some remarks on the show apparently angered a Federal cabinet minister. The CBC replaced Cohen as host: Cohen had been a member of the Communist Party and this was the era of McCarthyism. Cohen in fact went to England to look for work in 1954. Cliff Soloway, the producer of *Fighting Words*, launched a counter-attack. He wrote to the members of the audience who had protested Cohen's dismissal, urging them to express their opinion through letters to the newspapers. After an absence of six months, Cohen was back as chairman.

television the position which had been occupied by the critic and/or commentator on the network was, as we have already seen, to suffer a change in emphasis as well. If not entirely stilled, then the critic's voice was to become increasingly and effectively muted by programming policy. Nathan Cohen, having in a few short years established himself as Canada's foremost journalistic critic, now found himself fighting a rearguard action to defend the critical standards he had worked so hard to develop in himself and inculcate into audiences and performers, readers and listeners, and, perhaps most significantly, in other critics working in the media:

". . . if the critic really cares about drama, and he lives in a place like Canada, he will campaign for the development of a Canadian theatre, a Canadian drama," Cohen said in a 1956 broadcast.

"We have no Canadian drama to speak of — that is to say, no plays about Canada and Canadian life — and until such times as we do, the whole dramatic foundation will be built on sand.

"We have a theatre of sorts, but for the most part it is a swaddling thing, with no identity or spirit, hobbled by timidity expressed most crassly by the search, from Stratford down to the littlest theatre groups, for something better, and more daring.

"What they need now are plays which will enlarge their vision, teach them their craft, and challenge their capacities to the limit.

"What kind of plays are these? They are not the classics, with their cobwebs of tradition or gimmicks for directors, nor are they the commercial packages from Broadway and Shaftsbury Avenue.

"They are new plays, or at least plays new to us . . . plays from France and Germany and off-Broadway and

Ireland and the rest of the world . . . plays that will put actors on their own, because they will have no models to work from, to imitate.

"When our actors get to appear in such plays, we will again get the excitement and dynamics which the New Play Society had in its early days, and Jupiter, for it is these companies which gave us an inkling of that the Canadian theatre might be, vital, exploratory, human, and blessed with an ensemble style in which the play itself was the star.

"We've been misled into the belief that decor is the thing in theatre. It isn't. Acting is.

"However much lighting and scenery, makeup and music are emphasized, the playgoer comes essentially to see the actors, because what really makes it theatre is the presence of those men and women on stage who bring the whole affair to life before his eyes.

"And until these facts are grasped and applied, the critic is bound to agitate for them — because without its own acting style, and ultimately its own plays, the dramatic movement will never really sink roots in the Canadian soil, or among the Canadian people.[177]

From 1956 through 1958, Nathan Cohen continued his regular broadcasts several times a week, and took on the additional chore of working as a story editor for the CBC's Drama Department, selecting scripts for television programs, and acted as moderator of his own weekly dramatic series, *Cohen's Choice*.

As a CBC story editor, Cohen was responsible for selecting some forty stories for presentation each season, and he frequently found himself in the curious position of having to approach an author whose work he had already criticized severely in one of his broadcast reviews with the suggestion that the play could be adapted to television. He saw no particular contradiction in this, and invariably explained that while his role as a critic demanded the highest standards he could apply to judging a play, his role as a story editor was to get plays on the air.[178]

Although Cohen found the experience stimulating and creative, he was frequently disappointed with the way in which some of the plays he had chosen were presented, and with the ivory-tower attitude of CBC producers with whom he worked.

For example, "The number of plays which have been written by Canadians about men or women who actually work for a living is infinitesimal, even though they form one of the largest single blocs of the population," Cohen once explained.

"I remember once, when I was a TV script editor for the CBC, novelist and playwright Hugh Garner submitting an hour-long script about a man who worked as a lineman for Hydro.

"It was a good play, but it was turned down categorically by the five producers among whom it was circulated.

"Finally, one of them said to me, 'What do we know about working people? You can't expect us to do plays about people we don't understand.'

"It never seemed to occur to him that the weakness was his, that the onus was on him to go out and find out something about such people.

"Poor Garner was thoroughly discouraged however, and just gave up on the whole idea of trying to write for TV."[179]

In a letter to Robert Weaver of CBC Radio Arts, Cohen admitted that he was "shaken" by at least some of the offerings on *Cohen's Choice*. The director, he said, "did a careless and superficial job. I was demoralized by the whole thing."[180]

Cohen in fact developed some rather strong feelings about CBC producers — particularly for television — and argued that their domination of the broadcasting scene was to a large extent responsible for the apparent inability of the CBC to develop performers with much stature of their own:

"The real way to build interest in shows is by focussing on people, and by giving those people a chance to reveal themselves," Cohen commented:

"For quite obvious reasons, because they enjoy the dominance it gives them, because they don't want to share or yield the spotlight, the producers on CBC-TV are, as a group, unable to grasp or apply this fact. And until this fact is really understood, and its lesson learned, CBC-TV in news, drama, or any other category you care to mention, will remain essentially neutral and yes, uninteresting."*[181]

Cohen did make some exceptional discoveries during this period, however, notably that of playwright Arthur Hailey. He was so impressed with Hailey's first play, Cohen remembered, that he succeeded in persuading CBC producers to buy it without having read it, and the critic assisted in polishing Hailey's first three plays for production.[182] Hailey, of course, went on from his original job as editor of *Canadian Bus and Truck* magazine to become the highly successful author of novels, and saw the original play, *Flight Into Danger*, repeated on both television and film.

Another Cohen "discovery," in 1958, was an obscure

---

* The extent to which this criticism still applies can be seen in a recent commercial for a CBC "special" featuring the Royal Winnipeg Ballet, in which the entire emphasis is on producer Norman Campbell. Not one of the Ballet's star performers received so much as a mention.

professor of English Literature at the University of Toronto named Marshall McLuhan whose media-
philosophy interested the critic. Cohen recalled in 1966
"a television interview I did with him eight years ago,
when he was, so to say, my private discovery, and just
before the program started, to discourage him from the
use of jargon, I leaned over and said "Now, remember,
Marshall, we are going to talk basic English for the next
half hour...[183]

During 1957 and 1958, Cohen returned to regular
newspaper journalism, writing a weekly theatre column
for the Toronto *Telegram*, and continued to contribute
articles over the years to a variety of periodicals including *Queen's Quarterly, Tamarack Review*, and the British
publication *Dancing Times*.

In 1959, Cohen joined the Toronto *Star* as drama critic
and Entertainment Editor (a post which he held till
1965), and also reviewed films regularly for the paper's
television supplement *Star Week*.

In his own career, and despite his identification during
its last twelve years with the monolithic Toronto *Star*
surprisingly early in that career, Cohen was able to
prove that a journalist, working solely within the
confines of popular journalism, could become a critic of
enormous intellectual influence and, in his own way, one
of the architects of our cultural consciousness.

Cohen had already made his reputation as a broadcaster and freelance print journalist before he began working for the *Star*, and his reviews for that paper were
merely a continuation of his critical standards and attitude to his work which he had already established by
1959. Thus without in any way diminishing the paper's
importance in providing Cohen with a forum which was
to result in his gaining international respect — a condi-

tion which in itself is relatively unique for a Canadian journalist — it is fair to say that the Toronto *Star* hired an already successful critic to take over their entertainment pages.

It is equally accurate to suggest, particularly with reference to the later years of his career, that Cohen was able to retain the quality of his criticism despite the limitations of working for the *Star*, rather than because of any tendency of that paper to encourage the type of criticism he insisted on practising. Even so, Cohen's later copy in both printed and broadcast format was to become increasingly reportorial, rather than exclusively critical in the sense that it was in his early broadcasts and writings in *The Critic*.

Because of continuing limitations on the amount of time and space available to him, as well as the *Star's* propensity towards "items columns" which dealt with what various personalities in the arts were doing, rather than why or how effectively they were doing it, an enormous amount of the later material crossed over the line into gossip column writing. Cohen, who in his college days professed to hating gossip columns, once explained why he was later to find it necessary:

"I am not making a plea for the kind of gossip column in which Walter Winchell and the late Dorothy Kilgallen specialized," Cohen insisted, "but I do think that there should be a place in the newspapers for telling us what's happening in the world of entertainment and society and politics and business and fashion and among our foreign language groups... the behind the scenes marginalia and facts which get lost and don't belong in the regular coverage.

"One reason such columns haven't really caught on, perhaps, is that the authors were too lazy. They relied too much on the press release and on information that comes over the telephone. There was too little digging."[184]

Cohen, however, refused to limit his "gossip writing" to the comings and goings of theatre people, and insisted on dealing with what was happening behind the scenes of the press itself, and as always, he turned commentary into criticism:

"What's news?" Cohen asked his listeners on July 28, 1970. "In the *Star* the other day I mentioned how the newspapers, and for that matter the radio and TV stations, had ignored Secretary of State Gérard Pelletier's recent statement about a global budget for all the cultural departments that came under his jurisdiction. I thought it was a pretty important story and shouldn't have been ignored.

"Here's another example. For a couple of weeks now the *Telegram* has been going on about a couple of minor, and quite ordinary, changes in the news department of the CBC . . . the departure of some people . . . reshuffling of positions . . . things of that nature.

"From the way the *Telegram's* entertainment department goes on about these matters, they seem of cataclysmic importance.

"In fact they are absolutely ordinary, routine . . . the kind of thing which happens daily on any newspaper and no one thinks about it.

"On the other hand, I haven't seen any explanation in the *Telegram* for the mysterious disappearance of Jim MacPherson as its drama critic.

"After the death of Ralph Hicklin, who handled both drama and dance, ballet was delegated to the music reviewer, Ken Winters, and the theatre was turned over to MacPherson.

"It was the second time MacPherson had been given a

fairly responsible post. A year ago he was given a daily column to replace the one that Sid Adilman had been writing. MacPherson did it for a few weeks, and then announced that it was too much of a strain on him and begged to be released.

"On the drama beat he did it for a couple of months and then he took the holidays due him. The funny thing about that was that he decided his holidays would fall at the time of the Stratford and Shaw festivals, which are key events in the drama daybook. He went off to England . . . and when he came back, well after the expiration of his official holidays MacPherson advised the powers-that-be that he was resigning altogether from the Tely.

"No one at the paper forced him to resign . . . he wasn't pressured into it.

"Now wouldn't you say that's an interesting story?

"You can bet your life though that you'll never see a word about it in the *Telegram*, or in any of the other Toronto papers for that matter.

"There is a tacit agreement that, save in exceptional circumstances, the papers don't report internal shakeups going on among them, while they do report what's happening in magazines, or in radio, or in TV.

"But why? This is the kind of thing that always makes the press look sanctimonious and hypocritical in the eyes of its critics.

"And do you know something? The critics are right."[185]

Cohen, who was himself working for a paper about which there was, he said, "a standing joke in Toronto newspaper circles that no paper equalled the *Star* when it came to staff turnover and bad morale"[186] found such hypocrisy particularly galling.

As a journalist, Cohen was exposed to a mass of press

releases and publicity flackery, but rather than use the material to simply fill up space in his daily columns, as is so often the practice, he frequently turned it back on the hucksters:

"I want to warn you about a half-hour film called *Canada At 8:30* which has been getting a fair amount of publicity," Cohen announced in a 1971 broadcast.

"This movie purports to be a documentary about the theatre scene in this country. In specific details it is already out of date... Plainly and simply the film was made by a motor car company, which takes great pains in its press releases to let you know that it has done something of great moment in making the film.

"But the total cost of the film comes to no more than perhaps $90,000 or $100,000, the price of an expensive one-minute TV commercial.

"Beyond that, the film does nothing, absolutely nothing, to help the cause of the theatre in this country.

"It would have been much more useful if that same money had been divided among our regional theatres, or if the company had set up an organization for distributing funds annually to professional theatres in Canada, doing original plays."[187]

Cohen once remarked: "Show me someone called a critic who thinks his job is to evaluate how the public will respond, and I will show you at best a cretin and at worst a shill.

"My job is to report how I responded... what I liked, what I didn't like, and above all why.

"Anyone can have opinions.

"The mark of useful criticism is the reasoning that produces the opinions however negative or unpopular they may be.

"It doesn't worry me when I'm with the majority...

and it worries me even less when I am one of a small minority in my response.

"I not only know what I like, but why."[188]

As a columnist for the largest newspaper in Canada, he had to fight to maintain his integrity as a critic, as a journalist, and as a person, with as much vigour as he had shown in the days when he first began developing a critical and journalistic style in the Mount Allison *Argosy Weekly*. Ultimately, it is a credit to both the Toronto *Star*, whatever its shortcomings in covering the arts, and to Cohen's remorseless insistence on honesty in reporting and criticism, that he succeeded so well.

Backed by the *Star*, which he described as "an enlightened newspaper" in its attitude to national coverage,[189] Cohen began the almost incessant travel to centres of theatre across the country which was to confirm his position as Canada's first truly national drama critic, as well as making regular forays to the U.S., Europe, and even the Far East, from where he reported on international developments in the arts.

Always a reporter, Cohen's articles, and more particularly, his broadcasts, invariably contained as much colour and description of the areas he visited as they did commentary on the arts, and made fascinating listening for his stay-at-home audiences, even in subsequent reminiscences:

"When I visited New Delhi in 1965," Cohen remembered, "nothing prepared me for the fact that it was considered quite proper for people to stop in the middle of the street and urinate, or move their bowels...

"The more I travel, the more I realize that the travel books omit as much as they include about a city."[190]

And his reminiscences generally contained some intriguing little glimpses into the critic's personality as well:

"The first time I went to Paris, the first thing I did after registering in my hotel was to rush to the American bookshop on the left bank and buy all those forbidden books I'd been hearing about for years," Cohen recalled. "What a disappointment Henry Miller's books were. Far from being the great literary achievements I'd always been told they were by critics I trusted, they turned out to be the reminiscences of a Brooklyn boy who couldn't get over the thrill of living in gay Paree. . ."[191]

After a trip to the Bahamas, social-critic Cohen couldn't resist commenting on the absence of black dealers at the Paradise Island casino, and comparing the gamblers he'd seen there with similar breeds in Belgrade and Monte Carlo, adding, however, that: "I don't really qualify as a witness of the best locale for the gambling fraternity or the psychology of the gambler.

"Call it my Jewish-Presbyterian background . . . my firm belief that man is entitled to earn only what he makes by the sweat of his brow . . . but the gambling urge simply doesn't apply to me . . . although in all honesty watching some of the hundred dollar bills changed into chips, and lost by players with a toss of the shoulder, certainly caused my brow to sweat."[192]

"The worst part of traveling is the homecoming," Cohen once said.

"I don't mean being home . . . I mean getting adjusted to being home. What time is it? It makes no difference, I'm seven, eight hours behind . . . constitutionally I'm still in Europe and I'm trying once again to rearrange my sleeping habits."[193]

While Cohen's international travel broadened his cultural perspective, it did little to improve his opinion of much of European theatre, or its critics.

"The more theatre I see in England the more hilarious I find the opinions of the critics," he commented after one such visit, in 1970:

"It's true American critics may not be the most stylish in the world, and are certainly impressionable. But by comparison to their English counterparts the American critics are the embodiment of resistance to fickle fashion and modish caprice.

"It's just amazing how many bad actors come in for showers of commendation in the so-called quality London press... how many middling playwrights... how many mediocre and turbid productions.

"And if you think I'm talking about Sir Laurence Olivier and *The Merchant of Venice*, you're absolutely on target.

"One of the most preposterously bad shows I've seen in years, and one of the most hysterically overpraised.

"Well, Olivier is a great actor, and is entitled to his mistakes. But that's no excuse for Jonathan Miller's joyless, upside-down, utterly pedantic interpretation..."[194]

Travelling incessantly throughout Canada, Cohen, who was increasingly to draw other critics from the daily press in his wake, remained staggered by the sheer distances between the country's cultural centres:

"What a huge country this is..." he remarked in a broadcast from Edmonton. "How great the distances are.

"Even with travel by jet planes cutting down enormously on the time it takes to get places, the mileage involved getting from one Canadian centre to another staggers the mind..."[195]

Despite his always frail health, Cohen continued his

travels across Canada even after he had given up the post of *Star* entertainment editor in 1965, and subsequently added the task of lecturing on theatre aesthetics and history at York University to his already overloaded agenda. In a letter written to Arnold Spohr, artistic director of the Royal Winnipeg Ballet, in 1970, Cohen gave a hint of his punishing schedule, and of some of the toll it was taking on a man who had suffered a lifelong heart condition:

"You know the sensation of being on a treadmill," he wrote. "Well what with the theatre and dance on a non-stop basis, the problem of doing a weekly television show, two radio broadcasts a day and doing a lecture series for York University on theatre aesthetics, I really have been going full speed.

"But I must be doing something right because, despite everything I have not suffered any chest pains and in general I feel quite genially disposed. . ."[196]

Cohen continued his grinding schedule of cross-Canada and foreign travel to the U.S. and Europe throughout the year, but by February of 1971, he was writing to Sidney Newman, head of the National Film Board of Canada, that:

"My chest pains have returned at an alarming rate. In the old days I would suffer and pace the room. But now, with the movies-til-dawn we get from Buffalo, I grit my teeth, go down to the basement and watch festivals of Deanna Durbin films instead."[197]

By February 24, 1971, Nathan Cohen realized he was seriously ill after he suffered an attack in his hotel room in Edmonton, where he was covering a series of new theatre productions:

"I'm sorry we couldn't have dinner, but I really was in bad shape," he wrote to an old friend. "Went back to the room and I gulped pills madly and finally knocked myself out.

"When things like this begin happening to me, then I know my doctor is not joking and that he is not just putting me into the hospital for an enforced rest."[198]

There is something oddly touching, and even a bit eerie, about Nathan Cohen's final piece of criticism, a mini-review of a Toronto production with the title *Where Do We Go From Here?* It was as if Cohen was remembering back to one of those first productions he had reviewed, as well as thinking about his own future, when he wrote on March 12, 1971:

"The show, which opened last night is a collection of songs and sketches.

"Formally speaking, it might be called a review. Call it whatever you like. It is a fluttering of dead, yellow leaves on a host of subjects which have already been handled far more provocatively and pointedly in dozens of other shows that have been seen in Toronto.

"Among the twenty-seven numbers in the program, three in a kinky sex vein are not entirely devoid of humour. Another number about a mechanical Indian has a story line which anyone who has seen *Little Big Man* will appreciate.

"But that's very meagre nourishment for a sum effort.

"As entertainment *Where Do We Go From Here?* points to just one answer: This way to the Tomb."[199]

Fourteen days later, Nathan Cohen, journalist, critic, iconoclast and man-of-culture, died without regaining consciousness after open heart surgery at St. Michael's Hospital in Toronto.

The man who had always looked venerable beyond his years had finally reached the ripe old age of 47.

During his lifetime, the editor of the "show business

Bible," *Variety*, had ranked Cohen alongside Kenneth Tynan and Walter Kerr as "one of the five best drama critics in the world,"[200] and other internationally known personalities frequently asked for and received advice on their own work from the Canadian critic.

The influential U.S. drama critic Eric Bentley, for example, forwarded to Cohen a copy of his book *A Time To Die* with the observation: "You saw the contents once before and criticized same, and I took action and improved them . . . or did I?"[201]; and after reading a critique of his performance in *Hamlet*, crusty British actor Richard Burton, without a trace of sarcasm, called Cohen "the only brilliant critic in North America."[202]

Cohen had described the production as "an unmitigated disaster."

And after Cohen's death, the tributes which poured in included plaudits from many people who had been his competitors and adversaries, as well as admirers. "A lot of my own career is directly attributable to his taste and judgement as a critic," said Sydney Newman. "He was an extraordinarily rich person — there is no equivalent to him in this country."[203]

Broadway producer Alexander Cohen asserted that aside from certain New York critics and one in Boston Nathan Cohen was "the only critic worth paying attention to on the North American continent."[204]

Robert Fulford, one of the few Canadian journalist-critics to carry on in the Cohen tradition of comprehensively dealing with Canadian cultural development said: "He didn't seem to agree that, just because yours was a second-class culture, you should necessarily approach it with a second-class cast of mind. Why you, a Canadian, could even question Arthur Miller."[205]

In a moving and gentlemanly tribute, fellow Toronto

critic and man-of-the-theatre Herbert Whittaker confessed: "I was often made aware that I could never live up to the character Nathan has established for our profession — that of the irascible, disapproving, castigating and powerful foe of all that is frivolous and false in the theatre.

"In the darkness, after the curtain falls," Whittaker said, "I shall miss a great colleague and the contributor to the theatre of a special highly individual integrity."[206]

New York *Times* drama critic Clive Barnes called Cohen one of the continent's most knowledgeable critics: "He will be sadly missed," Barnes said, "particularly because he was an extraordinarily honest man."[207]

The tribute Cohen himself would perhaps have appreciated the most came from another *Times* drama critic, Walter Kerr, who described his death as "a serious loss to the theatre," and added, "I admired his work very much and respected him as a newspaperman."[208]

But, in terms of Canadian cultural development, it is still left to former National Gallery director Alan Jarvis to have uttered the most pertinent tribute: "The loss of Nathan Cohen," as Jarvis said at the time, "is immeasurable. Although he is known primarily in the world of theatre, his contribution to so many other fields of our creative life will only be judged at some future time."[209]

9

THE DISTORTED IMAGE

Teddy Kollek, the mayor of Jerusalem, once remarked that he was "constantly being asked why we still insist on spending large sums of money in Israel on 'frills' such as the arts, drama and the dance, and museums, instead of using the money to buy more arms. What they don't seem to realize," Kollek said, "is that it is precisely because we continue to develop such cultural resources that we can retain our sense of perspective, our humanity, and even our sanity, in the face of all those weapons."[210]

A country may actually *require* the development of a superior culture, not simply as an economic or intellectual plaything for a minority who can afford it, but as an adjunct to the growth, maturity, and even possibly the survival of the nation as a whole. It was perhaps this ideal of the humanizing potential of art which, more than anything else, informed Cohen's almost single-minded pursuit of excellence.

The standards of theatrical and cultural criticism which Nathan Cohen had consistently and relentlessly developed during the formative years of the period from the 1940's to the mid-1950's were, as I have suggested, to remain the firm foundation of his subsequent criticism; and that period can be characterized as one which gave birth to a critic who occupies a unique place in Canadian journalistic history, and deserves a prominent one in Canadian cultural history as well.

Even if one were only to consider Cohen's attempts to upgrade Canadian standards of critical appreciation, interest in the arts and national consciousness during those years, one would hope that his place would be secure.

Regrettably, and rather shamefully, this is not the case.

In a 1969 article on Canadian culture in the influential British publication the *Times Literary Supplement*, Cohen was singled out as "a good example of a local aberration . . . whose success depends upon pandering to a basic Ontario prejudice, the tendency to criticize too much without ever questioning the standards for evaluation, a prejudice understandable in a society which has gobbled up culture greedily without ever producing any of its own."[211]

That such a commentary tells us more about the patronizing attitude of Britons toward Canadian culture than it does about Nathan Cohen ("the tendency to criticize too much without ever questioning the standards for evaluation"!), goes without saying. But at least it was made while Cohen was alive, and capable of replying.

However, only five years after Cohen's death, a Canadian critic, John Hofsess, wrote an article praising a talented but relatively obscure Canadian actress:

"'Nothing good will ever come out of Canada!' Nathan

Cohen shouted at her two weeks before he died. 'If you want to amount to something, Miss Jackie Burroughs' — his voice seething with steamboat pressure and hiss — 'You'll go to New York and *try* to be accepted by the Actors' Studio. . .'

"She had gone to his office at the Toronto *Star* to reproach him for missing a 'great Canadian play,'" Hofsess continued. "Something called *How the Company Went to an Island, What Happened and Who Came Back,* in which she had recently appeared at the National Arts Centre in Ottawa.

"'Don't you care about Canadian culture?' she asked him.

"Cohen replied apoplectically by pounding his desk. He hated moment to moment people with nothing but fads for ideas; even without seeing this particular play with its preposterous title, he knew it was probably a grueling trifle that would be buried and forgotten in another week.

"Burroughs was relieved by his rage, his lack of reason, to see how touchingly vulnerable he was behind the mask of Canada's Foremost Drama Critic.

"She loves confrontations. She likes to see the veneer of social politeness wear thin and the madness underneath pierce through."[212]

To anyone who knew and worked with Nathan Cohen, Hofsess' cliché-ridden description of an irascible old Pooh-Bah, wheezing, hissing, and apoplectically pounding his desk, is as authentic as a portrait of him suddenly leaping to the desktop and executing a neat *entrechat*.

As Patrick Scott, who took over from Cohen as Entertainment Editor of the *Star,* and who was himself no mean critical duelist, has put it: "He had been entertainment editor before me; he was the older man; his

knowledge of virtually every facet of the entertainment
world and its inhabitants was vastly greater than mine,
his own reputation was much larger and more solidly
rooted . . . he could, had he chosen to, have 'put me in my
place' with formidable ease and dispatch.

"But that was not Nathan Cohen's way."[213]

Yet the more earnestly self-serving critical parvenus
in Canada will undoubtedly continue to use the dead
Nathan Cohen as a target, just as they were forced to
regard him as paradigm, while he was alive.

It may be just, as well as fitting, to allow Cohen's
widow, Gloria, a word of reply to the distorted legend
which now seems to surround the life's work of her late
husband. In a letter to the editor of the *Canadian Theatre
Review*, Mrs. Cohen responded to an article which in-
sinuated among other things that he had waged a critical
campaign against the Crest Theatre in order to enhance
his own reputation:

"It seems that in death as well as in life, my late
husband, Nathan Cohen, continues to be a thorn in the
side of the theatre community and its hangers-on," Mrs.
Cohen wrote.

"If you had taken the trouble to ask me about the Crest
and Nathan, you would have known how he welcomed
the new theatre. You would have realized how hopeful he
was for the professional theatre community, how op-
timistically he looked forward to a rise not only in the
number of theatres, but in the quality of theatre production in Toronto, and, eventually, in Canada.

"There was only one thing Nathan attacked — and
that was amateurism, or its equivalent, incompetent
professionalism. When he attacked the Crest, it was
never because of any latent opposition to the Davis
family — a family, incidentally, he much admired — but

because the productions deserved such criticism. That seems to be so simple a reason that the Crest aficionados/apologists still refuse to believe it. Nathan had a great love for theatre, and because of that love, he was thoroughly honest, thoroughly objective, thoroughly impartial. He paid theatre in Canada at that time a great compliment — he took it seriously.

"The fact that he was 'a Maritime working-class Jew' in no way motivated his remarks. He did not have to look for a reputation by attacking the Crest.

"Far from it. He had won a singular reputation years before — from the very start of his career in criticism — by virtue of the fact that he approached his work — criticism — not for himself or reputation but for the sake of theatre.

"In the Crest, he looked for greatness, even less, mere satisfaction — and too often, he found dross. When the Crest, or the Davises, individually, deserved praise, he gave it unstintingly, wholeheartedly, without reservation of any kind. Witness his review of *The Three Sisters*.

"I am only too sadly aware how thrilled he was with that production, how bright and vivid it remained in his mind so that, to the day he died, he could rekindle his hope for Canadian theatre with its memory.

"Nathan was indeed a Maritime working-class Jew, but he was an aristocrat among critics. There was no reverse anti-Semitism whatsoever in his approach to the Crest, or to any theatre, and if the Crest failed to draw the Jewish community support generally, it failed to do so because of its woeful frequency of inadequate productions.

"On the foundations of the criticism in Canada which Nathan single-handedly, and I must admit single-mindedly, built, on the professionalism which he espoused, the base for a truly professional theatre in Canada was laid. It is unfair, unjust, untrue and petty to label his work, even implicitly, in the ignominious and shameful way your Ross Stuart article (CTR 7) suggests."[214]

With regard to the Crest Theatre controversy, which to this day looms large in the minds of some theatre-buffs, if not theatregoers, Cohen did indeed render generous praise to many Crest productions, among them Stanley Mann's play *The Gift of the Serpent,* which he described as "The best play written by a Canadian to date. It warrants the most generous popular support,"[215] but he became quickly disenchanted with the calibre of theatre being presented by the Crest, and his reasons for doing so could still serve as a warning for future generations of Canadian actors.

In a broadcast in 1966 discussing the resignation of founder/director Murray Davis from the Crest, Cohen commented:

"The Crest was virtually run on the proposition that theatre is, in and of itself, a good thing. Quite possibly so. But there are forms of dramatic presentation besides live theatre, and in our day and age live theatre has to prove itself, has to give people something different and better than they can get elsewhere, has to create, if I may take advantage of Martin Buber's phrase, an I-thou relationship, a 'we-need-you' yes, but also 'you-need-us' sense of obligation. . ."[216]

Cohen viewed Davis' resignation as "the best thing for the theatre, which he founded with brother Donald and sister Barbara Chilcott.

"His going," Cohen said, "marks the end of an era in our theatre ... and of a generation which, with all its good intentions, was out of touch ... out of touch with what's happening in theatre, what's going on in Toronto, and with the place of theatre in today's scheme of things..."*217

What Cohen was saying, particularly in his reference to the late Martin Buber, was simply that if the worker in live theatre was rapidly becoming unnecessary to the public — even as a prime source of entertainment — then he should keep striving to discover a method of *making himself necessary* to that public by convincing them of his unique contribution to its culture, rather than simply indulging himself in the heady atmosphere of performing — and expecting or demanding that the public turn out in support on general principles.

That this lesson was largely lost on the devotees of the Crest, and continues to elude Canadian artists as a whole is evidenced by the fact that while theatre groups have continued to flourish in the country, their social and cultural impact on Canadian life is virtually nil, outside of the coterie groups which continue to support them. In her book on the Dominion Drama Festival, for instance, Betty Lee glowingly quotes statistics which she says officials of the Festival — which changed its name to Theatre Canada — cited to "help underline its claim that

---

*Prior to this period I was myself involved with acting in the highly improvised group-theatre atmosphere of George Luscombe's Toronto Workshop Productions and, at the time, young actors of my acquaintance vehemently shared Cohen's conviction that the air of what we considered bogus theatricality which surrounded the Crest and — in our view — most conventional theatres, was decidedly musty, to say the least. As for ourselves — we performed in the basement of a hat factory and, to no small degree inspired by Cohen, felt we were building the future of Canadian theatre.

Presumably even today, the lineal descendants of those dedicated actors from Hart House who stormed into Cohen's CBC studio in 1949 protesting his "destructive reviews," or even the potential heirs to the mantle of Jackie Burroughs, who manfully carried on the tradition of confrontation in 1971, would be on the march once again — if there were a critic around capable of stirring that much response in their righteous breasts, an event which appears increasingly unlikely.

community theatre is still as much the lifeblood of true Canadian drama as it was in Bessborough's day." According to Samuel French Ltd., Miss Lee writes, "Canada in 1972 boasted 500 Little Theatre Groups, 10 amateur childrens' theatre groups, 1,239 high school drama groups, 120 university drama groups, 100 fraternal drama groups, and an unaccountable number of church drama groups.

"It is estimated the groups boast a total of 31,000 active members and that their productions reach an audience of 2,790,000 or approximately one-tenth of the Canadian population. In that year, the latest count of professional or semi-professional companies totalled between 50 and 60, a spectacular increase during the 1950's and 60's which the DDF itself publicly applauds."[218]

In conclusion, Miss Lee, herself a former movie critic for the Toronto *Globe and Mail*, quotes "spokesmen" for the amateur organization whom she says insisted "The professionals simply can't see the woods for the trees" — which in a bush-league of those proportions, is hardly surprising.

Perhaps the most vivid example of the present-day local, let alone national impact of the DDF is contained in the opening paragraphs of Miss Lee's book:

"It was somewhat of a jolt to members of Theatre Canada's national executive when they walked into their Saskatoon hotel rooms that Sunday, May 21, 1972, to find their annual festival had been upstaged by a Regina dog show.

"Hotels in Saskatchewan distribute a provincial entertainment weekly called *Sight and Sound* to inform visitors of the province's current happenings. But instead of the 39-year-old celebration of Canadian theatre dominating the front cover of the magazine, the classy canines collected prime billing."[219]

As to Canadian professional companies, Toronto Workshop Productions, one of the relatively few Canadian theatre groups to have established an international following — at least to the extent of being invited to perform in European countries — found that when it recently took its successful ensemble production of *Ten Lost Years* (a comedy-drama-musical pastiche of the Depression years in Canada) to London, the critics had praise for the players but, if one is to believe the reports carried by the Canadian Press, neither understood what the play was about, nor cared to.

Further, if one is to take the word of the eminent dance critic Clive Barnes of the New York *Times*, Canada's National Ballet — on which the incomparable Celia Franca lavished so much dedication and energy — is now chiefly useful as a prop to help decorate the talents of Rudolf Nureyev or one of the other expatriate European superstars:

"In the case of the National Ballet of Canada, which is now at the Metropolitan Opera House, we see an almost extreme example of star consciousness, for the National Ballet of Canada is here simply and solely because Nureyev wants to dance with it. Without Nureyev — or, say Baryshnikov — the company would not be viable at the Metropolitan Opera House any more than the Australian Ballet could have brought *The Merry Widow* to New York the other month without Fonteyn. The test of this is simple enough. A few years ago when Nureyev was injured, a whole Canadian season at Washington's Kennedy Centre had to be cancelled.

"The dependence of the National Ballet of Canada on guest artists has been criticized. A young Canadian critic, John Fraser, in these pages a year or so ago reported widespread unhappiness among dancers being treated almost as scenery. The startled and furious response from members of the company — both men and women — was immediate. They affirmed their love for Nureyev and their belief that he was doing an important job for the company.

"Certainly, Nureyev has done a great deal to make the Canadians an internationally recognized company; yet as the Canadians already know to their cost, too much dependence on guest artists can be damaging.

"This season in Toronto the company was relying very heavily on the presence of Baryshnikov to sell out its season. Unfortunately, Baryshnikov was injured, ticket money had to be returned, and eventually the season was only narrowly saved by the rapid engagement of two other superstars, Fernando Bujones and Peter Martins."*[220]

One notes that it was the Canadian dancers — who had presumably been complaining to Fraser in the first place — who quickly pulled the rug out from under the critic, and that it was a Canadian audience, in Toronto, which threatened to withdraw its support from its own National Ballet, without the foreign superstars. All of which, one suspects, goes to prove that we may have indeed continued to develop a representative brand of Canadian theatre after all; that is to say, it remains, as in the past, to be considered by non-Canadians as notable for its lack of distinction, in form or content, at home or abroad, when taken on its own merits.

It is all the more curious and disheartening, therefore, to see the figure of Nathan Cohen, who did so much, who fought so hard, and who argued so eloquently for the establishment of those very artistic, social and national

*Barnes modified this view during the National Ballet's successful appearance in New York in July of 1977. He remarked on the ability of the Canadians to hold their own without the assistance of its guest superstar, Rudolf Nureyev. However, the bulk of his review is taken up with the performance of an American dancer with the Company, Peter Schaufuss.

standards which might at least stand a chance of adding some distinction to Canadian culture, portrayed in the late 1970's as a man who impeded the country's cultural development — or worse, who chose to ignore its potential. Such deprecation of Cohen's Canadianism, and concentration on his evident disappointment with the accomplishments of Canadian theatre is often done in a way which wilfully disregards the reasoning behind Cohen's theatrical criticism, and ignores his early and almost fanatical dedication to the development of a distinctive Canadian culture.

When the critic remarked, with regard to the lack of magnetism of Canadian actors, for example, that: "The fact is that whether it's on stage, or in television or cinema, the overwhelming majority of our actors are faceless blurs; they come and go, and no one really notices them; and this is one of the prime reasons so much of Canada's theatre falls on barren ground,"[221] he also added: "I think they are inhibited by unimaginative direction and by the lack of plays in which they can really find themselves." And in 1966, when he seemingly reversed himself on his assessment of the Americans, Cohen was still reacting logically, according to his own experience:

"I take absolute exception," he said in 1966, "to the double standard that prevails in judging American culture.

"When it comes to say, Great Britain or France or the Soviet Union, we praise them for the best they give us, not the worst... whatever its depths, the United States has cultural peaks that we are privileged to enjoy."[222]

"It is a matter of plain fact," Cohen added in a university lecture in 1970, "that when you live in a small country — a great many talented people in all professions will move to a neighbouring country which is bigger.

"That's what happened in the theatre world, and the only comic aspect of it is the way in which, in a vain attempt to stimulate some kind of national pride, we have tried to identify these emigrants as our own to this day. . .

"Lorne Greene is a good actor who has achieved continental and international fame for his performance as the patriarch in *Bonanza*. He is considered an intrinsic American type. It is not from any wish to offend our sensitivity that people in the U.S. think of Christopher Plummer as an Englishman. Our rankling at such attitudes to 'our' actors, our persistent lament that we keep losing our best people are classic symptoms of the envy and resentment which afflict a small country alongside a big one."[223]

Actually, what had finally come to afflict the man who had so frequently stated: "I go along with people who say that Canadians are as good as anyone else, I just want them to prove it to me,"[224] was not a loss of that faith — it was simply a loss of patience.

After twenty-four years of fighting against the current, Nathan Cohen apparently realized that the majority of Canadians accepted the Americanization of their culture, in economic and social, if not rhetorical terms, and any future consideration of Canadian cultural development would have to be regarded in that light. Two decades of chronicling a Canadian theatrical environment which remained, despite its bright post-war beginnings, primarily "a recurrent cycle of unnatural expectancy, gross exaggeration of slim talents, and frustrating disillusionment," had done their work. One might as well make the best of it.

But if Cohen was a realist who disliked false and baseless nationalism, he was also a visionary whose dreams died hard. His vision of a Toronto cultural renaissance, for instance, could well apply to all of Canada:

"I have a dream for Toronto," Cohen explained in 1967, Canada's Centennial Year, ". . . a dream which as a critic of the lively arts I am honour bound to hope will come true in the next hundred years.

"It's a dream in which Toronto recaptures its dynamism of a few years ago and begins to bulge at the seams once more with forms of play and players that will command admiration and joy the country and the world over.

"It's a dream in which that tattered mausoleum, the CNE, is torn down and converted into a year-round science and pleasure fair . . . where we are taught and entertained and excited.

"It's a dream in which every second club has a revue style show, using local talent, but of such sparkle and sophistication that you can bring visitors from anywhere and they too will be diverted and amused.

"It's a dream in which we have three repertory play companies . . . one specializing in the world's classics . . . another in new drama . . . a third in experiment . . . and all three are functioning all year and playing to packed houses.

"It's a dream in which there is so much talent about that our TV stations devote about fifty per cent of their program time to local variety and drama programming, and the ratings justify the prime time scheduling and the cost.

"It's a dream in which the CBC is again the hub of venturesome productions . . . and our motion picture people, instead of talking about the movies they are going to or could make if they had the money, actually make movies . . . and they turn out to be professional and pleasant . . . not masterpieces, who needs masterpieces?

"It's a dream in which every part of the city has its Yorkville . . . its colourful neighbourhood where, in the summer, you can sit at a table outside and have an apertif or a coffee and watch the girls go by in their summer dresses . . . and the world is lovely and cheerful and this is a wonderful city to live in.

"You think that's too fanciful a dream? I don't agree.

"In fact that's what I *believe* is really going to happen fairly early in the next century with this city. . . The slump of the moment will be overcome and Toronto again will be back on that jumping, galvanized track."[225]

The dream was perhaps less glorious than it had been in the beginning. Cohen was now asking "Who needs masterpieces?" when he had once spoken of a Canadian theatre which he hoped would produce "plays with poetic truth and insight, which become part of a people's life, its culture." But it was still a fine dream, and it is in that ebullient, positive, and creative spirit that Nathan Cohen should be remembered.

SELECTED
BIBLIOGRAPHY

Books:

Agee, James. *Agee on Film*. McDowell, Obolensky, New York, 1958.

Algren, Nelson. *Notes From a Sea Diary*. Fawcett Crest Books, Greenwich, Conn., 1965.

Allan, Andrew. *Andrew Allan: A Self-Portrait*. (Introduction by Harry J. Boyle). Macmillan of Canada Ltd., Toronto, 1974.

Bate, Walter Jackson, ed. *Criticism: The Major Texts*. Harcourt Brace & Co., New York, 1952.

Beckerman, Bernard and Siegman, Howard, ed. *On Stage 1920-1970. New York Times Theatre Reviews*. Quadrangle Books, New York, 1973.

Caute, David. *The Illusion: An Essay on Politics, Theatre and the Novel*. Harper Colophon Books, New York, 1971.

Doherty, Brian. *Not Bloody Likely (The Shaw Festival: 1962-73)*. J.M. Dent & Sons (Canada) Ltd., Toronto, 1974.

Edwards, Murray D. *A Stage In Our Past (English Language Theatre in Eastern Canada From the 1790's to 1914)*. University of Toronto Press, Toronto, 1968.

Farb, Peter. *Man's Rise To Civilization*. Avon Books, New York, 1969.

Ferguson, Max. *And Now . . . Here's Max*. McGraw Hill Co. of Canada Ltd., Toronto, 1967.

Gilmour, G.P., ed. *Canada's Tomorrow*. Macmillan of Canada Ltd., Toronto, 1954.

Glover, Elwood. *Elwood Glover's Luncheon Dates*. Prentice-Hall of Canada Ltd., Scarborough, Ont., 1975.

Grogan, Emmett. *Ringolevio*. Little, Brown & Co. Ltd., Toronto, 1972.

Guthrie, Tyrone and Davies, Robertson. *Renown at Stratford.* Clark, Irwin & Co. Ltd., Toronto, 1953.

Guthrie, Tyrone, Davies, Robertson and MacDonald, Grant. *Twice Have The Trumpets Sounded*. Clark, Irwin & Co. Ltd., Toronto, 1954.

Guthrie, Tyrone, Davies, Robertson, Moiseiwisch, Tanya, and Neel, Boyd. *Thrice The Brinded Cat Hath Mew'd*. Clark, Irwin & Co. Ltd., Toronto, 1955.

Kael, Pauline. *Reeling*. Little, Brown & Co. Ltd., Toronto, 1976.

Kilbourn, Wm., ed. *A Guide To The Peaceable Kingdom*. Macmillan of Canada Ltd., Toronto, 1970.

Lee, Betty. *Love and Whiskey: The Story of The Dominion Drama Festival*. McClelland and Stewart Ltd., Toronto, 1973.

Malraux, André. *The Voices of Silence*. Granada Publishing Ltd., St. Albans, Herts., 1974.

Marcuse, Herbert. *One Dimensional Man*. Beacon Press, Boston, 1964.

Moore, Mavor, co-ordinator. *The Awkward Stage* (The Ontario Theatre Study Report; The Province of Ontario Council for the Arts). Methuen, Toronto, 1969.

Raby, Peter, ed. *The Stratford Scene 1958-1968*. Clark, Irwin & Co. Ltd., Toronto, 1968.

Sheed, Wilfred. *Max Jamison*. Paperback Library, New York, 1971.

Simon, John. *Movies Into Film*. The Dial Press, New York, 1971.

Sontag, Susan. *Against Interpretation*. Dell Publishing Co. Ltd., New York, 1969.

Spengler, Oswald. *The Decline of the West*. Alfred A. Knopf, New York, 1939.

Richler, Mordecai. *The Incomparable Atuk*. Panther Books, Granada Publishing Ltd., London, 1972.

Tarr, Herbert. *The Conversion of Chaplain Cohen*. Avon Books, New York, 1963.

Toynbee, Arnold J., Kahn, Louis I., Michelson, Annette, Skinner, B.F., Seawright, James, Burnahm, J.W., and Marcuse, Herbert. *On The Future of Art*. The Viking Press, New York, 1970.

Magazine and Newspaper Articles:

Ashley, Audrey M. "Good Critics Hard To Find, Conference On Arts Told." *The Ottawa Citizen*, July 19, 1976.

Barnes, Clive. "Guest Stars Add More Than Glitter." *The New York Times*, August 1, 1976.

Brown, John Mason. Review of original production of *Death of a Salesman*. *Saturday Review of Literature*, February 26, 1949.

Cohen, Mrs. Gloria. "Letter to the Editor." *Canadian Theatre Review* (CTR 8), Fall, 1975.

Denison, Merrill. "Nationalism and Drama." *Canadian Theatre Review* (CTR 8), Fall, 1975.

Garebian, Keith. "Stage Two: Myths Macro and Micro." *Books in Canada*, June, 1976.

Hofsess, John. "The Burroughs Trip." *The Canadian Magazine*, June 19, 1976.

James, Geoffrey. "The Pattern Cutters." *Time*, May 6, 1974.

Kramer, Hilton, Review of Sir Kenneth Clark's *The Romantic Rebellion*. *The New York Times*, August, 1975.

Lambert, J.W. "Don't Strip To The Buff." *The London Sunday Times*, August 15, 1976.

McCaughna, David. "Nathan Cohen In Retrospect." *Canadian Theatre Review* (CTR 8), Fall, 1975.

Richardson, Jack. "Persons of the Drama." *The New York Times Book Review*, June 20, 1976.

Shils, Edward. "Mass Society and Its Culture." *Culture For The Millions* Norman Jacobs, ed., pp. 1-27.

Stoffman, Daniel. Obituaries of Nathan Cohen. Toronto *Star*, March 26 and 27, 1971.

In addition, I have consulted the files of the Toronto *Star* and, of course, the majority of the material in the text is taken from the private papers of Nathan Cohen, now in the Public Archives, Ottawa, Ontario, referred to in the Notes as "Cohen Archives."

NOTES

In the following pages, the Cohen Archives are referred to with the letters CA.

CHAPTER ONE

1. Interview with Jeremy Brown on radio station CKFM in 1970. Quoted in Toronto *Star* Obituary, March 6, 1971.
2. Ibid.
3. CA: undated broadcast script on 1948/49 theatre season.
4. CA: CKFM script, Sept. 8, 1969.
5. Brown Interview quoted in Toronto *Star*, March 26, 1971.
6. CA: CKFM script, June 30, 1967.
7. Brown Interview quoted in Toronto *Star*, March 26, 1971.
8. Ibid.
9. Ibid.
10. CA: Mount Allison *Argosy Weekly*, April 4, 1942.

11. CA: Ibid., May 19, 1942.
12. CA: Ibid., undated, Nov., 1942.
13. CA: CKFM script, Dec. 23, 1966.
14. CA: Mount Allison *Argosy Weekly*, undated article, Dec., 1941.
15. CA: Ibid., May 19, 1942.
16. CA: Ibid., March 21, 1942.
17. CA: Ibid., March 28, 1942.
18. CA: Ibid., March 28, 1942.
19. CA: Ibid, May 19, 1942.
20. CA: CKFM script, May 19, 1967. (The *Argosy Weekly* article Cohen refers to is not among those in the Cohen Archives.)

CHAPTER TWO

21. I am indebted to Toronto *Star* staff writer Daniel Stoffman, who wrote Cohen's obituary, for much of the biographical material in this section. Conversation in November, 1975.
22. Toronto *Star* Obituary, March 26, 1971. None of the *Gazette* material is available in the Cohen Archives.
23. CA: *Obiter Dicta*, the Osgoode Hall publication to which Cohen still periodically contributed. Article is dated only 1947.
24. Brown Interview quoted in Toronto *Star*, March 26, 1971.
25. David McCaughna, "Nathan Cohen in Retrospect," *Canadian Theatre Review* (CTR 8), Fall, 1975.
26. Toronto *Star* Obituary, March 26, 1971.
27. David McCaughna, "Nathan Cohen in Retrospect," (CTR 8), Fall, 1975, p. 30.
28. CA: *New Voice* "Editor's Notebook," May 29, 1947.
29. CA: *Wochenblatt*, August 20, 1946.

30. Herbert Tarr, *The Conversion of Chaplain Cohen*, p. 296.
31. CA: filed under *Wochenblatt*, Dec. 12, 1946.
32. CA: Ibid., Jan. 23, 1947.
33. CA: filed under *Canadian Jewish Weekly*, Vol. 8, No. 419.
34. CA: filed under *Wochenblatt*, April 3, 1947.
35. CA: filed under *Canadian Jewish Weekly*, Vol. 8, No. 376.
36. CA: Ibid., Vol. 8, No. 386.
37. CA: Ibid., Vol. 8, No. 391.
38. CA: CKFM script, March 14, 1966.
39. CA: Toronto *Star*, Jan. 8, 1970.
40. CA: Letter to Sean Mulcahy, Nov. 27, 1970.
41. CA: CKFM script, Nov. 21, 1967.
42. CA: filed under *Canadian Jewish Weekly,* Vol. 7, No. 369.
43. CA: CKFM script, Nov. 21, 1967.

CHAPTER THREE

44. Quoted in Murray D. Edwards, *A Stage In Our Past*, p. 170. Edwards adds: "Almost a hundred years later Canada was still too young to create a theatre of its own."
45. Quoted Ibid., pp. 29–30. Edwards, in fact, introduces his book by saying: "Most people with a knowledge of Canada's cultural past will agree with Nathan Cohen when he says, 'Theatre as something of value to a discerning public has never counted in the life of English-language Canada,' and adds that the information in his book was "not collected in the hope of proving Cohen and the other deductive writers wrong." (p.ix).

46. Ibid., p. 29.
47. Ibid., p. 37.
48. Ibid., p. 39.
49. Ibid., p. 39.
50. Ibid., p. 170.
51. *Ottawa Citizen*, July 19, 1976, p. 61.
52. CA: Nathan Cohen, "Theatre in Canada: An Expendable Commodity," lecture given at York University, 1970. Cohen adds: "There are some people who can recall the period when, with just half the population we have now [1970], there were five or six legitimate theatres in English Toronto, and a flourishing Yiddish theatre."
53. CA: Ibid.
54. CA: Ibid.
55. CA: Ibid.
56. Quoted in Betty Lee, *Love and Whiskey: The Story of the Dominion Drama Festival*, p. 100.
57. Ibid., p. 100.
58. Merrill Denison, "Nationalism and Drama" (1929). Reprinted in *Canadian Theatre Review* (CTR 8), Fall, 1975, pp. 74-78.
59. Ibid., pp. 77-78.
60. Quoted in Betty Lee, *Love and Whiskey*, p. 113.
61. Ibid., p. 283.
62. Ibid., p. 180.
63. Ibid., p. 129.
64. Ibid., Introduction, p. ix.
65. Andrew Allan, *Andrew Allan: A Self-Portrait* (Introduction by Harry J. Boyle), pp. 1-2.
66. Ibid., p. 71. He adds: "There were obvious limits to the scope of a broadcasting career in Canada in the 1930's."
67. Ibid., p. 111.

68. Ibid., p. 116.
69. Quoted in Betty Lee, *Love and Whiskey*, p. 291.
70. Quoted in Wm. Kilbourn, ed., *A Guide to the Peaceable Kingdom*, p. 298.
71. Quoted Ibid., p. 330.
72. Peter Farb, *Man's Rise To Civilization* p. 58.
73. Ibid., p. 58.
74. Quoted in Wm. Kilbourn, ed., *A Guide to the Peaceable Kingdom*, p. 303.

CHAPTER FOUR

75. Mordecai Richler, *The Incomparable Atuk*, pp. 51-52.
76. CA: CKFM script, April 13, 1966.
77. This is remarked on by virtually every writer to discuss the subject, most recently David McCaughna, "Nathan Cohen in Retrospect," *Canadian Theatre Review* (CTR 8), Fall, 1975.
78. Jack Richardson, "Persons of the Drama," *The New York Times Book Review*, June 20, 1976.
79. CA: filed under *Wochenblatt*, Feb. 1, 1947.
80. CA: Ibid., Feb. 13, 1947.
81. CA: Ibid., Feb. 24, 1947.
82. CA: Ibid., April 10, 1947.
83. CA: Ibid., April 10, 1947.
84. CA: Ibid., May 8, 1947.
85. CA: filed under *Canadian Jewish Weekly*, Vol. 7, No. 369.
86. CA: filed under *Wochenblatt*, June 19, 1947.
87. Conversation between Cohen and the writer on anti-Semitism in the arts, 1968.
88. CA: filed under *Canadian Jewish Weekly*, Vol. 8, No. 324.

89. CA: Ibid., Vol. 8, No. 383.
90. CA: Ibid., Vol. 8, No. 389.
91. CA: Ibid., Vol. 8, No. 390.
92. In his essay "Nathan Cohen in Retrospect" (CTR 8), Fall, 1975, David McCaughna points out that Cohen "took the theatre as well as his duties as a critic more seriously" than other critics of the period, "and it was that — as well as his insistence that because of the decentralized nature of the Canadian theatre that a theatre critic in this country had to travel — which made him Canada's first truly national drama critic." (p. 27.)
While this is undoubtedly true, it can be seen that Cohen took a "national" view of the theatre — in both the aesthetic and physical sense — long before his employment or income permitted him to do much actual traveling.
93. CA: filed under *Canadian Jewish Weekly*, Vol. 8, No. 416.
94. CA: The clipping containing the announcement also features a photo of Cohen as a chunky, rather round-faced young man, sporting a button-down collar and a natty, pencil-line moustache.
95. Cohen remarked on this to the writer, and the same observation is quoted in David McCaughna's essay (p. 30) and the Jeremy Brown interview on CKFM radio.

CHAPTER FIVE

96. CA: CBC script, Sept. 29, 1967.
97. CA: Ibid.
98. CA: "CBC Drama Item," Nov. 30, 1948.
99. CA: *Across the Footlights*, Dec. 12, 1948.

100. CA: Ibid., undated, Dec., 1948.
101. CA: Ibid., #1, undated, Dec., 1948.
102. CA: Ibid., Jan. 16, 1949.
103. CA: *The Theatre Week*, Jan. 30, 1949.
104. CA: Ibid., Feb. 6, 1949.
105. CA: CKFM script, Jan. 2, 1969.
106. CA: Ibid., July 2, 1970.
107. CA: *The Theatre Week*, announcer's outro, Feb. 27, 1949.
108. CA: Ibid., Feb. 20, 1949.
109. CA: filed under CBC script, Feb. 25, 1966.
110. CA: Ibid.
111. CA: *The Theatre Week*, March 6, 1949.
112. CA: Ibid., April 3, 1949.
113. CA: Ibid., April 17, 1949.
114. CA: *Across the Footlights*, undated, April, 1949.
115. CA: *The Theatre Week*, undated, April, 1949.
116. Toronto *Star* Obituary, March 26, 1971.
117. Conversation with the writer, and remarks in Toronto *Star* Obituary, March 27, 1971. Luscombe also believes: "There are no critics writing in Toronto since Nathan Cohen died."

CHAPTER SIX

118. Mavor Moore (co-ordinator) *The Awkward Stage*, pp. 181-182.
119. CA: *CJBC Views the Shows*, Nov. 27, 1949.
120. CA: Ibid., Dec. 18, 1949.
121. CA: Ibid., May 6, 1951.
122. CA: See items of July 23, July 24, Sept. 3, Sept. 27, Nov. 14, Dec. 3, 1950 as some example of broadcast scripts.
123. Max Ferguson, *And Now . . . Here's Max*, pp. 84-85.

124. CA: filed under CKFM script, Aug. 29, 1966. On McGeachy's death, Cohen also writes: "Our world is just a little smaller and poorer for his death."
125. CA: CKFM script, July 14, 1970, on James Bannerman's death.
126. Christopher Young, head of Southam News Services, quoted in Audrey M. Ashley, "Good Critics Hard To Find, Conference On Arts Told," *The Ottawa Citizen*, July 19, 1976.
127. CA: CKFM script, April 27, 1967.
128. Andrew Allan, *Andrew Allan: A Self-Portrait*, p. 131.
129. CA: *Critically Speaking*, Jan. 15, 1950.
130. CA: *The Critic*, Vol. 1, No. 9, 1951.
131. Toronto *Star* Obituary, March 26, 1971.
132. CA: *The Critic*, Vol. 1, No. 4, Sept., 1950.
133. CA: Ibid., Vol. 1, No. 5, Oct., 1950.
134. Keith Garebian, "Stage Two: Myths Macro and Micro," *Books in Canada*, June, 1976.

CHAPTER SEVEN

135. CA: *Critically Speaking*, May 20, 1951.
136. CA: *The Critic*, Vol. 1, No. 10, June, 1951.
137. CA: *CJBC Views the Shows*, June 17, 1951.
138. CA: CBC script, Dec. 9, 1951, in reference to *My Dear Children*.
139. CA: CBC script, July 13, 1951.
140. CA: *CJBC Views the Shows*, Sept. 30, 1951.
141. John Mason Brown, *Saturday Review of Literature*, February 26, 1949.
142. CA: *CJBC Views the Shows*, Nov. 11, 1951.

143. Quoted in David McCaughna, "Nathan Cohen in Retrospect," (CTR 8), Fall, 1975. McCaughna, who has presumably read the script, calls the play "a rambling, poorly focussed tale." There is no copy in the Cohen Archives for reference.
144. Toronto *Star* Obituary, March 26, 1971.
145. CA: Letter to Sergei Sawchyn, general manager of the Royal Winnipeg Ballet, Nov. 25, 1970.
146. Toronto *Star* Obituary, March 26, 1971.
147. Ibid.
148. Ibid.
149. CA: CKFM script, Aug. 2, 1967, as a prologue to a review of Stratford's *Antony and Cleopatra*. Cohen adds: "I want to tell you that it's been a long, long time since I made as many notes as I did in Stratford the other night..."
150. CA: CBC script, Dec. 28, 1952.
151. CA: Ibid., May 3, 1953.
152. CA: Ibid., June 28, 1953.
153. CA: *The Critic*, Vol. 2, No. 2, Oct. 27, 1953.
154. David McCaughna, "Nathan Cohen in Retrospect," (CTR 8), Fall, 1975, pp. 34-35.
155. CA: CBC script, July 16, 1953.
156. CA: Ibid., July 19, 1953.
157. CA: Ibid., Aug. 9, 1953.
158. CA: Ibid.
159. CA: Ibid., Jan. 10, 1954.
160. CA: Ibid., Aug. 16, 1953.
161. CA: Ibid., Jan. 31, 1954.
162. CA: *The Lively Arts*, March 14, 1954.
163. Hilda Neatby, "Cultural Evolution," in G.P. Gilmour, ed., *Canada's Tomorrow*, p. 188.
164. Hilton Kramer, *The New York Times*, August, 1975.

165. David McCaughna, "Nathan Cohen in Retrospect," (CTR 8), Fall, 1975, p. 36.

CHAPTER EIGHT

166. Tyrone Guthrie and Robertson Davies, *Renown at Stratford*, pp. 28-29.
167. Ibid., p. 47.
168. Tyrone Guthrie, Robertson Davies and Grant Mac-Donald, *Twice Have The Trumpets Sounded*, p. x.
169. CA: *CJBC Views the Shows*, July 11, 1954.
170. Tyrone Guthrie, Robertson Davies, Tanya Moiseiwisch, and Boyd Neel, *Thrice The Brinded Cat Hath Mew'd*, p. 17.
171. Peter Raby, ed., *The Stratford Scene 1958-1968*, p. 6.
172. CA: *CJBC Views the Shows*, July 24, 1955.
173. Quoted in David McCaughna, "Nathan Cohen in Retrospect," (CTR 8), Fall, 1975, p. 35.
174. Andrew Allan, *Andrew Allan: A Self-Portrait*, p. 138.
175. Ibid., pp. 138-140.
176. CA: CKFM script, June 2, 1970: on the eve of Sinclair's 70th birthday.
177. CA: *CJBC Views the Shows*, Jan. 1., 1956.
178. Toronto *Star* Obituary, March 26, 1971.
179. CA: CKFM script, filed as "standby" program. Undated, Feb., 1970.
180. CA: Correspondence: letter to Robert Weaver, date unclear. The director referred to is Esse W. Ljungh.
181. CA: CBC script, March 11, 1966.
182. Toronto *Star* Obituary, March 26, 1971.
183. CA: CBC script (unidentified) March 29, 1966.
184. CA: CKFM script, March 29, 1966.
185. CA: CKFM script, June 3, 1970.

186. CA: CKFM script, June 20, 1967.
187. CA: CBC "Assignment" script ("stand by"), Feb. 1971
188. CA: CKFM script, Jan. 12, 1966.
189. CA: CKFM script, Aug. 12, 1970.
190. CA: CKFM script, Oct. 13, 1969.
191. CA: CKFM script, Dec. 7, 1967.
192. CA: CKFM script, Sept. 8, 1969.
193. CA: CKFM script, Jan. 23, 1967.
194. CA: CKFM script, May 29, 1970.
195. CA: CKFM script, Oct. 28, 1966.
196. CA: Correspondence: letter to Arnold Spohr, Nov. 27, 1970.
197. CA: Correspondence: letter to Sydney Newman, Feb. 18, 1971.
198. CA: Correspondence: letter to Joseph Schockter, Feb. 24, 1971.
199. CA: Toronto *Star*, March 12, 1971.
200. CA: Toronto *Star* Obituary, March 27, 1971.
201. CA: Correspondence: letter from Eric Bentley, Dec. 10, 1970.
202. Toronto *Star* Obituary, March 27, 1971.
203. Ibid.
204. Ibid.
205. Ibid.
206. Ibid.
207. Ibid.
208. Ibid.
209. Ibid.

CHAPTER NINE

210. Interview with the writer in 1973.
211. Toronto *Star* Obituary, March 26, 1971.

212. John Hofsess, "The Burroughs Trip," *The Canadian* magazine, June 19, 1976.
213. Toronto *Star* Obituary, March 26, 1971.
214. Mrs. Gloria Cohen, "Letter to the Editor," *Canadian Theatre Review* (CTR 8), Fall, 1975.
215. CA: CBC script, May 8, 1955.
216. CA: Ibid., Feb. 18, 1966.
217. CA: Broadcast script, Sept. 12, 1966.
218. Betty Lee, *Love, and Whiskey,* p. 303.
219. Ibid., p. 15.
220. Clive Barnes, "Guest Stars Add More Than Glitter," *The New York Times*, Sunday, Aug. 1, 1976.
221. CA: CBC "Assignment" script, June 3, 1966.
222. CA: CKFM script, November 3, 1966.
223. CA: Undated lecture manuscript, York University, 1970.
224. CA: CBC script, June 1, 1959.
225. CA: CKFM script, July 1, 1967.

INDEX

Index

Johnson, Bernard, 212
Julius Caesar, 148, 227
Juno and the Paycock, 45, 85-6, 100, 115-6, 117
Jupiter Theatre Company, 154, 155, 222, 235

Kanin, Garson, 150
Kaplan, Henry, 128
Karr, Jack, 206
Kay, Arden, 81
Kelley, Barbara, 78
Kerr, Walter, 248, 250
King, Alan, 57
King, Charmion, 92
King Lear, 178, 227
Kingsley, Sidney, 205
Knapp, Bud, 35, 60, 78, 81, 83, 97
Koestler, Arthur, 205
Kollek, Teddy, 250
Kramer, Hilton, 221*n*
Krassovka, Nathalie, 142
Kubrick, Stanley, 80
Kyd, Thomas, 132

Langham, Michael, 227-8
Laughton, Charles, 210, 227, 229
Lee, Betty, 56, 58, 256
LeRoy, Kenneth, 138
Lescot, Marc, 49
Levin, Bernard, 52
Lewis, Wyndham, 63
Light Up the Sky, 129
Little Big Man, 247
Lockerbie, Beth, 213
Logan, John, 118
London Little Theatre, 205
Love and Whiskey, 56, 257-8
Luscombe, George, 72, 152, 256*n*

Macbeth, 95, 114-5
McCance, Larry, 60
MacDonald, Rose, 69, 76
McGeachy, J.B. "Hamish", 160-2, 163, 165
McKee, Alex, 71, 86
McLaughlin, Col. R.S., 57-8
Maclean's, 188
McLeod, Norman, 160

McLuhan, Marshall, 238
MacPherson, Jim, 240-1
Mallett, Jane, 60, 71, 97
Man in the Blue Moon, The, 81-2, 87
Mann, Stanley, 255
Maria Chapdelaine, 186
Markle, Fletcher, 60, 71, 72
Marlowe, Christopher, 89, 227
Martins, Peter, 259
Massey Report, *see* Royal Commission on National Development in the Arts, Letters and Sciences, report of
Massey, Vincent, 53, 54-5, 57, 118, 215-7
Merchant of Venice, The, 87-9, 245
Mews, Peter, 72, 97
Miller, Arthur, 201, 248
Miller, Henry, 244
Miller, Jonathan, 245
Mr. Bolfry, 75-6, 83
Mister Roberts, 204
Mrs. Moonlight, 195
Monday Magazine, 160
Montreal Repertory Players, 106
Montreal Star, 118
Moore, Dora Mavor, 47
Moore, Mavor 154-5, 158, 159, 172-7, 181-2, 206, 215, 222; as actor, 72, 76, 83; as director, 86, 97, 115-6, 149; as playwright, 98-9, 166, 168
Morgan-Powell, S., 118
Morse, Barry, 60
Mould, Willie, 6
Mount Allison University, 6, 7, 22-4, 24*n*; fire at, 13-4
Movies Into Film, 33*n*
Mulcahy, Sean, 45
Murray, Claire, 72, 83

Narrow Passage, 174
National Arts Centre, 252
National Ballet of Canada, 215, 258-9
National Film Board, 27, 192, 246
Neatby, Hilda, 221
Needles, William, 61, 171
New Liberty, 188
New Play Society, 61, 84, 91, 99, 106, 154, 173-5, 176, 179, 222, 235; productions by, 35, 44, 45, 70-2, 73,

Index

Henrietta, Circus Star

Henrietta, Circus Star

By Syd Hoff

GARRARD PUBLISHING COMPANY
CHAMPAIGN, ILLINOIS

109536

Henrietta, Circus Star

"The circus is in town,"
said Mr. Gray.
"I think I will go see it."

Henrietta heard him.

"I've never been to a circus,"
she thought.

"Maybe I'll go along."

When Mr. Gray wasn't looking,
Henrietta jumped
into the back of the truck.
He didn't know
that she rode into town with him.

"Hurry! Hurry! Hurry!
The big show is about to begin,"
said a man selling tickets.

Mr. Gray got in line
to buy a ticket.
Henrietta got in line behind him.

"You can't go in
unless you pay,"
the man said to Henrietta.

"I don't have any money,"
Henrietta told the man.
She walked away.

She walked around
to the back of the tent.
Henrietta slipped in
when no one was looking.

She saw an open door.

Henrietta peeked inside.

It was the clowns' dressing room.

"Look who's here,"
said the clowns.
"Would you like to be
a clown too?"

14

"Yes," said Henrietta,
"if I can stay
and see the circus."

The clowns put a big nose,
shoes, and a hat on Henrietta.

"And now," said the ringmaster,
"here are the funniest clowns
in the world."

Out came Henrietta
and the clowns.

Everybody laughed at them.

Mr. Gray was laughing too.
"Don't you know me?"
asked Henrietta.
But he did not hear her.

Henrietta did tricks
with the clowns.
She let them
squirt water on her.

Then the clowns
threw pies at each other.

"I don't want
to get hit with a pie,"
said Henrietta.
She flew away.

She landed
on an elephant's back.

The elephant stood
on his two back legs.
Henrietta walked out
on his trunk.

"Do you like it out there?"
asked the elephant.

"Yes, I can see
what's going on,"
said Henrietta.

She saw a bear on roller skates.

"I want to do that,"
said Henrietta.
She flew down
from the elephant.
She put on roller skates, too.

But Henrietta
had never been on skates before.
She skated into a big cage.
Out came the lions and tigers.

30

They saw Henrietta.

They growled.

They opened their mouths wide.

They wanted chicken for dinner.

"I only train lions and tigers,"
said the trainer.
He tossed Henrietta
out of the cage.

Henrietta landed
on a teeter-totter.
"Maybe I can rest here,"
she thought.

But an acrobat jumped down
on the teeter-totter.

Henrietta flew up
into the air.

She landed
on a high bar.

"And now, you will see
the daring young man
on the flying trapeze,"
said the ringmaster.

Henrietta jumped off the bar.

She flew out into space.

At the same time
a man swung over
from another bar.

He caught Henrietta
in the air.
"Your hands are cold,"
said the man.
"Those are my feet,"
said Henrietta.

The man let go.
Henrietta fell into a net
and bounced out.

She bounced
into the mouth of a cannon!

"You're just in time,"
said a man.
"The human cannon ball
is not here today."

"I'm not a cannon ball,"
cried Henrietta.
The man lit a match.
Boom! Boom!
Henrietta shot out of the cannon.

Her nose, hat, and shoes flew off.
She landed in Mr. Gray's lap!
"Why, Henrietta,
what are you doing here?"
asked Mr. Gray.

"I've been clowning around,"
said Henrietta.
"And I got to see the circus.
But now I'm tired
and ready to go home."
"I'm ready too,"
said Mr. Gray.

46

He bought Henrietta a balloon.

They rode home together.

DATE DUE

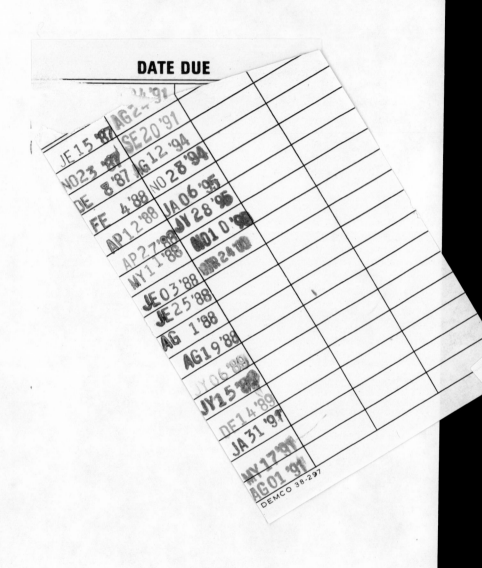